OVER SHAP TO CARLISLE

The Lancaster and Carlisle Railway in the 20th century

OVER SHAP TO CARLISLE

The Lancaster and Carlisle Railway in the 20th century

Harold D. Bowtell

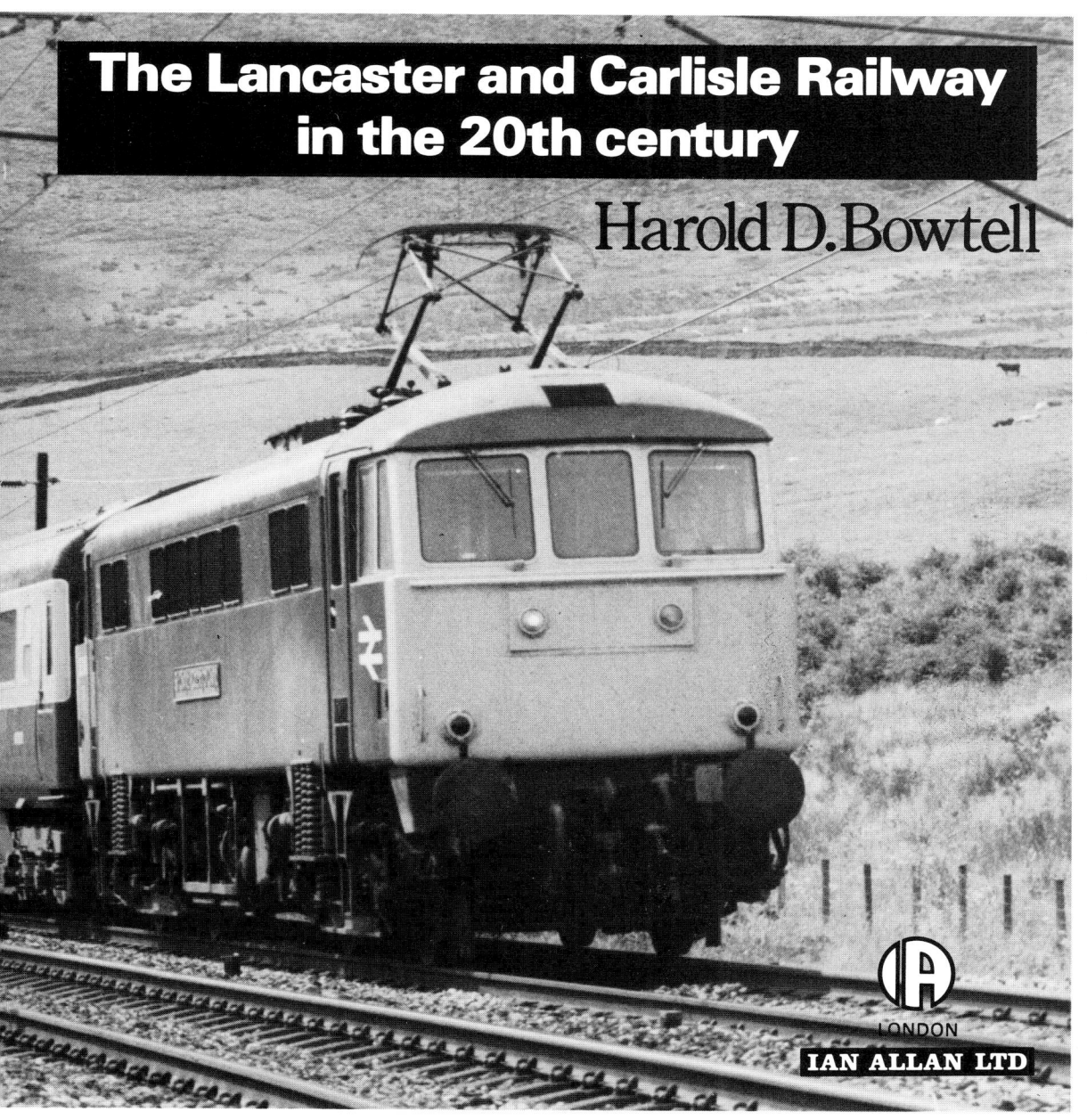

LONDON

IAN ALLAN LTD

First published 1983

ISBN 0 7110 1313 6

Published by Ian Allan Ltd, Shepperton,
Surrey; and printed by Ian Allan Printing Ltd at
their works at Coombelands in Runnymede,
England

Half title page: *Ajax*, a 'Scot' of 1927, is tearing southward over
Dillicar troughs, into the Lune gorge, early in its career. The
L&NWR type of engine shed plate '29' is clearly seen,
indicating a Carlisle (Upperby) engine. *J. W. B. Hext collection*

Title page: Class 86 No 86.248 threads the Lune gorge with a
Euston-Glasgow express in August 1982. *D. E. Canning*

LE RAILWAY: MAIN LINE.

CONISTON 7A

KESWICK

WIGTON

CARLISLE

GESWR

CR

NBR

M&CR

CALTHWAITE

CK&PR

PENRITH

NBR

CR

NBR

LONGTOWN

BRAMPTON TOWN

GREENHEAD

WINDERMERE

SHAP SUMMIT

SHAP

NER

NER

APPLEBY

NER

LITTLE SALKELD

NER

TEBAY

LOW

NER

N

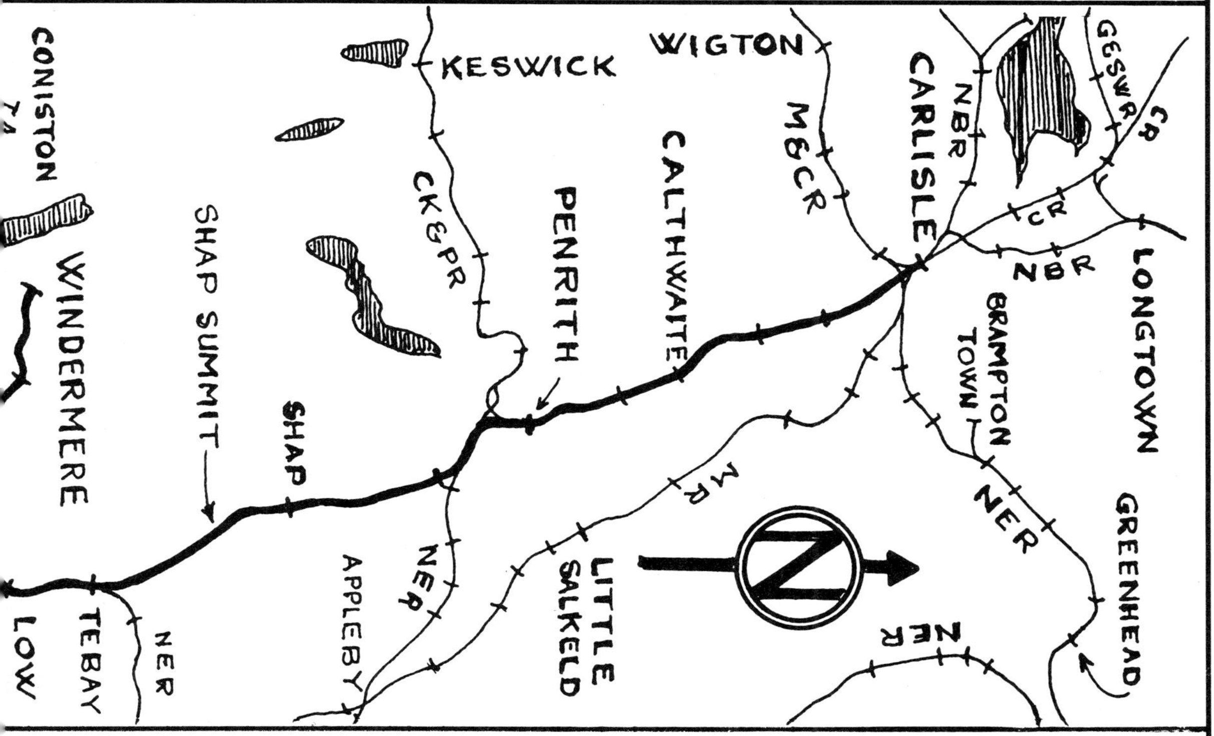

ED TO SHOW DETAIL BUT
L PICTURE OF THE LINE. | ARTHUR CHAMBERS,
JANUARY 1982.

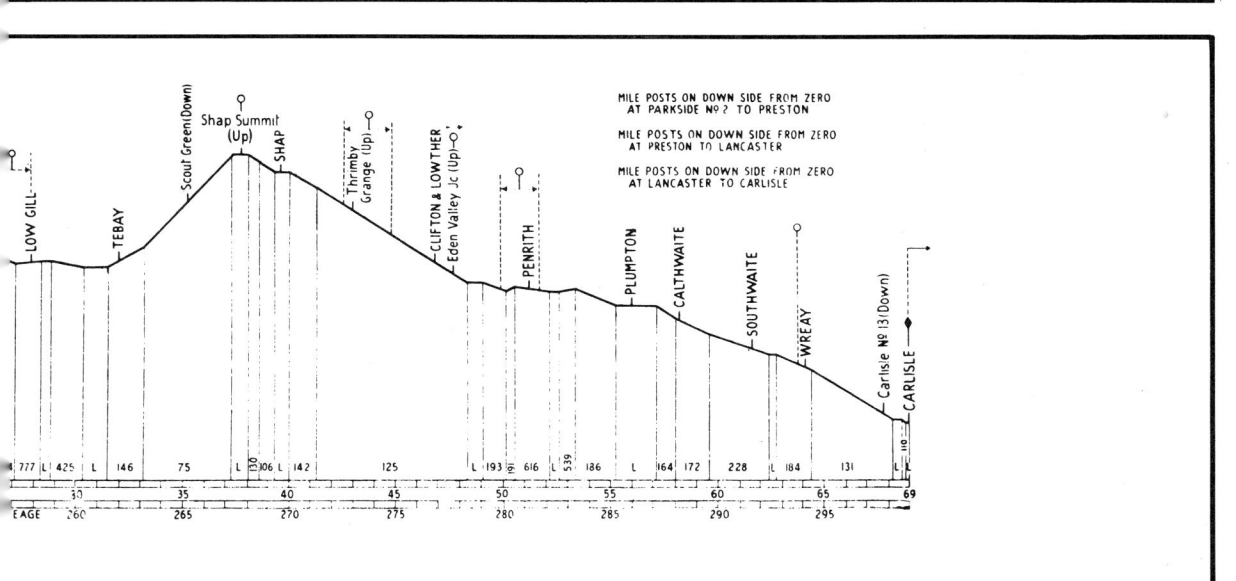

MILE POSTS ON DOWN SIDE FROM ZERO
AT PARKSIDE Nº 2 TO PRESTON

MILE POSTS ON DOWN SIDE FROM ZERO
AT PRESTON TO LANCASTER

MILE POSTS ON DOWN SIDE FROM ZERO
AT LANCASTER TO CARLISLE

LOW GILL

TEBAY

Scout Green (Down)

Shap Summit (Up)

SHAP

Thrimby Grange (Up)

CLIFTON & LOWTHER

Eden Valley Jc (Up)

PENRITH

PLUMPTON

CALTHWAITE

SOUTHWAITE

WREAY

Carlisle Nº 13 (Down)

CARLISLE

777 L 425 L 146 75 L 130 L 142 125 L 193 616 559 186 L 164 172 228 L 184 131 L 110

30 35 40 45 50 55 60 65 69

EAGE 260 265 270 275 280 285 290 295

Contents

Contents continued

Preface

The Preston to Carlisle main line and its Windermere offshoot were styled 'homely and self-contained in atmosphere, with various families well represented and signalmen who wasted no margins and kept express passenger traffic moving'. That was written by a lifelong enthusiast and railwayman, who as a young man well knew the line and its people in the opening years of the century.

Another great character vividly recalls his first trip, as a schoolboy travelling alone from Liverpool to Scotland, in a through carriage of the Lancashire & Yorkshire Railway Company. At Preston, an ancient Crewe saddletank locomotive quickly transferred the Liverpool vehicles to a Manchester-Glasgow/Edinburgh train. Chief memories of the ensuing journey are of 'a thick white mist that shut out all except the lineside telegraph poles, and the constant patter of cinders on the carriage roof as a pair of "Jumbos" made their voices heard'. That was just before 1914.

My own first lone trip to Carlisle was likewise made in schooldays, in one of those boxlike, horsehair-seated L&YR contraptions. The locomotive coupled directly ahead was not the then familiar 'Lanky Claughton' or 'Royal Scot', but unsuperheated 4-4-0 *Cyclops*. It has always astonished me that the 'box' did not go on fire that September morning; there was such a violent and terrifying deluge of unburned coals rattling down on its wooden roof, as the 'Precursor's' unhappy driver struggled to control his fierce steed on the slippery ascent to Grayrigg. When enjoying a thrilling electric run up the winding hill, I also recall with pleasure the sharp crackle of a pair of 'Princes' making those climbs with the Manchester-Glasgow. If looking out in late evening to see the lights of the last down Carlisle winding its way confidently into the fells, it is pleasant to remember the unmistakable deep beat of a L&NWR 'Claughton' climbing, muffled, through the woodlands and then in full cry on to the open fellside.

Let us look more closely at the Carlisle and Windermere roads; they are well worth it!

Kendal, Westmorland   *Harold D. Bowtell*

Left: Impressive pile: the Park Hotel on East Cliff, Preston, drawn for the L&NWR in late 19th century.

Introduction to the Lancaster and Carlisle Railway in the 20th century

The railway from Preston to Carlisle, 90 miles of route, and the diverging line from Oxenholme to Windermere, 10 miles, were made up from:

(1) The Lancaster and Preston Junction Railway (L&PJR), opened from Preston to Lancaster on 26 June 1840, with terminal arrangements in the North Union Railway's station at Preston and in their own station at Lancaster Penny Street (alt: Greaves; and later known as Lancaster Old).

The L&PJR came under the management of the Lancaster & Carlisle Railway (below) by agreement of 13 November 1848, which was ratified by Act of 1 August 1849, with amalgamation following in 1859.

(2) The Lancaster & Carlisle Railway (L&CR), opened from Lancaster to Kendal Junction (later: Oxenholme) on 21 September 1846 (formally) and 22 September 1846 (for public passenger traffic), also opened from Kendal Junction onwards to Carlisle on 15 December 1846 (formally) and 17 December 1846 (for public passenger traffic).

The L&CR was from the first linked to the L&PJR at Lancaster Old Junction, almost a mile south of Lancaster Castle station.

(3) The Kendal and Windermere Railway (K&WR), opened from Kendal Junction (Oxenholme) to Kendal on 21-22 September 1846, in conjunction with the route from Lancaster, and from Kendal to Windermere on 20-21 April 1847.

The K&WR was leased to the L&CR in 1858, formalised by Act of 1859.

The L&CR, comprising these three constituents, was itself leased to the London and North Western Railway (L&NWR) in 1859 and finally vested in that Company in 1879.

With the L&NWR, the routes passed to the London, Midland and Scottish Railway (LMS) on the main 'railway grouping', 1 January 1923, and the LMS became part of British Railways on nationalisation, 1 January 1948.

The special importance of the railway route from Preston to Carlisle was the linking with other railways at Carlisle, not only those already existing there in 1846, but especially those which were being formed in Scotland. The particular partner of the L&CR/L&NWR was always the Caledonian Railway (CR), whose routes from Carlisle to both Edinburgh and Glasgow were opened

throughout on 15 February 1848. The CR too passed to the LMS group on 1 January 1923.

At Preston, the prime object was to link up with an existing route from London Euston, then via Birmingham, Grand Junction line (but very soon directly via Nuneaton), Stafford, Crewe and Newton(le Willows). This in turn connected at Newton with the original Liverpool and Manchester Railway. By the time that our Preston-Lancaster-Carlisle/Windermere railways were complete, in 1847, Euston-Preston was part of the then newly formed amalgamation, the London and North Western Railway — with one qualification, which has relevance to our story.

This qualification concerns the North Union Railway (NU), owner of the lines from Parkside (on the Liverpool-Manchester line of the L&NWR), and Bolton, to Preston (NU station); these two converged at Euxton Junction, some $5\frac{1}{2}$ miles south of Preston NU station. The NU was leased in 1846 to the Grand Junction Railway and the Manchester and Leeds Railway and these became respectively L&NWR and Lancashire and Yorkshire Railway (L&YR), so it was under the joint control of these two major Companies. The NU was eventually absorbed by them jointly under Act of 1888, and in 1889 — Bolton-Euxton Junction became L&YR property (and part of their Manchester-Preston route) and Parkside-Euxton Junction became L&NWR property (and part of their Euston-Carlisle route).

Also in 1889 a L&NWR/L&YR Joint Committee was established to be responsible for:

(1) The NU line, primarily Euxton Junction-Preston NU Dock Street Junction (mainly operated by the L&NWR, although also of great importance to the L&YR).

(2) The Preston and Wyre line, commencing 10 chains north of the undermentioned Longridge Junction and extending to the Fylde (mainly operated by the L&YR).

(3) The Preston and Longridge line, commencing at Longridge Junction, 14 chains north of Dock Street Junction, and including Deepdale Goods (mainly operated by the L&NWR).

With this abbreviated version of often complex railway history, it is appropriate to study Preston as gateway to the railway route northward, then proceeding to a closer scrutiny of the railway to the Lakes, Shap fells and the Border City.

Infrastructure: Preston to Carlisle and Windermere

Presentation

A general map of the route and connections appears on the endpapers. With improvements of 1925-26, the route achieved its maximum development and complexity — as to track layouts, loop lines, profusion of signalboxes and stations. Progressive simplification set in from about 1932. The LMS operating department's line diagram, 1928 edition, has been reproduced photographically to illustrate each portion of the main line, supported by a *schedule* of the signalboxes in 1928 and followed by a *record* of main features as seen by the author. This record features the present-day scene but also looks backward to origins, changes and events in time past. Where available, the LMS 1928 enlargements of complex station areas are photographically reproduced. These are supplemented by our own maps of two interesting yard layouts in the Preston area, also one of Milnthorpe and one of Windermere.

The mileages quoted on the 1928 line diagram are unhelpful and the seemingly precise mileages shown in the schedule of signalboxes must be treated with reserve, as there are many inconsistencies between the versions in successive operating 'appendices'. However, indicative milepost distances are quoted in the left margin of the author's record of main features.

Bridges of significance structurally or as landmarks are touched on in the descriptive record. The brief details of their construction relate in general to the 1920s-30s (LMS period) and have not in all cases been up-dated with the strengthening of underline structures and raising of overline ones which took place in the 1960s and especially c1970-71, prior to electrification.

Dates of alteration or closing of lines, stations or yards are normally quoted with effect from (wef) the first business day following the alteration, thus usually from a Monday. The signal and telegraph department (S&T) usually report the *actual* date of a change but, for consistency, S&T changes carried out on Saturdays and Sundays are shown in the schedule and record wef the Monday following (with * indication against this date). Intermediate block signals are shown as IBS and are colour-lights unless stated otherwise. PB denotes taking over of functions by the centralised power boxes (located at Preston and Carlisle), wef dates quoted in 1972-73.

The 'infrastructure' is concluded by reproduction of the route layout controlled by the power boxes, most of which route was electrically worked from May 1974. Subsequent changes are few and are mentioned in the record. The progressive and complex curtailment of goods yard facilities is not set out but interested readers are advised to consult Mr C. R. Clinker's register of closed passenger stations and goods depots, 1830-1977, and supplements, for an authoritative account.

Signalling, Preston to Carlisle and Windermere

Under a contract of February 1867 with the L&NWR, Saxby & Farmer undertook construction of primarily brick-built signalboxes, containing lever frames to operate points and signals, with integral interlocking. The work proceeded during 1867-72. Between 1870 and 1872, block instruments were installed in these boxes on the L&C section of the main line, in order strictly to impose a space interval between trains and supersede the less rigid system hitherto in force. The types of signalboxes encountered on this line were:

Author's key	Description of signalbox (alt: 'signal cabin')	Period built
'A'	Saxby & Farmer, brick, 'poky' windows, hipped roofs	1867-72
'B'	First Crewe styles, deeper windows, hipped roofs	1873-76
'C'	Webb (Crewe) standard, having gabled roofs	1877-1902
'D'	Later L&NWR (Crewe), still deeper windows, more overhang of eaves and roof ends, bargeboards prominent	1902-22 *et seq*
'E'	LMS pattern, based on MR, large windows, gabled, usually with frame placed 'back-to-front'	from c1929
'F'	LMS and BR boxes, rather similar, slab concrete flat roofs	from c1939
'G'	BR later boxes, flat-roofed, but of lighter construction	from c1957

L&NWR practice was to carry timber construction down to foundations on sites unsuitable for supporting a mainly brick-built structure. Occasionally, new timber and glazed/slated upper portions have been built on to old brick bases.

The older signals survived until the early 1900s, here and there. Their semaphore arms operated in a slotted upper portion of the post, sometimes with the spectacles and lamps lower down the post and often, at wayside blockposts, with an arm for each direction carried by one post. Replacements were of Crewe pattern with sturdy posts and varied configurations, using corrugated steel arms and handsome cast spectacles. Tall posts were a feature on winding routes, sometimes with co-acting (repeating) arms low down the post. There were miniature arms, calling-on arms and slow line rings, the last mentioned being removed rapidly from c1925. Splitting distants were largely eliminated by 1926. Upper quadrant arms came in from January 1928 and the LMS followed the LNER in painting distant arms yellow (with yellow glasses) from about the same time. IB signals replaced the small boxes and their semaphores on the L&C, between 1932 and 1949; they were usually worked from the box in rear, often battery-powered and approach-lit, but continuously lit as public power supplies came within reach. Colour lights replaced isolated distants (those not on the same post as a stop signal) on the difficult Oxenholme-Shap Summit section during 1942-49 and the process was completed on the L&C in 1954. Detonator-placers were early a feature of the small blockposts. Track circuits (TCs) and their corollaries were installed from about 1910 but rapidly extended by the LMS. The automatic warning system (AWS) was installed rapidly, around 1960-61.

TCs are now installed throughout the section, along with colour-light signals and motor points, associated with illuminated diagrams and route-setting, in the two power boxes.

Preston and its immediate approaches

Signalboxes — 1928

(1) Boxes directly controlling and closely affecting the West Coast Main Line (WCML) through Preston, all then being ex-L&NWR structures. The names/numbers accorded to the boxes are in some cases from a slightly later period. Where station platform numbers are quoted in this schedule, they are from the period 1903-73. Types of boxes follow the author's key, *ante*. 'BP' signifies block-post. Suffix 'PB' indicates functions passed to central power box on date stated.

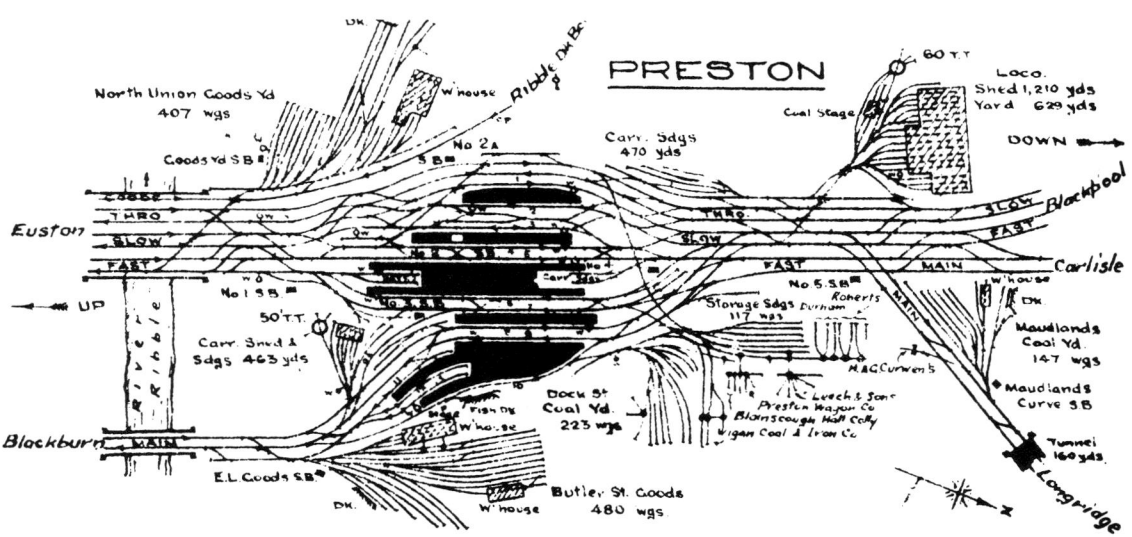

Miles/yards	Name/No	Location and type	Functions	Historical
	Farington Curve Junction	Between fast and slow lines, close against high overline bridge. L&NWR 'C'	BP, also controlled junction on west between L&YR routes from Liverpool/ E Lancs and slow lines.	Junction dates from 1/7/1891 but access from EL since 25/5/1908. Box closed 6/11/1972*PB. Layout little changed
763	Skew Bridge	Down side of cutting. L&NWR 'C'	BP, also (at one time) entry/ exit of pair of 'through lines' on west side of Preston layout and entry to single goods road on extreme west.	Layout with seven roads northward dated from opening of 1900-02 bridge. Box closed 5/2/1973*PB. See 1973-74 diagram for present usage of tracks.
1,069	Ribble Sidings	Up side of all WCML tracks. L&NWR 'C'	BP: Seven roads over bridge (down goods line leads to NU goods yard and docks branch); controlled access to Ribble Sidings on down side WCML.	Box replaced one of 1880 in course of the new works of 1900-02. This box replaced in 1949-50 by LMS 'E' type box 170yd south. Box closed 5/2/1973*PB.

The crossing of the Ribble follows: two roads originally ; three more downstream from 1880; two more, extreme downstream (west) side in 1900-02 widening

Miles/yards	Name/No	Location and type	Functions	Historical
581	Preston No 1	Up side of all WCML tracks, immediately south of station. L&NWR 'C', long and tall	BP controlling main lines at south end of station.	Replaced shorter box immediately to its south in 1900-02 works. Box closed 5/2/1973*PB.
—	Preston No 1A ('Goods Yard')	Down side, just south of watertower and opposite No 1. L&NWR 'C', with projecting operating floor	Controlling adjoining NU Yard (Christian Road); also BP for electric train staff to Strand Road on branch.	Box closed 5/2/1973*PB.
—	Preston No 3	Up side of NU layout inside station and south of plat 7, with access from 7 to EL lines passing to east of it. Partly under station roof. L&NWR 'C'	Local movements.	Box closed 13/3/1972*PB.
—	Preston No 2 ('Station Box')	Overhead box on narrow island plat 3-4 (1-2 from 1973), towards south end but within NU station.	BP, controlling main lines including scissors in centre of station but could switch out to allow working from No 1 to No 4 box.	Box closed 16/1/1961*.
—	Preston No 2A ('Preston Goods', alt: 'Preston Goods Lines')	On gantry over dock branch cutting, to west of the pair of 'through lines'. L&NWR 'C'	BP, controlling 'through lines' on west of layout. Could be switched out to allow working from No 1 box to No 4.	Box closed 17/5/1971*.
378 (from No 1)	Preston No 4 ('Dock Street', alt: 'Dock Street Jn')	Between down and up fast lines just north of station, sleeping car dock and Fishergate overline bridge. L&NWR 'C', long and low	BP, controlling main lines, both NU and EL, at north end of station, also access to Corporation St/Dock St coal yards to north east of station.	Direct lead from down 'through' to Corporation St across entire layout was taken out c1955, after which no access to yard from line west of old plat 6 road. Box closed 5/2/1973*PB.
389	Preston No 5 ('Maudlands Junction')	Up side, north of station and just south of Longridge branch junction with slow lines. L&NWR 'C'	BP, controlling crossovers in main lines, Longridge junction and divergence of Fylde and L&C routes.	Box closed 5/2/1973*PB.

Continued overleaf

(2) Other signalboxes, in the immediate Preston area, in 1928, on lines with joint L&NWR and L&YR characteristics.

Name	Location
Maudland Viaduct	Down side of the four tracks of the Fylde (Preston and Wyre) route. Box closed *5/2/1973 PB
Maudlands Curve	Down side of Longridge (Preston and Longridge) branch, by canal, where Maudland goods station lines trail in. Box closed 1965 (following fire damage, wef 17/5/1965, a temporary cabin existed for a time).
Deepdale Junction	Down side of Longridge (Preston and Longridge) branch, east of tunnel, where Deepdale yard line trails in.
Strand Road	At the level crossing on the Preston Docks branch, working with electric staff from Preston No 1A and westward into Ribble Navigation (Preston Corporation) territory.

(3) Signalboxes in the immediate Preston area on the former L&YR (ELR) lines.

Name	Location
East Lancashire Goods Yard	On the east of the EL line, where the lines from the EL side of Preston station converged with those from Butler Street goods station before crossing the L&YR Ribble bridge.

Others on lines south of the Ribble.

The Ribble Bridges at Preston

The former North Union Railway — WCML — approaches Preston station from the south over an embankment, then by the actual bridges which complete the crossing of the broad valley of the Ribble, close to its estuary. From the railway, the seven lines of way provide an integrated layout but in fact there are three bridges, side by side, located between MP21$\frac{1}{4}$ and MP21$\frac{1}{2}$:

(1) Original bridge, being the upstream portion today — masonry abutments and piers (three in the river bed) supporting five elliptical masonry arches, each of 120ft span — built 1835-38 and opened October 1838. This bridge has always carried two roads, being from 1880 the up and down fast lines, in fact bi-directional since 1973.

(2) Second bridge, the central portion today, of generally similar construction and dimensions, being effectively a widening on its downstream side of the 1838 bridge, in order to carry three additional roads — built 1877-79 and fully opened August 1880. The tracks were up and down slow (both bi-directional since 1973) and up 'through' (known as 'up goods' since 1973).

(3) Third bridge, being the downstream structure and more readily distinguished. Its construction is on sandstone abutments and piers but the one pier in the river bed carries hollow steel columns to support the spans. The latter are of steel lattice girders, and floorplates, with inner girders in five spans, face girders in three spans; the two main spans are over the river, each 275ft, and the subsidiary northern span, on land, is 120ft. The construction of this bridge was announced in November 1895,

authorised by Act of July 1896 — which also embraced widening works through the station. The lines over the bridge were brought into use in July 1900, but associated layouts, platforms and resignalling followed; completion around 1902, with full opening in 1903, ensued. The tracks carried were 'down through' (known as 'down goods' since 1973) and a single goods line, known by 1955 as the 'shunting line', available for up and down movements between Ribble Yard Ground Frame and 1A box, connecting then as now to the NU yard and the docks branch.

Downstream, the L&YR's West Lancashire Railway used a bridge which went out of use by normal passenger trains in 1900 and carried modest goods traffic until 1965.

The L&YR's East Lancashire Railway approach to Preston was over the EL bridge of 1850, just under a quarter mile upstream of the NU bridges. The use of the EL bridge and approach was run down progressively; the Southport passenger service ceased in 1964 with severing of the former WLR route, the Liverpool Exchange express route to Preston was virtually cut at Ormskirk in 1970; in 1968 local passenger trains from Colne, Nelson, Burnley and the Copy Pit line from Yorkshire were diverted to approach Preston by Farington Curve Junction and the NU route. Butler Street goods station closed in November 1971 and the ensuing remodelling completed the process, in May 1972.

The Main Line Passenger Station at Preston — down to 1970

The passenger station as we know it today had its origins in the highly inadequate NU station, with buildings soon established on the west side, and the EL station alongside to eastward, with its buildings on the east side. The NU and EL tracks converged in the tunnel to the north of the stations. The tunnel was crossed at its northern end by Fishergate. Major reconstruction was carried out during 1877-80, with partial use in September 1879 and full use in July 1880. This date corresponds with the second NU Ribble bridge and with most of the signalboxes in use in the 1920s (schedule, *ante*) and indeed until 1973. Central to the station of 1880 was the broad main island platform, 1,225ft long, with the long range of buildings upon it, having a small bay at its north end and two longer bays at the south. This is the platform so well known from 1903 to 1973 as Nos 5 (down side) and 6 (up side) and now as 3 and 4. Refreshment and dining rooms were here, and accommodation for operating staff. The Post Office sorting was above the catering facilities and is now in the southern end of the block, reconstructed as Preston remains a focal point for mails and a principal call for the West Coast postal special trains. A short wooden island platform to the west was replaced in 1888 by a more permanent one, still rather narrow and windswept, namely 3-4 in 1903 and nowadays 1-2. The platforms to eastward of the main island were essentially those of the L&YR (EL, or 'Butler Street') portion of the station. The L&YR absorbed the EL in 1859 but the old name still survives in the 1980s.

Immediately north of Fishergate overline bridge, widening was effected, westward of the original viaduct, in order to carry northward to the Fylde line's divergence the improvements made to the bridges and station. As a result, from May 1882, there were five running roads on the curve north of the station to the vicinity of No 5 (Maudlands Junction) box and four roads past the engine shed, one pair for the Fylde (to which widening was extended in 1889) and the other pair for trains bound for the L&C route. Just as the Bill (Act of 20 July 1896) for the third stage bridge and station enlargements was awaiting Royal Assent, disaster struck early on 13 July 1896. The first portion of the 8.00pm (12 July) down Highland express from Euston ran from Crewe with 2-4-0 'Jumbos' No 2159 *Shark* piloting No 275 *Vulcan*; there were nine (alternatively quoted as eight) vehicles, mostly eight-wheelers of presumably the non-bogie type, including four sleeping carriages. The schedule was 112min non-stop from Wigan to Carlisle, a creditable timing until the diesel and electric days. The nominal speed limit round Preston curve, of 13 chains radius with a small portion of seven chains, was 10mph. This limit was commonly interpreted liberally but on this occasion there was serious misjudgement and it was greatly exceeded, followed by a disastrous derailment. The occurrence gave impetus to plans for fresh improvements north of the station. Land and property were purchased from Fishergate northward on the west side. Included was a tram depot, which had opened on to Fishergate, and the works finally obliterated Dock Street, which was originally crossed transversely by the L&C of 1846 : note 'Dock Street signalbox' (No 4) and 'Dock Street coal yard', near the canal basins or dock. Around 1900, the acquired lands on the west of the

railway were reclaimed, right up to Pitt Street, with retaining wall, piling, filling and construction of 'Dock Street viaduct' (bridge No 3 of the L&C section). The Lancashire County Council buildings today occupy the opposite side of Pitt Street and overlook the twice widened formation — where six roads were achieved on the somewhat-realigned curve and these ran directly to the four roads for the Fylde and two for Lancaster. The date of completion over Dock Street viaduct and the reclaimed ground is a little obscure but thought to be in 1903-04. There were adjustments of layout here in the 1970-73 remodelling.

Reverting to the station itself, the combined improvements which took shape in 1900-03 involved the provision of a new island platform, 1 and 2, with yellow brick buildings implying L&YR influence, first brought into regular use in summer 1903 and providing for, primarily, those L&YR Manchester-Blackpool trains which called at Preston. This platform was lost to the passenger station in the 1973 version and given over to parcels and mails, with also more restricted rail access. The 'through lines' were provided west of these new platform roads in the 1900 works; in substitution, a pair of 'goods lines' between the 'yellow brick island' and the surviving passenger platforms have been contrived (1973). The changes of 1903 gave a station with islands, west to east. Nos 1-2 (mainly for L&YR Manchester-Fylde coast trains), 3-4 (chiefly for L&NWR secondary services and portions of combining trains), 5-6 (principal WCML trains), 7-8 (moving into L&YR/EL territory and 9 (just inside the 'EL' easterly wall). Platform 7 gave access south alternatively to NU or EL bridges. In c1880 the L&NWR had erected a Francophile booking hall on a high level facing the Fishergate approach, in use today. The L&YR much later, in the decade before 1914, built a separate high level hall for the EL side, in yellow brick and gilt lettering. No 10 platform was added outside the EL wall of the station, a through platform line, and appeared on a plan of 1926 but was taken out of use in c8/1967. Scissors crossovers on each side of the main island improved flexibility of working and the pilot engine which stood at the south end was in instant readiness to deal with combining of trains or movement of stock in the station of 1903-73. The down side crossovers (between 4 and 5 platform roads) were removed c1961.

The Park Hotel, Preston

The railway hotel was a joint venture of the L&NWR and L&YR, a handsome building on a superb site — the cliff to east of the NU approach lines, overlooking the Ribble valley and with convenient access to the main island by an oblique footbridge across the tracks. The hotel opened in autumn 1882 but it passed out of railway use in World War 2. Reconstruction was considered in 1945 but it was sold to the County Council for £85,000, finalised in September 1950, and it is used for offices. This is a shame, as it could be an asset to Preston, an important county, commercial and industrial town which does not appear to be blessed with a single presentable hotel in its centre.

Preston Passenger Station Today

A major remodelling of the railway layout at Preston was planned during 1969-70 and took place in 10 stages between July 1970 and May 1972, the power box taking over signalling, by colour-light signals, in February 1973 to replace nine boxes and two shunting frames; 805 levers were superseded. During the interim stages, the number of points worked by the mechanical boxes had been brought down from 201 to 94, in readiness for the take-over. The passenger platforms were reduced from a nominal 13 to six; the islands 3-4, 5-6 (main) and 7-8 are the ones retained, renumbered respectively 1-2, 3-4 and 5-6. With the EL bridge closed and some local services discontinued over a period of many years, much of the remodelling is logical. It was, however, visualised in 1969-70 that the express train services would be electrically hauled through Preston, without the need to combine or detach portions or to change engines. This was a 'counsel of perfection', which from the very first day in May 1974 has never been approached. The practice has been both to combine/divide trains *and* to change engines. The reasons have been mainly economic, predominantly failure to electrify between Manchester and the north, either by the straight and simple route via Parkside or the devious and complicated one via Bolton and Chorley. In consequence, since electrification of the Preston-Carlisle-Glasgow route in 1974, Manchester-Scotland trains have commonly been held for 15-25 minutes while the manoeuvres at Preston are carried out. Oh for the return of that lively station pilot engine which did duty for 70 years, or even its predecessors back to the opening of the Lancaster and Carlisle Railway!

Preston Docks Branch

The branch leaves the WCML on the down (western) side of Preston station and — largely descending at 1 in 29, or thereabouts, is a single line, formerly under the control of 1A and Strand Road boxes. It originated in 1846 as a NU route to convey coals from Wigan pits to quays on the Ribble, for shipment. The construction of Albert Edward Dock of Ribble Navigation, property of Preston Corporation, came later, contemporary with that of the Manchester Ship Canal. Opening of the dock was in July 1892 and the branch line was adapted to give access to the private lines on the dock estate. In 1898, the Railway Clearing house showed:

NU goods line, 14 chains	NU signifying
NU and Preston Corporation	joint property of
Joint, 39 chains	L&NWR and L&YR
Remainder of branch —	
Corporation property	

The Corporation dock closed in October 1981 and plans are being formulated for redevelopment of the dock estate. However, an oil terminal is retained, this being for storage, and distribution by road; accordingly, in 1981, two company trains are worked on most days, one direct from Stanlow and the other from Lindsey (Lincolnshire) via Copy Pit and the EL line to Farington Curve Junc-

tion, with corresponding empty tanks out via the docks branch. The branch is not electrified, so diesel locomotive haulage applies. The operating arrangements at Strand Road are being simplified, 1981-82.

Corporation Street/Dock Street coal yards

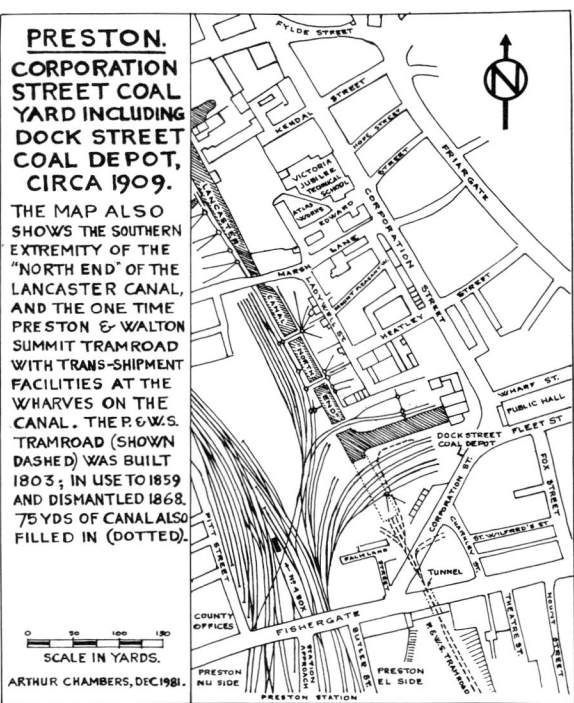

PRESTON. CORPORATION STREET COAL YARD INCLUDING DOCK STREET COAL DEPOT, CIRCA 1909. THE MAP ALSO SHOWS THE SOUTHERN EXTREMITY OF THE "NORTH END" OF THE LANCASTER CANAL, AND THE ONE TIME PRESTON & WALTON SUMMIT TRAMROAD WITH TRANS-SHIPMENT FACILITIES AT THE WHARVES ON THE CANAL. THE P.&W.S. TRAMROAD (SHOWN DASHED) WAS BUILT 1803; IN USE TO 1859 AND DISMANTLED 1868. 75 YDS OF CANAL ALSO FILLED IN (DOTTED). SCALE IN YARDS. ARTHUR CHAMBERS, DEC 1981.

A diagram is presented of these yards, as they were, on a site north-east of Preston station and Fishergate. It shows how they were intimately related to the southern basins of the Lancaster Canal. Coals from Wigan pits were initially brought north by craft on the Leeds and Liverpool Canal but the relevant branch of that canal never crossed the broad Ribble valley. There was transhipment to tramroad wagons for the final stage of the journey to Preston, culminating in an ascending route not far from the Park Hotel site, then skirting the EL's Butler Street depot, tunnelling under Fishergate and so reaching the Lancaster Canal's basin, from which onward shipment could be made. It is understood that traffic by the tramroad ceased in 1859, possibly as late as 1862. Its cessation was probably due to competition as the pits progressively developed their own railway systems and links with the L&NWR. Thus developed coal traffic from Bamfurlong Sidings to Ribble Sidings, Preston, whence it was 'tripped' to (inter alia) the Corporation Street/Dock Street coal yards. Coal was then distributed locally and some transferred to canal craft and sent north, competing with the L&NWR's own through coal trains from the Wigan area to as far afield as Kendal; the gas works at Kendal received coal by canal until September 1944, after which a little commercial traffic by a canal continued as far as Lancaster until 1947. Corporation Street/Dock Street closed as a coal depot from 11 November 1968 and the layout was simplified during the staged remodelling of 1970-72; odd vehicles such as a saloon are stabled here. The Railways' divisional offices and control office (embracing also, from 1981, the Carlisle control area) have been erected virtually on the abandoned canal basins.

Deepdale yard, trailing off the P&L line in Preston's environs, was a goods depot of L&NWR/L&YR but survives as a coal concentration depot, in replacement of the Corporation Street/Dock Street complex. The Longridge line itself closed to passengers from 2 June 1930 and then progressively to freight, culminating in total closure beyond Courtaulds No 2 ground frame wef 16 October 1967, closure of Courtaulds' Red Scar tyrecord factory (opened 1939) in March 1980 and a last working to Ribbleton in August 1980. In September 1981, a stop block was put in to terminate the branch 500yd east of the level crossing at the trail-back to Deepdale depot.

Other goods depots in Preston

References, including various closures, have been recorded for Butler Street L&YR/EL goods, West Lancashire (Fishergate Hill), Corporation Street/Dock Street and Deepdale (individually, *ante*). Greenbank and Oxheys are mentioned in the next section, being on the L&C route northward from Preston. Maudlands, the Preston & Wyre (L&NWR/L&YR) depot, has suffered a painfully slow decline to final closure in July 1981. Since electrification, Ribble Sidings have nominally been partially closed; typically, in 1981, they have been rusty and devoid of wagons. This leaves for mention NU yard (Christian Road), beside the passenger station; its functions are very limited indeed.

Engine sheds of Preston

These are discussed later, along with others serving the Lancaster and Carlisle route in the 20th century.

Preston (exc)-Garstang-Scorton (inc)

Signalboxes — 1928

Miles/yards	Name	Location and type	Functions	Historical
844 (from Preston No 5, in 1928)	Greenbank Siding (becoming Greenbank Sidings)	Down side, south of Aqueduct Street underline bridge. L&NWR 'C', with timber lower panels	BP and access to Greenbank yard on up side; also up and down slow lines northward, opened 1901-03	Replaced box on up side, central to sidings connections, in 1902. Box closed 10/2/1969.
744	Oxheys	Down side, north of Addison Road overline bridge. L&NWR 'D'	BP on fast and slow. Access to Oxheys cattle sidings (up) and Turner's coal sidings (southward, on up side). Later controlled Thorney Brook down IB signals.	Replaced box 40yd south on same side, 12/8/1923 to permit new overline bridge. That previous box was new 7/1903 to replace box on up side. Box closed 5/2/1973*PB.
1,732 (from 1903 site of Oxheys)	*Thorney Brook.*	*Down side, on south bank of Sharoe Brook.*	*BP on fast and slow.*	*Replaced previous box in 1902, owing to widening, but 'closed at present' by 1906 and demolished by 1910. Later: replaced by up and down IB signals.*
3/428 (from Oxheys in 1928)	Barton & Broughton	Up side, well south of station and overline bridge. L&NWR 'C'	BP controlling northern extremity of up and down slow lines, which opened 28/6/1903; also a down loop and up sidings. Later controlled Thorney Brook up IB signals.	Replaced box on same side but farther north, near Carter Lane overline bridge, in 1902. The siding and short loop on up completed 1907. Box closed 20/11/1972*PB.
2/1547	Brock	Up side, immediately north of station and the then level crossing. L&NWR 'D'	BP and protection of level crossing and station, also controlled siding down side to north of station and crossing.	Replaced (in 1917-18) early box, type 'A', which was on down side at north end of station. Box closed as block post 20/11/1972*PB but retained to control level crossing until crossing abolished on 14/2/1976.

Continued overleaf

Miles/Yards	Name	Location and type	Functions	Historical
1/1681	Garstang & Catterall	Up side, south of station. Lengthy box, L&NWR type 'C'	BP with up and down refuge sidings and down divergence to G&KER line, small yard on down. Latterly: Scorton south and north down IB signals.	See notes which follow. Box closed 20/11/1972*PB.
3/428	Scorton	Down side, south of station. No siding or crossover: four levers only.		Replaced box on down platform in early 20th century. Box closed 11/12/1932 and demolished by 8/1933. Replaced by IB signals (two sets each way by 1960).

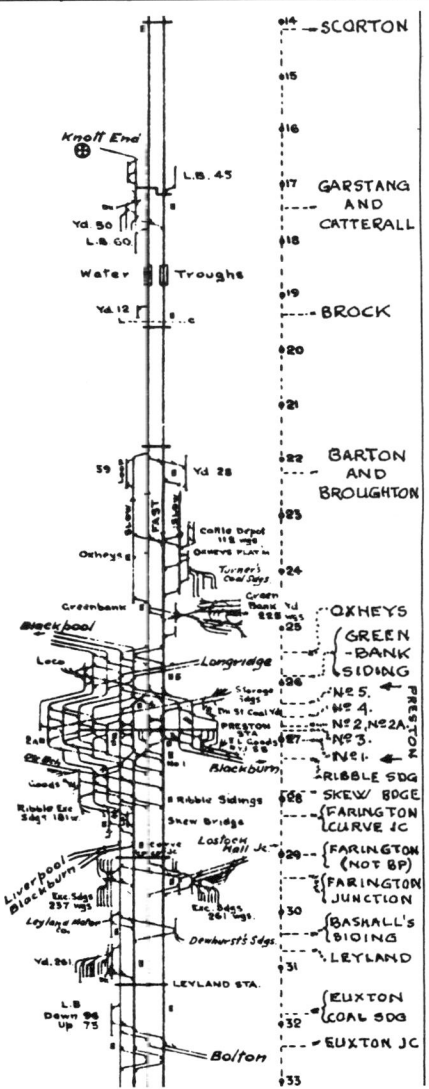

While reproducing the LMS line diagram of 1928 photographically in this and subsequent Figs, the titling to its right has been re-stated, for clarity.

Other features, in sequence, northward of Preston No 5 box, include:

dn — *Preston L&NWR engine shed*, site of.

dn — *Fylde lines* bear left, westward.

dn — *St Walburge's church*, with magnificent 303ft tall spire (and stone sleepers from the L&PJR in the lower portion of its tower), commands the junction.

up — *(concurrent with above):*
Maudlands Curve to former Preston & Longridge line, opened 1/6/1885.
Maudlands goods station, P&WR (L&NWR/L&YR) became progressively derelict and finally closed 7/1981.
Crossings on level over L&C/WCML by two tracks of P&WR and one of Maudlands Railway abandoned when the Maudlands Curve opened in 1885.

north of overline bridge (Pedder Street):

up — *Prominent Fylde Road cotton mill*, demolition commenced 1981.

beneath line — abandoned course of *Lancaster Canal* (Preston Corporation Street/Dock Street basins to Kendal). Navigation now starts at Ashton basin on NW side of Preston and extends to Tewitfield, NE of Carnforth.

up — *Greenbank Sidings*, site of the 'Greenbank Railway', believed first installed 1881 as private enterprise estate where the 'Railway' (directed successively by its agent, wharf master, manager) provided sidings, cranes and probably storage, for various coal merchants and others, eg Joseph Foster & Sons of Soho Foundry, adjoining. The 'Railway' employed two four-wheeled saddle tank locomotives. L&NWR took over 1/11/1906. Directories still showed 'Greenbank Branch Railway' in 1910 but by 1913 entry was 'L&NWRly, Greenbank branch'. A small locomotive was always kept at Preston by L&NWR/LMS/BR until site closed 1/2/1966. Site partially redeveloped in recent years.

MP1 up — *Aqueduct Mill*. Southern extremity of up slow line from Barton & Broughton was here, before curtailment.

up — *Turner's Sidings* (coal) were connected by an up independent line — subsidiary to Oxheys layout.

16

up — *Oxheys* had a wooden passenger platform on up slow: two up trains called around 8.00 in morning to set down on days when the cattle market was operating, practice ceasing early in 1925. In the 1890s two early passenger trains from Preston had called, implying a platform on down side in those days.

up — *Oxheys Livestock sidings*, closed 9/9/1968 — remains of the cattle docks clearly visible.

1¼+dn — *Oxheys box* was (from 1923) just north of the major overline bridge built 1924, carrying ring road (Blackpool road, A5085).

Up loop, as curtailed since 1969, converges here.

The additional down road (slow line) from Greenbank Siding box, via Oxheys, to Thorney Brook box was opened 30/7/1901 and onwards to Barton & Broughton opened 20/7/1902. The whole of the additional up slow line from Barton & Broughton to Greenbank Siding opened 28/6/1903, minuted as date of completion of widening, although the formal L&NWR-Board of Trade report on completion of the widening was not made until 3/1906. Additional siding works at Barton & Broughton were installed in 1907. In 1969 (by the end of August), the slow lines of 1903 were much curtailed, namely:

(a) up loop, entered at a point a few yards north of MP 2¼ in the outer suburbs of Preston (by motor points, worked from Oxheys box), with southern exit opposite Oxheys box, having mechanical points;

(b) down loop, entered northward of the up loop, at a point just south of Crow Hall bridge (MP4), by motor points worked from Barton & Broughton, with exit at its original northern extremity, having mechanical points worked from the nearby Barton & Broughton box.

The loops remain in this form, but controlled since 1972-73 by Preston power box.

3+ — *Lightfoot Green overline bridge*, built 1973, carrying motorway M55, connecting M6 with the Fylde.

3¾+ — *Pipe-bridges* carrying water mains across the line, these spans constructed 1926 and 1963 for the then Fylde Water Board.

dn — *curtailed down loop commences, converging short of:*

4¾+ *Barton & Broughton station*, closed (P) 1/5/1939. Early stone station buildings (down), with interesting houses immediately west of them.

4¼+ — *Barton viaduct*, three brick and stone arches, carries line over Barton brook.

5¾+ — *White Horse tunnel*, A6 road carried over the line.

7½ — *Brock station*, closed (P) 1/5/1939, preceded on up by:

Parlick Terrace — four L&NWR brick houses in improved style of c1900.

Old stone station house (up side).

No level crossing survives.

up — *Motorway M6* takes up parallel course.

near MP8 — *Brock water troughs* commenced, with plantation on down side, and ended just beyond *overline bridge*.

This is the first bridge with badger insignia, originally carved in stone, seen by a keen eye on the

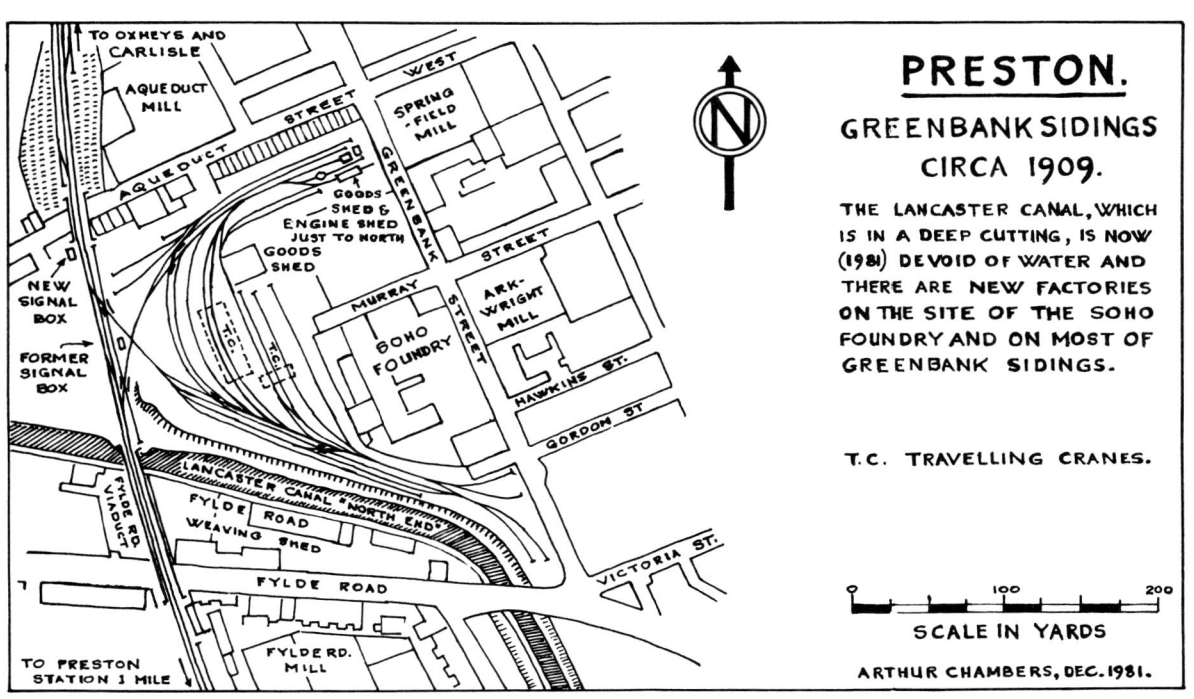

PRESTON.

GREENBANK SIDINGS CIRCA 1909.

THE LANCASTER CANAL, WHICH IS IN A DEEP CUTTING, IS NOW (1981) DEVOID OF WATER AND THERE ARE NEW FACTORIES ON THE SITE OF THE SOHO FOUNDRY AND ON MOST OF GREENBANK SIDINGS.

T.C. TRAVELLING CRANES.

SCALE IN YARDS

ARTHUR CHAMBERS, DEC. 1981.

capitals at carriageway level. Those on the inner faces may be inspected from the road which crosses the line. The badgers are the emblem of the Brockholes family, traditionally of Claughton Hall, nearby to eastward of the L&C line, but with the motorway now intervening. Replica badgers were set into artificial stone on rebuilding of the bridge during pre-electrification works.

8¾+ — *Whim underline bridge*, also with badger stones, best seen from the road (Stubbins Lane). These eight badgers were cast in fibreglass in moulds made from a survivor of the original phosphor-bronze animals.

9½ — *Garstang & Catterall station*, closed (P) 3/2/1969 (having survived the others on the Preston-Lancaster line).
See line diagram for layout and also table of signalboxes, *ante*.
The Garstang & Knott End Railway dated back to 1870, extended and retitled 1908, and its last portion closed in 1965. It had use of the outer face of the down platform and paralleled the main line northward for about a mile — its overbridge arches can be seen — before it headed west to Garstang

Town, where its main facilities were sited, and thence to Pilling and Knott End.
The G&KER was provided with a crossover connecting back into the down main line 1,520 yards north of Garstang box, wef 20/9/1942, so producing a lengthy down loop, with outlet through spring points.
The creamery, seen on up side north of station (site) was given access to former up siding. All buildings and layouts have been swept away, the main station building (up side) being demolished 1971—72.
The Kenlis Arms Hotel (up side, below) survives the destruction, also (immediately north of hotel) two blocks of L&NWR brick houses.

11+**up** — *Woodacre railway cottages* vanished and Woodacre Great Wood much reduced — motorway is very close.

12½+ — *Scorton station*, closed (P) 1/5/1939, had no sidings, timber platforms, house (gone by 1910) on up side — all swept away. Site is on embankment, followed by underline bridge. Motorway has borne away north-east, to skirt Scorton village and its attractive church.

Scorton (exc)-Lancaster Castle-Carnforth (exc)

Signalboxes — 1923

Miles/yards	Name	Location and type	Functions	Historical
2/898 (from Scorton in 1928)	Bay Horse	Up side, south of station. L&NWR 'A'	BP, with small goods yard on down, cattle on up. Latterly also Galgate down IB, Scorton North and South up IB signals.	Box closed 27/11/1972*PB.
—	*Galgate*	*In 1890, down side, about 120ft south of station, but replaced about that time by box of L&NWR type 'B' on down platform about 25ft south of buildings.*	*BP until c1890 (alt: 1903) but the replacement box only contained frame for minimum signals for limited protection in emergencies.*	*In 1905, listed as blockpost 'closed at present'. By 1906, listed as 'Galgate Booking Office'. Signals survived to 1910 or rather later. Up and down IB signals later installed.*
2/1429 (from Bay Horse, in 1928)	Oubeck	Up side, central to loops (about 250yd south of earlier box). L&NWR 'D'	BP, controlling up and down loops, mechanically. Latterly also Galgate up IB signals.	Replaced box with four working levers, which was on up side south of the overline bridge, in 1925-6. Box closed 27/11/1972*PB.
1/1696	Lancaster No 1 (form: Lancaster Old Junction)	Down side, just north of junction of old line and L&C line. L&NWR 'D'	BP, controlled divergence to Lancaster Old branch, also from branch to engine shed. Latterly also up IB signal in advance.	Replaced previous box (on up side at actual jn) in 1905. Shed closed 1934 and branch closed 14/8/1967 but retained as engineers' depot siding until late 1969. Box closed 8/1/1973*PB.
1347	Lancaster No 2	Down side, well south of station. L&NWR 'D'	BP, also goods loops (permissive), up and down, onwards to No 3; access to up sidings and down goods depot.	Replaced earlier box on nearly same site, in 1913. Box closed 8/1/1973*PB.

Miles/Yards	Name	Location and type	Functions	Historical
338	Lancaster No 3	South of station, between up and down fast lines. L&NWR 'C', long box	BP, controlling all running lines at south end of station.	Replaced earlier and smaller box (on up side), in 1902, in consequence of station re-modelling (three through roads became six). Box closed 8/1/1973*PB.
525	Lancaster No 4	Down side, well north of station and just north of divergence of branch to Glasson Dock/Lancaster Quay. L&NWR 'C' — tall and long box, with two men each shift (excl Sundays)	BP, controlling all running lines at north end of station, also jns to Glasson/Quay and MR Green Ayre branches also access to station bays; worked down IB *semaphore* signal 1,222yd in advance of down starter.	Concurrent with station re-modelling, it replaced, in 1901, a rather smaller box, also down side but just south of Glasson junction. Most of Glasson branch closed 7/9/1964 remainder removed in 1971. Box closed 8/1/1973*PB.
			There was a siding frame in NE embankment; the Green Ayre branch taken out of use, on 17/3/1976 and lifted by mid-1977.	
—	Lune Bridge	*Believed just north of bridge over river.*	*Early BP, with six levers.*	*Functions taken over by Lancaster No 4 by 1906 — note the down IB semaphore, ante.*
1/1302 (dubious mileage) from No 4 in 1928.	Morecambe South Junction	Down side, at junction of Morecambe line. L&NWR 'C'	BP, controlling junction. River Lune up IB *semaphore* signal (and distant for Lancaster No 4 below it) replaced wef 8/5/1960 by four aspect colour light signal.	Junction and box dated from 1888. Box closed 8/1/1973*PB.
1/232	Hest Bank	Up side, just south of station plat. L&NWR 'C' The 1958 box had 30 levers until the 1973 resignalling. From 12/1977 it has had TV coverage of Bolton-le-Sands crossing.	BP, with oversight of crossing and control of down bay and siding; also control of branch line to Bare Lane: in early 20th century by staff and ticket, later by L&NWR electric staff, later again by elec token; from 27/2/67* by direction levers and interlocked block, with track circuits throughout branch. Down IBS controlled.	Box replaced wef 22/12/1958 by new box on down side north of stn and crossing BR 'F', with reversed frame, 10 levers and gate wheel (better sited for control of gates). Box closed as BP 8/1/1973*PB, but retained as gate box, with signalman in charge.
1/591	Bolton-le-Sands	*Up side, just south of station and crossing. L&NWR 'B'*	*BP at one time but after 1888 entries were 'closed at present', ceasing by 1910.*	*Building survived in 1910. Distant signals retained, worked by platform levers — instruments in office, to provide some protection to crossing — but sigs replaced by IBS 9/5/1937.*

Other features, in sequence, northward of Scorton, include:

MP13+ — *Wyre viaduct*, 262ft long, with six semi-elliptical brick arches (sandstone clad), five of 30ft and one of 20ft span, carrying the railway over the river Wyre and a road; arches strengthened, 1927 and later.

15¼+ — *Bay Horse station*, closed (P) 13/6/1960. Station had a passenger subway. Structures all swept away but L&NWR brick house adjoining former up platform survives.

16+ — *Major overline bridge* of three spans, built 1961, carries motorway link road M6-A6 over the line.

16½+ — *Galgate station*, closed (P) 1/5/1939. Station had no crossover or sidings; there was a shelter on up side and substantial two-storey stone buildings on down, these last surviving to immediately pre-electrification, but since disappeared.

dn — Galgate basin on Lancaster Canal glimpsed beyond A6 road; branch canal to Glasson Dock and sea leaves Preston-Kendal waterway just south of basin and proceeds by descending locks.

16¾+ — *Galgate bridge*, lofty, in stone with skew brick arch, carries line over A6 road — village below on up side.

Conder viaduct, 265ft long, built in stone with six

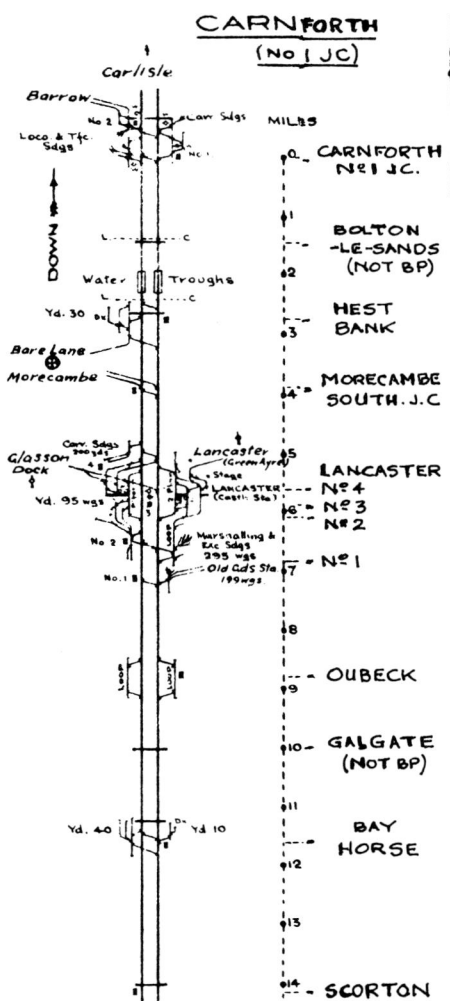

CARNFORTH
(No 1 JC)

↑ Carlisle

Barrow →
Loco & Tfc Sdgs

MILES

CARNFORTH
No 1 JC.

0

BOLTON
-LE-SANDS
(NOT BP)

1

Water Troughs

2

Yd. 30

HEST
BANK

3

Bare Lane
Morecambe

MORECAMBE
SOUTH. J.C

4

Glasson
Dock

Lancaster
(Green Ayre)
Stage
LANCASTER
(Castle Sta)

LANCASTER
No 4
No 3
No 2

5

6

Yd. 95 wgs

Marshalling &
Exc Sdgs
295 wgs
Old Gds Sta
199 wgs

No 1

7

8

OUBECK

9

GALGATE
(NOT BP)

10

11

Yd. 40   Yd 10

BAY
HORSE

12

13

SCORTON

14

---

brick arches of 30ft span and sandstone clad — carries line over the River Conder and the road westward to Glasson.

17¾+ — *Oubeck loops*, up and down — installed 1925-26.

up — *Bailrigg estate*, with Lancaster University, seen beyond A6 road.

up — *Oubeck House*, beside line, after overline bridge.

up — *Scotforth filter house* of Lancaster Corporation/ North West Water Authority, built 1913 and extended progressively between 1920 and 1971, is sited between WCML and A6 road; it often figured on lineside photographs of the 1920s.

19¾+dn — *Royal Albert mental hospital* in wooded grounds above the line.

dn — *Lancaster Old Junction*, site of No 1 box, slack over left hand curve.

up — *Course of the 'Old Line'* to Lancaster Old station,

closed (G) 14/8/1967 and finally in 1969, and abandoned, is seen descending on straight alignment.

up — *Engine shed and turntable* were between Old and L&C lines.

20+ — *Lancaster & Preston Junction Railway mileposts* were extended on L&C as far as Lancaster Castle station.

Ashton Road overline bridge (A588) is immediately followed (up) by prominent buildings and chapel of Ripley Hospital (an endowed school of 1864), now Ripley St Thomas Church of England School, with the school grounds to its north, beside the line.

20¼+ — *Lancaster Canal* (with Preston westward and Kendal eastward on the canal at this point) and Aldcliffe Road crossed by two-span bridge on stone piers.

20½+up — *Lancaster Castle sidings*. Very limited layout survives, and the restricted wagon-load freight facility (retained on closing Lancaster for general goods from 3/1/1972) was withdrawn wef 3/8/1981. In c1900, the layout here was extended to provide a bank of eight roads, plus accommodation for cattle traffic. Now, car-parking occupies a derelict area of the former layout.

dn — Yard is lifted, it was always restricted. Now car park.

Meeting House Lane overline bridge, six varied spans carry the road over the railway at entry to Castle station.

21/zero — *Lancaster Castle passenger station* (strictly: 'Lancaster' since 5/1969).

The main L&C station building of 1846 was on the down side — a symmetrical twin-gabled erection, with entrance from the carriageway on that side through three arches between the gabled wings, all in stone, with mullioned windows and leaded lights. Its style was akin to an Elizabethan manor house and is seen in the well-known contemporary print from the *Illustrated London News* and as a focal feature today. It is best viewed from *outside* the premises, on the down side. The first floor room under the northerly gable extends from front to back and has a handsome 'bulkhead ceiling' supported on timber trusses springing from the side walls. It is likely to have been the boardroom of the Lancaster and Carlisle Railway Company. Incidentally, when the lights are on in this room, a good impression of the ceiling structure can be obtained from a position on the up island platform. This 1846 building, and other original stations on the L&C, were designed by Sir William Tite, architect to the Company and distinguished in his profession.

Lancaster was the headquarters of the L&C and they commissioned a major extension, which extended the original down side building southward, almost to Meeting House Lane bridge. The drawings are signed by architect Thomas Worthington, then of 54 John Dalton Street,

Manchester and dated April-May 1858. The fine tower ('turret') with internal spiral stone stair is part of this extension, which included spacious and dignified offices for the engineer and locomotive superintendent and their respective staffs; these apartments were in grand manorial style. One may note that Thomas Worthington & Sons, with many public buildings to their credit, are the architects for the current restoration of Liverpool Road station buildings, of 1830, in Manchester.

The extended buildings were no doubt splendid for the offices of the Company and, with internal rearrangements such as those of 1906, retained much of their importance until 1969. A smaller area administrative headquarters of BR remains, with responsibilities extending to the Furness route. However, the facilities for the trains and their passengers were not so grand. The station had one down and one up running road, each with platform. On the down side, at its north end, was a single bay, shared by the Glasson Dock train (introduced 1883) and departures for Morecambe (from 1888, when the L&NWR reached that place directly from the south via Morecambe South Junction). The up platform, with castellated buildings generally in keeping, though less magnificent, had a bay at the north end which was used by arrivals from Morecambe and the modest number of Midland Railway trains which came up from Green Ayre station. Both platforms were very low. A pair of goods lines passed behind the up side station buildings. Patience ran out and in 1896 the Lancaster Borough Council represented to the directors of the L&NWR 'the danger and inconvenience caused to pasengers by reason of the totally inadequate accommodation provided at the Castle Railway Station'. They urged provision of a new and more convenient station at an early date. The Mayor, Town Clerk and colleagues were to follow this up with the general management of the L&NWR. One might note that the entrance to the station, being on the down side, was remote from the town, the greater part of which is to the east of the main line. Incidentally, the L&C bought land for a station hotel — facing the down side buildings across a roadway — in 1847 and the County Hotel was built by the L&NWR on this site in 1863-69 and may still be seen, although sold by the LMS in 1929.

Progress was rapid in the matter of the station. Work on site began in 1898 under Francis Stevenson, engineer of the L&NWR, a principal building contract being placed with Neill & Sons, of Manchester, in March 1899, other contracts following. Much of the work was completed in 1900, while full completion and opening to passengers was at the end of April 1902. The station took very much its present form, with four through roads, the outer ones having platform faces. Long bays were provided at the north on the down side,

for Glasson Dock (outer bay) and Morecambe (inner). The completely new up platform was an island, with a useful outer face for up trains; from about 1978, the signalling of this outer platform road has been made suitable for northbound departures, as well as southbound movements. To the east, a separate outer platform was constructed for the Midland trains. The 1846 and 1858 down side buildings were extended by seemly single-storey stone buildings at their north end, the most northerly being a pleasant refreshment room, now sadly lost as such. A compatible range of buildings was erected on the up island, including staff offices, spacious waiting room and good refreshment room, which happily is well maintained and helpfully run today. The site had to be excavated on the up side and an access road from Meeting House Lane was made on top of the bank, with a new upper level entrance hall and booking office, dated 1900 in its external stonework, this normally being the sole entrance in recent years and opening straight on to the new footbridge. The Furness Railway had running powers, the odd train from Barrow coming in until 1896. After this, they generally accepted Carnforth as their junction. In LMS days, some Furness line trains ran through to Lancaster and this practice has been general since the main line platforms at Carnforth closed in 1970.

A retrograde feature introduced in 1902 with the remodelled station and commented upon at the time was the severe slack for down trains entering the platform road. This is accentuated by the 1972-73 centralised resignalling; approach-controlled colour-light signals slow trains severely even before crossing the canal bridge.

North of Lancaster Castle station:

up — The Castle itself — with Court of Assize and prison — and the Priory Church are prominent on the eminence immediately eastward of the L&C main line.

up — The course of the single line to Green Ayre, where the station and the Morecambe-Wennington route of the MR are also abandoned, and landscaped, diverges to the east, descending, round the castle hill.

dn — The line to Glasson Dock, with its trail-back to Lancaster Quay, and linoleum works connections, is also abandoned (being lifted in spring and early summer 1971), but its course can be detected.

$0\frac{1}{4}+$ — *The Lune viaduct, Lancaster.*

This notable viaduct, popularly known as the 'Carlisle Bridge', has a total of 12 spans. On the south, there are seven arches, each of 32ft 9in span, built in stone with brick in the arches. On the northern shore, beside the river, is a stone arch of 32ft 6in span, over the MR line, which was opened on 12 June 1848 and closed to passengers on 3 January 1966, and totally closed wef 5 June 1967. Immediately north of it is a steel span of 60ft, having abutments of stone, with brick internally;

21

this crosses the Lancaster-Morecambe road A589, its span being increased to the present width for road widening in 1926.

Between the south and north approaches are the three longest spans, which cross the river Lune. Two masonry piers are based in the bed of the river. The three river spans were originally bridged by arches in laminated timber (quoted as each of 120ft span), with timber superstructure. These gave place circa 1866 to spans of wrought iron continuous girders, with (latterly in their life) rail bearers and floorplates of steel. The river crossing was again rebuilt — with trains running, at restricted speed — during late 1962 to 1964. Between 27 January 1963 and 24 March 1963 the up and down tracks were interlaced. The resulting three spans are respectively 127ft, 130ft and 126ft, and each comprises four deep steel girders, in parallel. Outriggers carry a footway, on the upstream (up) side. The securing of the structures for electrification, 1972-73, and their anchoring beneath the spans, was a task in itself.

MP1 — *'Vale Cottage accommodation bridge'* crossed the line immediately north of MP1 and was demolished in 1967; no trace is visible from trains and only on the down side can it be identified from the top of the cutting. It was a favourite vantage point of F. E. Mackay for photographs of down trains, many having been published, and it took the author many years (and some help) to identify the location. 'Vale Cottage' (in the 1840s), later 'The Vale', was a fine old stone-built farm amid meadows, and set off by the parkland surrounding Ryelands House. 'The Vale' is glimpsed in the photographs but now much disguised, being converted to a television warehouse and tightly surrounded by private and municipal housing developments of the 1930s. Even the up distant signal was moved out northward, after the Mackay era, so confusing the issue. See *The Railway Magazine* 1922/2 p435 (etc).

1¾+dn — *Morecambe South Junction* — double track, curving westward to Bare Lane, opened May 1888 (variously 13/5/1888 and 19/5/1888, perhaps postponed to the latter). The Heysham-Belfast nightly sailings were withdrawn wef 7/4/1975; Euston and Manchester connecting boat trains had run this way since 30/4/1928.

An earlier suspension of Lancaster-Morecambe traffic was on 2-3 October 1917. At 10.40pm on 1/10/1917 fire broke out at the Ministry of Munitions shell-filling factory at White Lund, south of the MR Lancaster-Morecambe line. Explosions occurred every few minutes for over eight hours. Disastrous destruction occurred at site. Bare Lane station (approximately 1½ miles away) suffered damage. A shell baseplate, weight 28lbs, was hurled 2¼ miles and landed on the L&C line near South Junction, embedding itself in the ballast.

2½+ — *'Coastal Road' overline bridge*, of two spans, built 1933, carries A5105, a new road of the 1930s from the A6 near Hest Bank to join Morecambe promenade, over the line. It is closely followed by 'Cinderella footbridge', built 1932, and charmingly named after the nearby children's home.

dn — *Bare Lane single track* (for Morecambe trains to and from the north) comes alongside as the WCML reaches the shore of Morecambe Bay. If clear, the vista over the bay extends to the westerly mountains of the Lake district.

3+ — *Hest Bank station*, closed (P/all) 3/2/1969, the down platform being quickly removed, and the single track from Bare Lane was extended over its site late in 1970. The up platform disappeared later. For years, up trains for Morecambe had to run past the box (then on up side, south of platforms) and set back *across down main* to the south-facing bay platform, departing thence for Morecambe. If too long for the bay, they were backed through the slip to the down main, and then left for the Morecambe branch. At last, in July 1934, a facing crossover was installed — certainly helpful in BR days, when 'Duchess' Pacific locomotives were liable to work Glasgow-Morecambe trains on summer Saturdays.

up — L&C station house survives, in blackened stone.

dn — Crossing keeper's house is of early architecture but not readily compatible with L&C style. Does it pre-date the railway? Residents Mr and Mrs Whittaker were respectively of the engineer's department and the last crossing-keeper. It is followed by the level crossing and the box of 1958, surviving (see schedule of signalboxes, *ante*). Camping coaches occupied the outer siding, to seaward of bay, in LMS and also BR days.

Probably unique was the windmill generator which stood on the banking between the railway and the shore, about opposite the earlier signalbox. It was erected experimentally by the LMS in the 1930s, believed to be on the initiative of a member of the station staff. Electric light was provided to the station, 'one-upmanship' in its day. If the wind was too high, the signalman had to cross the line and apply the brake, otherwise the impeller landed on the line. This landmark disappeared by about 1939. The present gate box has a windgauge; if over 65mph is registered, Preston power box staff are informed and drivers are warned to reduce speed, while the CMEE prays that the wires will not to be blown out of line and 'hooked down' by locomotive pantographs.

Hest bank water troughs were on the following straight.

4½ — *Bolton-le-Sands station*, closed (P/all) 3/2/1969.
It never had sidings. See schedule concerning the level crossing (now with lifting barriers) and the box.

up — L&C style twin gabled stone station building survives as a house.
The story is resumed in the approaches to Carnforth.

Carnforth-Oxenholme (both inc)

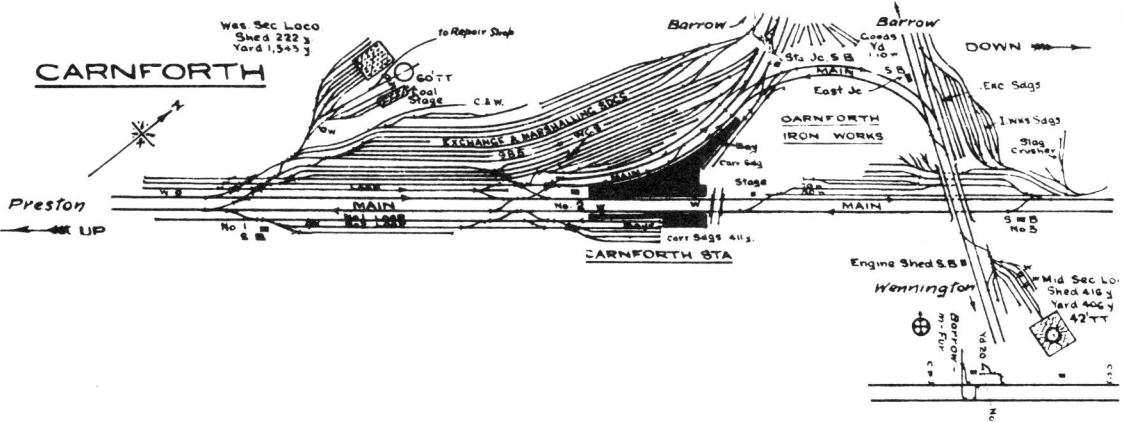

Signalboxes - 1928

Miles/yards	Name	Location and type	Functions	Historical
2/1365 (from Hest Bank in 1928)	Carnforth No 1 Junction	Up side, south of station and loops. L&NWR 'C', tall and lengthy.	BP, including control of south end of up and down loops, and entrance to engine shed. Up IBS controlled (later).	Replaced in 1938 by LMS 'E' type box, located 201ft 6in to its south. Box closed 22/1/1973*PB.
615	Carnforth No 2 Junction	Between down L&C main and Furness passenger line immediately south of station. L&NWR 'C', long and low.	BP on L&C, also on Furness line to Carnforth Station Junction box; and controlling north end of L&C goods loops. Later: entry to dn north loops and Yealand down IB sigs (when No 3 closed).	Replaced in c1938 by LMS 'E' type box, located on up side and 262ft 6in to its south. Box closed 22/1/1973*PB.
943	Carnforth No 3 Ironworks	Up side, just north of MR bridge over L&CR.	BP, and had controlled sidings on down when ironworks operated. Later: down IBS at Yealand controlled.	Opened only in summer by 1938 and 1939. Last regular opening 1939, but controlled two refuge sidings on down, believed in emergency use in 1940-41.
		Replaced 26/10/1941 by Carnforth North Ground Frame (on down side) and box removed. The ground frame was in turn replaced 20/9/1942 on slightly different site and then remained until 23/11/1969; at 20/9/1942, the two down refuge sidings became down loops, entry controlled by No 2 box.		
1/1550	Yealand	Down side, north of Dockacres skew underline bridge and Dale Grove overline bridge. L&NWR 'A' — very small	BP	Box closed 28/6/1943* and replaced by up and down IB signals.
	Burton & Holme	*Up side, north of station, at junction of mill branch, 2/520 from Yealand box.*	*BP, also controlled access to Goodacres Holme Mill long siding, trailing on up.*	*Replaced 1925-26 by Nos 1 and 2 boxes (below).*
2/778 (from Yealand in 1928)	Burton & Holme No 1	Up side, just north of previous box, which it replaced. L&NWR 'D'	BP, controlled south end of new up and down loops, installed 1925-26. Later: also Yealand up IB sigs.	Built 1925-26. Loops taken out of use 28/6/1971*. Box closed 14/5/1973*PB.
1243	Burton & Holme No 2	Down side, 1,243yd north of No 1 box. L&NWR 'D'	BP, controlled midway outlet points from up and down loops, also north end of loops.	Built 1925-26. Loops taken out of use 28/6/1971*. Box closed 28/6/1971*.
	Continued overleaf			

23

Miles/Yards	Name	Location and type	Functions	Historical
1/1252	Milnthorpe	Up side, south end of station. L&NWR 'B' (but unlike other boxes)	BP; controlling gunpowder exchange yard and (later) milk factory sidings (up side), also refuge siding and goods yard on down.	Latterly working down IB signals at Hincaster and Sedgwick. Box closed 14/5/1973*PB.
2/25	Hincaster Junction (nominally 'Hincaster' from 15/2/1964)	Down side, at convergence of FR single line from Arnside. L&NWR 'D'	BP; also controlled to/from Sandside, with electric train staff; and down sidings for gunpowder traffic. Controlled Sedgwick down IB signals from 1933.	Line to/from Sandside opened 26/6/1876 and closed 9/9/1963; junction removed 26/1/1964. Box replaced original one of 1876 in 1914. Box closed 20/3/1967* and replaced by IBs. Box removed by 9/1967.
1/873 (marginally suspect mileage)	Sedgwick	Down side, about 70yd south of underline bridge on lane to village (pair L&NWR cottages on the lane) four working levers.	BP	Shown 'closed at present' in 1913 but open 6.00am to 10.00pm Mon-Sat in 7/1925. Box closed 20/2/1933* and demolished by 8/1933 — replaced by up and down IB signals.
1/1167	Oxenholme No 1 (formerly: South box, No 1)	Down side, immediately north of overline bridge for Kendal-Skipton A65 road. L&NWR 'C', of 1882, tall, with view over bridge.	BP; controlled south end of up and down goods loops; and Sedgwick up IB signals from 1933 and Hincaster up IB signals from 1967.	Box closed 14/5/1973*PB.
644	Oxenholme No 2 (formerly: Yard box, No 2)	Down side, immediately south of overline bridge to south of station. L&NWR 'C' of 1882, tall, with view north over bridge.	BP; controlled north end of up and down goods loops, and sidings on up and down, also access to engine shed and to single line round west face of down platform.	Replaced 3/5/1943* (or 17/7/1943*) by new box of LMS 'E' type, on up side, about 100yd to north; new box long and low, with view *under* road bridge. New box took over work of No 3 wef 17/7/1943*
			Replacement box of 1943 closed 14/5/1973*PB, when access to Windermere line taken over by Carlisle power box.	
346	Oxenholme No 3 (formerly: Junction box, No 3)	Up side, just north of the up platform. L&NWR 'C' of c1882.	BP, controlled double line junction with Windermere line at north end of station and north end of single line round down platform.	Controlled Peat Lane down IB sigs from 1935. Box closed 17/7/1943* and repl by No 2.

Other features, in sequence, from Carnforth northward, include:

MP5¾dn — *Southern approach to Carnforth station*
After Crag Bank overline bridge — 15in gauge and standard gauge railways, adjuncts of Carnforth Steamtown, are parallel (the 15in gauge added to site in 1977).

up — site of Carnforth No 1 box.

up/dn — loops both sides were in constant demand for examination of freight trains; now the two down loops are bi-directional and their main use is staging of merry-go-round (mgr) coal from Maryport and Whitehaven to Fiddlers Ferry power station (near Warrington, on low level line to Widnes), essentially a 1981 development.

6up — Former L&NWR Company houses, 41 in two substantial terraces in Grosvenor Place, glimpsed on bank, with recent houses in foreground.

Until pre-electrification works, long footbridge crossed direct to site of the pre-1944 L&NWR
dn — engine shed.

dn — wagon shed survives as nucleus of carriage and wagon repairing/rebuilding venture, associated with 'Steamtown'.

6+dn — *Carnforth Steamtown*. The 1944 LMS engine shed, progressively developed since closure by BR in 1968 as locomotive museum under independent management. Coaling plant — a landmark. A new running connection put in 1980 under control of Carnforth Station Junction box into Steamtown to facilitate working of locomotives for steam-hauled special trains.

6¼+ — *Carnforth station*
Titled 'Carnforth-Yealand' until 1864, it was initially L&C of 1846, on present site, with its main building on down side (integrated in later

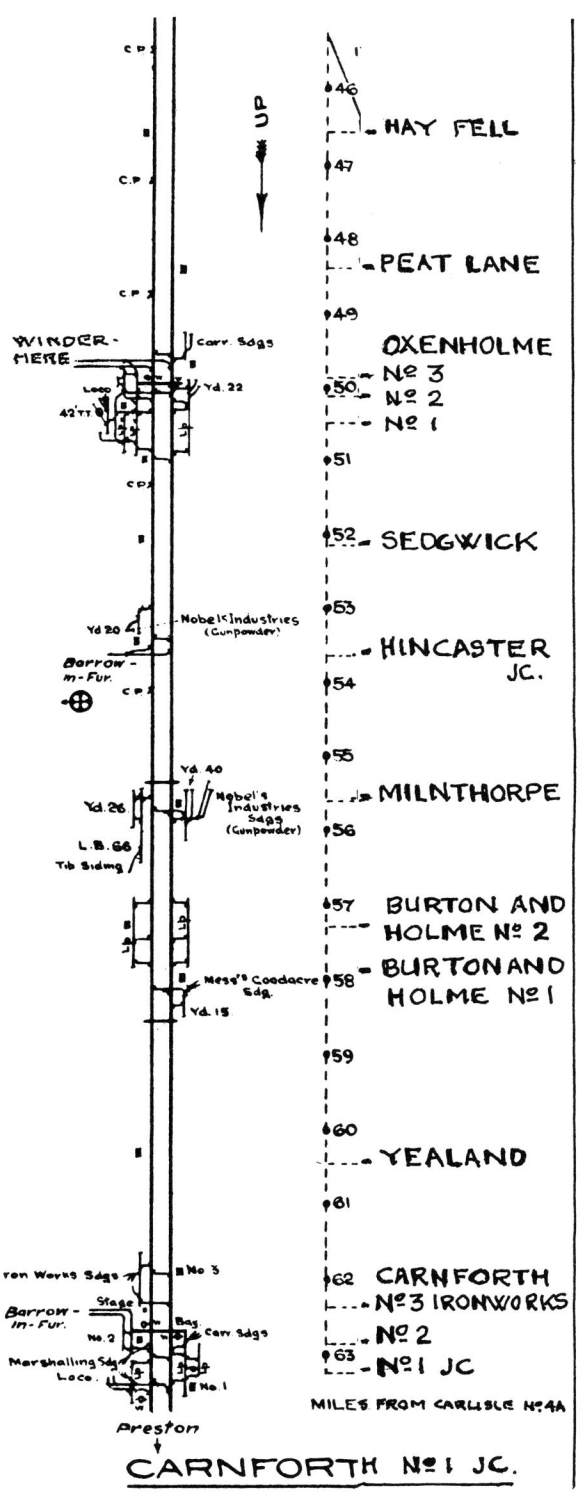

developments but still identifiable): styled 'Carnforth station-Hall Gate' on first edition of ordnance survey, 1845, published 1848.

The Furness Railway (initially as Ulverstone and Lancaster Railway) reached here and opened 1857.

The Furness and Midland Joint line (F&M), connecting from Midland Railway proper at Wennington, opened 1867 — a joint station resulted.

The station was remodelled 1880, as joint FR and L&NWR, with accommodation also for MR, and 'opened 2/8/1880' in its well-remembered form, with up and down L&NWR (L&C) main line platforms, up L&NWR bay, one diverging (curving) bi-directional FR platform and MR bay at its north end; there was a pleasantly-located refreshment room at the apex of the buildings, with vista southward. The L&NWR arms appeared in the masonry of a south-facing tower on the island platform.

The FR had a remarkable signalbox on the north end of their platform and happily the structure stands today, cleaned, with that Company's arms (carved in stone) in its north face and (formerly) a clock in the south face. It was replaced in 1903 by the FR's large 'Carnforth Station Junction' box, in use now (with L&YR frame) as a 'fringe box' relative to Preston power box. 'Carnforth F&M Junction' FR (with FR frame) is in use, beyond 'Station Junction', on Furness route.

In 1937, the LMS undertook major new works at Carnforth, under a Government loan scheme. Nos 1 and 2 boxes were replaced in 1938 (see schedule, ante). A new down Furness line platform, 890ft long, was commissioned on 3/7/1939, concurrent with commencement of the summer timetable. A new motive power depot (posh name for engine shed) was in the scheme but not ready until 1944 (see subsequent reference).

The up and down main line platforms of Carnforth station were taken out of use wef 4/5/1970, and their faces cut back, neatly. This speeds operation of the WCML but can render journeys between the Furness line, also the Midland line from Leeds, and the north highly inconvenient.

6½dn — *Carnforth Ironworks.* The works was north of the overline bridge (Warton Road) at the north end of the L&C platforms, on the down side. It extended practically to the line of the F&M, which it just ante-dated; opening was 1865 with three blastfurnaces. In 1871, Bessemer steelmaking plant came into production, believed out of commission by 1890, leaving pig-iron production. The lofty stone blowing-engine house stood close to the L&C, with the tall blastfurnaces north of it and parallel to the line. The works succumbed to the 1926 general strike and ensuing depression. There were six private locomotives in 1931, about the time when T. W. Ward Ltd bought the works and plant, for dismantling, scrapping and sales. The main entrance gate is seen on Warton Road, by the

25

road to Steamtown. After wartime use, Boddy Industries Ltd has established storage depots on site, with rail connection at the north end to sidings adjoining the F&M: locomotive No 23 *Merlin*, 0-6-0 diesel Hudswell Clarke No D761/1951, formerly of Port of Bristol Authority, Avonmouth, has been in evidence for some years until autumn 1981, on limited rail traffic.

dn — The two sidings beside WCML were adapted c1940, in order to stable and sort traffic brought 'rough' from Merseyside (etc), and they were converted in 1942 to loops and remained until 1969, being indeed used to an extent during electrification works. Until that time, it was nominally possible — though not for passenger traffic — to emerge from the F&M sidings to a north head shunt, set back into the 1942 loops, and then proceed via the outlet at the North Ground Frame to the down main line for the north; it was not a favoured practice.

up — *Carnforth Midland Railway 'roundhouse' engine shed* can be seen, in industrial use, beside the F&M line to Wennington and Yorkshire.

6¾+ — *River Keer bridge*, a modest structure carrying the L&C line over a stream flowing through low-lying meadows to Morecambe Bay.

up — *'Carnforth Level'*, the straight road to north of Carnforth, beside the L&C, which pre-dated the railway, as the Garstang and Heron Syke turnpike, now A6 road.

7dn — *Warton Crag* in view, with Warton village on its slopes.

8+ — *Dockacres underline bridge*, with skew stone arch, over A6 road, with separate reinforced concrete *overline* bridge in use since c1968 for southbound traffic.

8½dn — *Yealand box, site of:* the pair of L&NWR brick houses at right angles to line, behind the box, have also vanished.

dn — *Yealand Conyers village* a mile away, with Leighton Hall over the hill just behind it, and soon *Yealand Redmayne*, in the same direction.

up — *Lancaster Canal* briefly alongside, but it is here north of the limit of navigation at Tewitfield; the M6 road was so constructed as to allow only a culvert, not navigation, under the carriageway — at three places in a few miles.

10+ — *enter Westmorland*, nominally 'Cumbria' since 1974.

10¾+ — *Burton & Holme station*, closed (P) 27/3/1950.

up — *The Railway Inn* boasts a prominent upper quadrant semaphore signal.

up — Pair of L&NWR brick houses.

up — L&C stone station house carefully cleaned, privately occupied. The small stone warehouse, which adjoined the platform, is still in blackened stone. The rest of the station has long vanished.

up — Long siding (or branch) trailed in from north east direction, where Holme Mills of Goodacres are visible; in the 1930s, a van load of their product, coconut matting, was commonly despatched

nightly. Stone and timber were, earlier, traffics which had been despatched from Burton & Holme. Holme village is seen but Burton-in-Kendal, two miles south, is not readily seen from the railway.

up and dn — *The goods lines* from No 1 to north of No 2 boxes were put in 1925-26, taken out of use 1971 and then removed. The crews of goods trains 'put inside' at No 1 and run through to the north end of the down loop were seldom pleased when the signalman at No 2 let out a following fitted freight through the intermediate crossover to the down main and it proceeded ahead. (Similar comments apply on the 'up'.)

12-14½ — Route unusually straight! In 1898, the L&NWR had secured authority to carry widening from Burton & Holme through to Milnthorpe, but only the above-described works of 1925-26 were ever completed.

13+ — *Beela viaduct*, two skew arches, in brick and stone, each 35ft span, carrying the railway over the river Beela (alt spelling: Bela).

13½+ — *Milnthorpe station*, closed (P) 1/7/1968. See plan, also schedule of boxes.

dn — L&C stone station house/building survives, but blackened and neglected.

up — The former L&NWR No 3 siding ran into the nitrate warehouse for exchange of traffic with a tramway of 3ft 6in-4ft gauge and No 4 siding also permitted transhipment to the tramway, but in the

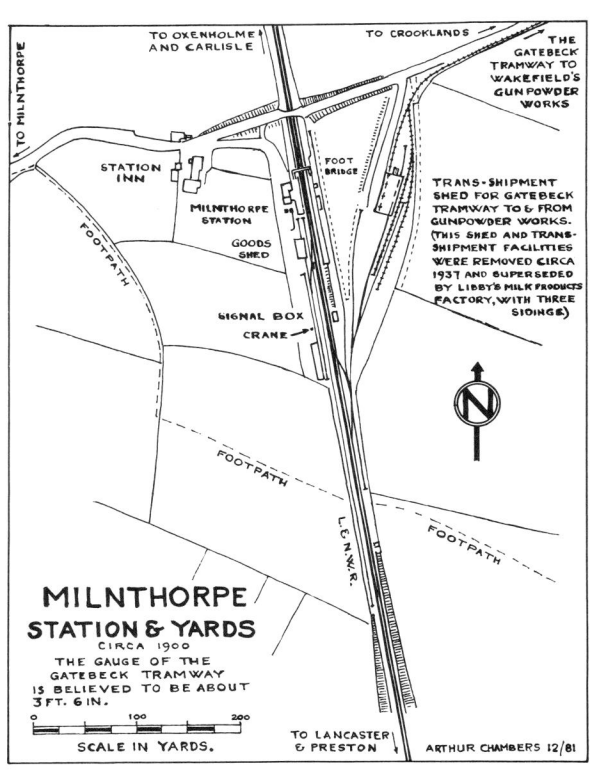

MILNTHORPE
STATION & YARDS
CIRCA 1900
THE GAUGE OF THE GATEBECK TRAMWAY
IS BELIEVED TO BE ABOUT 3FT. 6IN.
0   100   200
SCALE IN YARDS.

ARTHUR CHAMBERS 12/81

open. The horse-worked tramway was the property of W. H. Wakefield & Company, later Brunner Mond and ICI Ltd (Nobels Explosives). It extended for some four miles to Gatebeck gunpowder works, with branches intermediately to coal and timber wharves on the Lancaster Canal (Kendal section). The works operated from 1852 until 1936-37, when production ceased at Gatebeck, the last working Westmorland gunpowder works, and was transferred to Ardeer. The tramway was in use from 1874 until the end of production.

Libby's private sidings, three in number, came into use in the later 1930s, concurrent with the rundown of gunpowder activities; they were for dairy products; the factory remains active but no longer has rail connection.

Today, unsightly vehicles and impedimenta have been permitted to ruin the pleasant site, on up and down sides of BR's premier main line; a heavy vehicle testing station (up side) bears some of the responsibility.

14+ — *Rowells overline bridge*, prominent and lofty, with three arches, built in brick and stone and carrying a byroad.

15½ — *Hincaster Junction*, takes its name from a Roman camp.

dn — Course of FR single line from Arnside, in belt of trees, converges.

dn — Signalbox was at the junction, just before underline bridge.

up — Pair of L&NWR brick houses, beside the lane.

dn — Buildings of Nobels Explosives (ICI), where traffic was exchanged for the explosives Company, who conveyed it locally by road to and from their Sedgwick gunpowder works — which had its own internal tramway. Gunpowder activity seems to have commenced later here than at Milnthorpe and certainly ended earlier, but some general siding facility was continued at Hincaster until removal of the connections wef 15 July 1963. If very fortunate, travellers may glimpse a road-roller (steam) awaiting restoration or gleaming showman's conversion bound for a rally as the site is occupied for the business of Cyril and Max Woodend, steam enthusiasts. From here, Levens Hall is only a mile to westward, but not visible owing to the lie of the land.

15½+ — *Hincaster canal tunnel* passes beneath the line on the section north of Stainton basin and now devoid of water. Then, immediately north:

15¾+ — *Underline bridge* of two spans, in concrete construction with steel joist and concrete deck, built 1969, carries the line over the Windermere link road (from M6), A591.

17 — *Sedgwick*

dn — site of box, followed by underline bridge, crossing lane.

dn — pair of L&NWR brick cottages on the lane to village.

17¼dn — *Sizergh Castle*, distant 1¼ miles westward —

vista of the delightful part-fortified residence, a property of the National Trust.

18¼dn — *Natland village*, with church and green (below); and *Kendal town* (2½ miles).

19+ — *Oxenholme station*

The basic layout of the station originated in 1846, the L&C having an outer face to a down island platform, for the Kendal & Windermere Railway Company's trains; with, on the up side, a long range of typically attractive neo-Elizabethan stone buildings, two storeys high, which were completed in 1852. They have been cleaned and are well-kept today. The building style appropriately lies between the 'manorial defensive' (Lancaster) and 'gamekeeper's cottage' (Burton & Holme, Milnthorpe, and others). Many leaded lights survive.

The first real remodelling was in c1880-82. The Kendal-Old Hutton road was diverted to cross the line by the overbridge to the south, involving particularly awkward bends. This cleared the way for southerly lengthening of platforms. Buildings erected on the island included a small but useful refreshment room at the south end of the block and facing the subway. The present booking office and small hall were added to the L&C up side buildings at that time or a little later — together with more protective walling and roofing, as the site is exposed, often wet and windblown from the west. Three new signalboxes and new signalling, with distant signals only pulled off for a clear road right through, emerged from the same scheme.

The northern double-line junction — between main and Windermere lines — dated from the same period and was used by most through trains to and from Windermere, although down Grange-Kendal locals often used the back down platform. A stiff climb and curve were involved if coming off the Windermere line to the up main platform with, for example, the morning 'Club train' to Manchester or a full train for London. Note from schedule that the work of the north box was taken over in 1943 by a new No 2 box. The northern double line junction was taken out of use wef 13/5/1968, this being the Monday following the securing of the points. Changes on the Windermere line are mentioned later.

In 1975 the down main line platform was greatly lengthened to the north, out across the site of the double line divergence; this ended the tradition of down expresses drawing up twice. Now, 12 vehicles are accommodated comfortably. A neat little building was substituted on the down island and, since spring 1978, a free-standing buffet-bar (which arrived 'packed in strong box', placed by crane) provides an all-year welcome, under cheerful management. The up platform was lengthened at the north end over the site of the onetime No 3 box and beyond, in the territory of a former pair of carriage sidings. The station, with clear and informative announcements, is notable for its tidiness.

South of the station, the engineering department's mechanical equipment is marshalled in the small up yard, ready for early morning, or Sunday, line occupations. The down loop is little used in daytime but the up loop is well used. In the latter days of No 2 box, one night an exceptionally long double-decker car-carrying train was put inside on the up, the guard riding contentedly with the driver of the diesel locomotive. An up sleeping car train duly overtook, and the car train departed. Next morning, all the door handles of the passenger train were found in a neat heap.

Signal relay rooms are on the down side, south of the station at ground level. Nearby can be seen the steps and wicket gate giving access to the road bridge and used by generations of steam locomotive men on their way to and from the engine shed.

Oxenholme took its name from the farm — which survives — below the station. The village is above the railway to southward and first developed as two railway communities. L&NWR brick terraces of 12 and 13 houses faced one another at 'Helmside', near No 1 box and the Skipton road; there was a mission hall, also a reading room, by that road. Another block was built much nearer the station and eventually the two were linked by road and more development ensued. The former Company houses remain.

Nowadays, while the Windermere connecting DMU trains are usually well loaded, many passengers from Kendal and a wide rural catchment area drive to Oxenholme station and use the car parks.

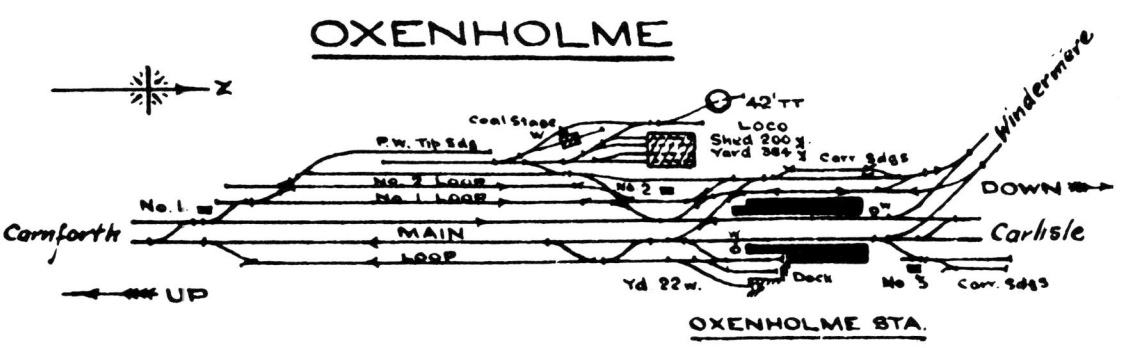

Oxenholme (exc)-Shap Summit (inc)

Signalboxes - 1928

Miles/yards	Name	Location and type	Functions	Historical
1/868	Peat Lane	Up side, about 40yd south of underline bridge over original Kendal-Sedbergh road: L&NWR 'B'. Believed four working levers.	BP	Box closed 25/3/1935*and replaced by up and down IB sigs.
1/1535	Hay Fell	Down side, to north of overline bridge for Kendal-Appleby road and of cottages. L&NWR 'A': four working levers.	BP	Box closed 2/5/1949* and demolished, replaced by up and down IB sigs.
1/1223	Lambrigg Crossing.	Up side, just south of minor crossing, with house opposite on down. L&NWR 'A'.	BP and crossing box. Trailing crossover by late LMS days; also facing crossovers since pre-elec'n work. Controlled (in due course) Hay Fell and Peat Lane up IB sigs and (in rear) Hay Fell down IB sigs.	Box closed as BP 30/4/1973*PB. Crossing closed, with lane diverted, 18/4/1977*. Box retained 1981 to work facing and trailing crossovers, as required.

Miles/Yards	Name	Location and type	Functions	Historical
1/364	Mosedale Hall Crossing	Down side, just south of crossing of byway. L&NWR 'B', unusual structure.	BP, and crossing box.	Box closed 5/6/1967* and demolished by 19/8/1967 — no substitute signals (accommodation crossing retained in 1967).
1426	Grayrigg	Down side, well north of station and set back. L&NWR 'D'	BP, controlling small down sidings and up and down loops; also Low Gill down IB signals (and Dillicar IB sigs) from 3/4/1967*. (Refuge siding on down, before conversion to loop.)	The up and down loops were installed 1925-26 and box replaced a small one of L&NWR 'C' type. Box closed 30/4/1973*PB.
1/1422	Low Gill Junction	Up side, at convergence of Ingleton route with main line, north of station. L&NWR 'C' of 1890	BP for main and Ingleton lines, supplemented by ground frame on Ingleton line. Controlled Dillicar down IB sigs from 1933.	Ingleton line finally out of use from 26/7/1966: plain line replaced junction 13/2/67*. Box closed 3/4/1967* and repl by IB sigs.
	Low Gill Yard Ground Frame (with its sidings and connections) on Ingleton branch taken away early July 1963.			
2/128	Dillicar	Down side, north of MP30. Structure used main parts of former Dillicar Ballast Siding box: four levers.	BP	Probably dated from 1891 at this site, replacing Dillicar Fell box and Dillicar Ballast Siding box. Box closed 30/10/1933* and repl by up and dn IBs.
1/1299	Tebay No 1 (previously: Tebay South, No 1)	Down side, midway along the down loop, south of station. L&NWR 'D'	BP; and controlled down loop; also south end of station, exit from up yard and (from 1933) Dillicar up IB sigs. Also controlled Low Gill up IBS from 1967.	Replaced box which had been on down but about 240yd further north, when down refuge siding converted to down loop in 1925-26. Box closed 16/4/1973*PB.
518	Tebay No 2 (previously Tebay Junction, No 2)	Up side, immediately north of up platform. L&NWR 'C'	BP; and goods junction for NER single line at north of station; also NER passenger single line (with train staff from No 3). Tebay North down (only) IB sigs installed 1/2/1943*, 1/630 to north.	Replaced 1/12/1952* by new box (BR 'G') some 70yd to north, in angle of main and NER lines. Box closed 16/4/1973*PB: its base retained as relay room for power signalling.
—	*Tebay NE Yard, No 3 ('Tebay East' and 'Tebay Yard' were earlier NER titles)*	*Beside NER line, on its north side. Constructed to NER design.*	*Controlled east end of both goods and passenger single tracks from No 2; also east end of up yard and the marshalling sidings for traffic to NER.*	*NER route to Kirkby Stephen closed 1/1962, but box closed 12/1/1965.*
2/1700	Scout Green	Down side of 1 in 75 Shap Incline. L&NWR 'A': four working levers (gate lock added 1948)	BP; and level crossing. Scout Green IB sigs (dn only) installed 27/4/1942* 1/650 to north, and controlled.	Box closed 16/4/1973*PB.
2/935	Shap Summit	Between up main and up loop. L&NWR 'D'	BP; with up loop and refuge siding, also down granite quarry sidings and (later) Manchester Corporation sidings, down side.	Replaced L&NWR box ('C' type), which was set into wall on dn, when up refuge siding converted to loop in 1925-26. Box closed 2/4/1973*PB.

Other features, in sequence, northward of Oxenholme include:

19¼+dn — *The Tidey spot:* the favourite vantage point of that noted photographer of locomotives and trains in motion, Gordon Tidey, was on the down side banking, where the main line climbs away from Oxenholme on 1 in 178 — soon 1 in 104 — and the Windermere line, with its vista, drops away. His views were southward, the trains climbing north towards him. The very tall L&NWR up home signal by the old No 3 box, with distant for No 2 (also 'slotted' from No 1) below it and a repeating pair of arms lower down the post, was prominent through the years until, in August 1941, it was replaced by a post 20ft less in height and carrying one pair of upper quadrant home and distant arms.

19½-20 — *Inner and outer up distants.* The combination of consistently fast running, on the level and especially downhill, with constant curvature and problems of sighting, led the signal engineers of the L&C section to place signals thoughtfully, often to provide very tall posts, also to provide inter-working between boxes which were close together. One notes, above, that at Oxenholme on the up line, the 'slotting' (by interdependent balance weights on the post) ensured that the distant signal seen in Mr Tidey's viewfinder would not come off until both Nos 1 and 2 signalmen had pulled their relevant levers. In order to give extra protection to the station and junction, No 3 (the north box) was provided with up inner and outer distants, the outer distant being almost opposite MP 20, about 850ft south of the main road overline bridge. This practice gave good, and dual, warning of a signal stop ahead and it also helped flexibility of working; if a driver sighted the outer distant at danger and made a first brake application, he might still find the inner distant cleared — it served also as an outer distant for No 2 box, where the signalman could have cleared a preceding goods train to the loop in the seconds available, so enabling our express driver to release his brakes and pass the station at around 60mph, accelerating. Practices changed and are likewise exemplified here. From April 1943, No 3's up main inner distant was taken away and the up main outer distant was superseded by a continuously-lit colour-light signal, 1,649 yards in rear (north) of the up main home, also controlled as an outer distant for No 2; this gave excellent visibility and braking distance, but not the same flexibility of working. Incidentally, it anticipated the elimination of No 3 box, an economy effected a few months later.

20+ — *Hatton Skeid overline bridge,* stone, with brick arch — reconstructed for electrification — carries the 'new' Kendal-Sedbergh road, A684. Then follow, in wooded cutting, Birklands 1 and 2 accommodation bridges in close succession, con-

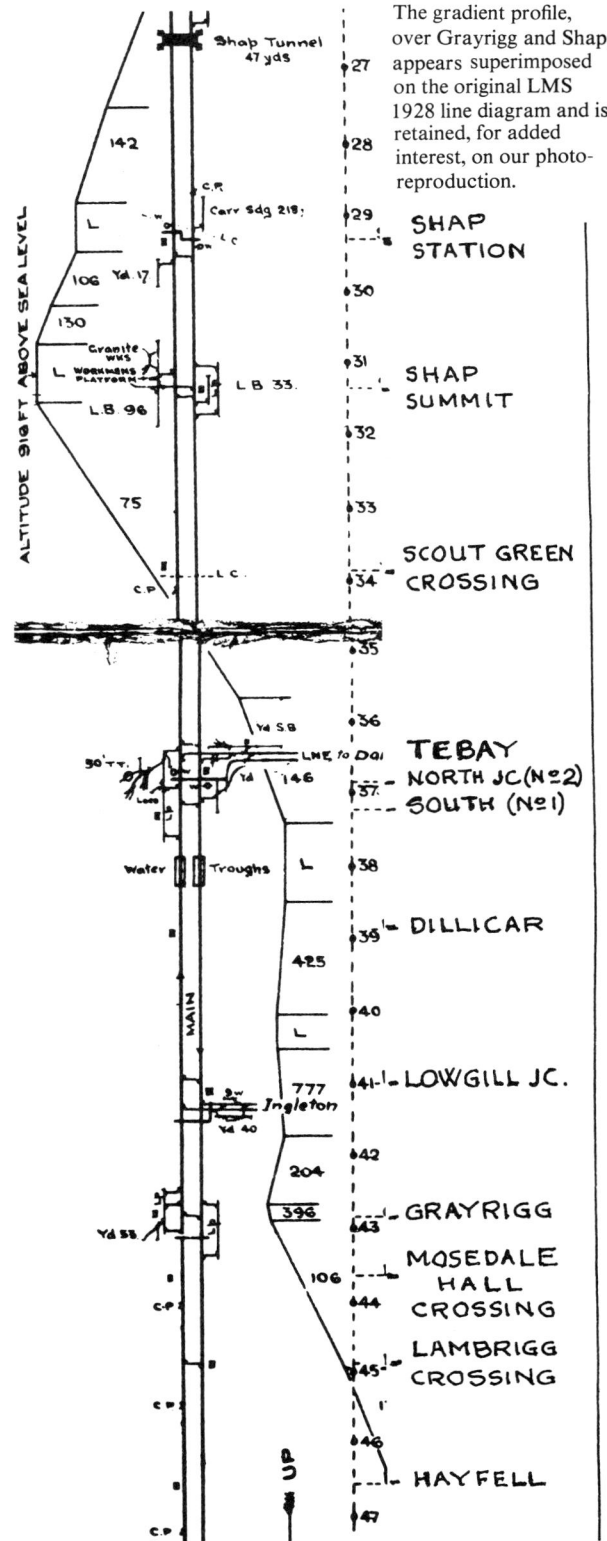

The gradient profile, over Grayrigg and Shap, appears superimposed on the original LMS 1928 line diagram and is retained, for added interest, on our photo-reproduction.

necting Castle Green and Singleton Park. Emergence is at:

20½+ — *Peat Lane*. The signalbox, pre-1935, was on the up side just before the bridge carrying the railway over onetime 'Peat Lane', now 'Sedbergh Road' but long superseded by the new A684 for through traffic. This bridge was notable. It had steel trough girders and floorplates and a span of 25ft across the carriageway between stone abutments, but when rebuilt in that form it had been permitted to retain its side members — presumably not load bearing — with their cast inscriptions picked out in white for road users to see:

LANCASTER AND CARLISLE RAILWAY 1846

The bridge was again reconstructed, in July 1965, but this time philistines were in command of the engineering department; the old cast side members were destroyed. Had the job been done five or six years later as part of the pre-electrification works, the bridge would have received the same careful consideration as the many other handsome civil engineering and architectural structures between Weaver Junction and Carlisle.

up — The steep hill road under Peat Lane bridge is known as the '*Greyhound Hill*', because of the Greyhound Inn a half mile away at the hill top. The inn existed as licensed premises in the 1840s and 1850s, but not significantly before or after those decades, although even now it can readily be recognised as a typical hostelry for carters, drovers and other wayfarers. *Paddy's Lane* parallels the L&C line — on the hillside above the railway — from near the site of Oxenholme No 1 signalbox to that of Hay Fell box and passes both the Station Inn (above Oxenholme) and the Greyhound (that was). This was a very old 'way' indeed, possibly back to Roman times, and traceable northward over the fells to emerge in Tebay gorge, near Borrow Bridge, but it probably gained its name in the mid-1840s, when the 'Paddies' who had come to build Joseph Locke's masterly Lancaster and Carlisle Railway were encamped on the slopes of Hay Fell, below Benson Knott, and would trek daily from shanty town to working sites.

up — The tiny signalbox at Peat Lane was perched so precariously on the railway embankment that one of the signalmen became alarmed by the close passage of certain up trains and would retire to the hill pasture behind the box; he eventually secured a transfer. The up fitted freights of the 1920s and 1930s, made up of short-wheelbase four-wheeled vans and container trucks, were particularly terrifying when passing at close quarters at 60 or 70mph.

dn — *Broom Close plantation* and (up) *Birds Hill farm*, followed by:

dn — wide view of Kendal, Kendal fell beyond and the Kent valley, traversed by the Windermere line, and Lakes mountains more distant.

21¼+ — *Thirlmere aqueduct*, first commissioned 1894 from Thirlmere to Prestwich, near Manchester, passes beneath the line.

22up — *Benson Hall (farm)*. *Paddy's Lane* close at hand and *Benson Knott* above.

22½up — *Hay Fell* open slopes give place to deep rock cutting through rock and Kendal-Appleby road overline bridge, A685.

dn — *Rock Cottages*, formerly occupied by a ganger and a platelayer and their families, now modernised as one white house.

dn — Site of Hay Fell box adjoined, just north of the cottages.
Very severe eastward curvature brings the L&C line from a generally south-to-north alignment to one generally west-to-east for the next few miles.

24 — *Docker viaduct* (alt: *Docker Garth*), with six arches of 47ft to 50ft span and length 370ft, in stone and brick, crosses the valley of Fiddlers Gill, with new byroad beneath, replacing the road which formerly crossed the railway at Lambrigg.

24¼+up — *Lambrigg Crossing box*. This is an early L&NWR/Saxby & Farmer type signalbox (see schedule), retained to operate facing and trailing crossovers. It acquired a new name sign in 1981. The trailing crossover dates back a good many years and, incidentally, permitted a lagging or failed bank engine to be crossed to the up road and returned to Oxenholme. The level crossing was closed after electrification.

dn — L&C handsome stone house at Lambrigg was presumably built for the short-lived Grayrigg station, in use August 1848-November 1849, and stood close beside the line at the crossing, but was demolished c1974.
The Lambrigg signalman had to be very much on the alert, owing to topography and curves marring visibility. The next box north was little over a mile away. At one time, a policeman, turned railway bobby (signalman) was regularly in Mosedale box; he was very particular and constantly sending 'stop and examine' for fast up freights. As this warning was belled, the train would be approaching Lambrigg's distant signal and the Lambrigg man had barely time to throw the distant on, then the home, and also stop any traffic on the down — ascending — road. Seldom was anything found amiss with the train.

25½dn — *Mosedale Hall Crossing box* (see schedule); demolished; crossing now closed. Moresdale Hall (note spelling differed) is hidden away on the up side.

26up — *Grayrigg Railway Cottages*, a pair of L&C houses, in stone, once occupied by a pw foreman and a signalman, and families, now stand somewhat disconsolate.

26+ — *Grayrigg station*, closed (P) 1/2/1954.

dn — Platform was short, with L&C stone building/stationmaster's house (strictly, the station and building post-dated the L&C, being opened in

31

1861). Refuge siding was beyond the dn platform, northbound, converted to a loop (for freight or passenger use) in 1925-26, and this down loop 'moved' in the up direction in the later 1960s. The station building has been demolished since electrification.

up — Loop also constructed 1925-26; it passed behind the up platform, the shelter on which was pulled down soon after closing; that platform was removed in 7/1965. Both loops remain.

dn — The 1926 box stood well beyond the station, set back pleasantly against trees, but leaning over backwards — due to having been built on soft peat.

Grayrigg was a country station, typically remote from the village which it barely served, apart from when schoolchildren went on outings or families on holiday. Local women would take the train to Kendal, carrying butter and eggs to sell in the market. Farmers would order a wagon of coal and 'control' would arrange for it to be detached from a down mineral train. The resident stationmaster, who had charge of Lambrigg, Mosedale and Grayrigg boxes, had a peaceful life, with little goods traffic and passenger income about £35 monthly in winter, £100 in summer, in the 1930s. He was however responsible for the safety and expedition of *all* the Company's traffic while it was on line within the compass of his station and signalboxes and he played his part in single-line working. 'Hot boxes' occurred about once a fortnight, usually being grease lubricated axleboxes on private-owner wagons, spotted by the signalmen. One summer day, 'stop and examine' led to the down 'Royal Scot', streamlined 'Pacific' on 14 bogies, being brought to a stand. An axlebox on the leading coach was nearly white hot. The short siding off the down loop was in defective condition and quite unfit for the heavy locomotive, so the vehicle was detached, drawn forward, uncoupled, brakes released and gently kicked back into the siding, the engine back on to the train, and away with only 11 minutes stay, including transfer of passengers and removal of the carriage headboard. Two inspectors came with all speed from Derby works and expressed the view that, if the vehicle had not been detached, the whole train would have been derailed on the northward descent from Shap. There was cause for quiet satisfaction on the part of the staff concerned.

Dr Tice F. Budden, of Dorking, with 40 years at Scotland Yard to his credit, along with railway photographs back to 1889, liked to stay at Arnside, then travel via Oxenholme to Grayrigg and set up his tripod in a favourite spot; he used a large camera and black hood, with a white board near the box as marker — as the train passed it, his shutter was released.

Curvature commences at Grayrigg, to bring the route to a generally south-to-north alignment at Low Gill. Just beyond the site of Grayrigg signal-box, the M6 motorway breaks in on the peaceful scene with:

26½ — *Grayrigg motorway bridge*, single skew span, built 1968-69 and creating a 'tunnel'. This is bridge BR 90, and the original overline bridge 90, carrying a lane, was demolished 27/10/1968 to make way for it.

26¾ — *Overline bridge of three lofty spans*, built 1968-69, to replace two lanes which lost their bridges due to incursion of the motorway.

27+up — *Beck Foot* hamlet visible below, from near the bridge over B6257; then:

up — *'Old station house'*, single storey, close beside the line — a pleasant residence, with small garden: believed to be part of the original L&C station of Low Gill, closed 15/9/1861 on opening of the resited station.

The Howgills — delightful hills to view in all weathers, and to clamber upon, can be seen ahead of a northbound — literally, westbound — train from Docker viaduct onwards, and now they are close at hand, with *Low Gill viaduct* of 11 arches handsome against this backcloth. It carried the L&C-promoted double track L&NWR route to Sedbergh and Ingleton (and onwards by MR to the West Riding). This line was opened 24/8/1861 (G) and 16/9/1861 (P), closed 1/2/1954 (regular P), 1/10/1964 (actual) and 7/12/1964 (officially) to G, 26/7/1966 (finally). Incidentally, the intention had been to make a triangular junction with the L&CR main line, in the vicinity of Beck Foot and 'Old Station House'.

27¾+ — *Low Gill station*, opened 16/9/1861; closed to regular passenger traffic for Ingleton line 1/2/1954, to main line and all traffic 7/3/1960, and since swept away.

The station layout was all on a left hand curve for main line trains, northbound, and was exceedingly elongated to accord with the final plans of 1859-61 for the junction arrangements, also further easing of curvature and modifications c1890. A broad, curving island platform was the final outcome, with modest buildings, in stone, and sunken garden beds; up main line trains used one face and arriving trains from Ingleton the other, the two outer platforms being undistinguished. Indeed, the timber built platform for departing branch trains was narrow and low, provided with a set of movable steps to aid passengers in boarding trains. A solicitor changing here took to moving the steps for himself, slipped on one occasion and sustained injury; the resulting legal case went against the Company and the unlucky stationmaster earned disfavour with higher authority.

up — An attractive terrace of 10 stone houses of 1860, built for the L&C, stands somewhat below the level of the main line and a little south of the station; they provided snug homes for a compact group of 'railway families' for many years but all are now in private occupation, with only one or two railwaymen among the owners. A former school building adjoining the houses is also now a residence.

up — The signalbox of 1890 (see schedule) was well north of the station, at the point of final convergence of routes.

From Low Gill northward to Tebay, the route of the L&C line is in the upper valley of the Lune, with gorge and cuttings.

approx 29½up — *Dillicar Fell Cottages.* A terrace of three railway houses, closely facing the railway, but demolished many years. They were reached only by a steep cart road down from the Kendal-Appleby road, the cart road now being lost due to motorway engineering on the valley side below the main road and a little above the WCML. The two end cottages were occupied by pw men but the middle one became unoccupied and was then used for tools and shelter by pw staff; on Mondays, they were liable to find that a tramp had kindled a fire in the grate during the weekend. It is believed that the cottages were all empty by the time that Dillicar box closed in 1933.

There was at one time (in the last century) a box called 'DillicarFell' and one would expect it to be near these cottages.

after 30dn — *Dillicar box.* This small box was also very isolated, with no proper access except by the lineside. It probably dated from c1891, when it was reported that 'Dillicar Ballast Siding Cabin is to be moved about 300 yards on the Tebay side of the site occupied by Dillicar Fell Cabin'. This reference is obscure, as the actual site of Dillicar box was about a half mile north of the Dillicar Fell cottages. The box closed in 1933 and stood for a few years, in use as a shelter for staff.

30½+ — *Borrow Beck viaduct*, with three arches of 45-46ft span, in brick and stone construction, 68ft above Borrow Beck, tributary of the Lune. The viaduct also crosses the lane to Borrowdale, now reconstructed as part of the Sedbergh to Tebay by-road.

30¾+ — *Appleby Road underline stone arch bridge* remains, but is not now in use by the road.

dn — *Borrow Bridge railway cottages*, group of three, were immediately north of the bridge, beside the line, but demolished during motorway construction, 1968-70. At one time, a ganger, a sub-ganger and others lived here.

approx 31 — *Dillicar water troughs* were hereabouts. They were renewed as late as 1961. Tebay No 1 box's down distant was a tall signal by the troughs, sometimes known as 'the green star' to enginemen. The tall signals on the L&C section of the L&NWR were epitomised by a 'true tale' from the L&NWR in the Chilterns; after a pleasant evening, a railway enthusiast friend was being seen off homeward towards London and waxed lyrical about the quiet setting and the clarity of one bright star in particular — his host had gently to point out that it was the back light in a tall 'distant'.

31½+ — *New overline viaduct* carries Kendal-Appleby road over M6, WCML and River Lune to reach Tebay village. This replaces 'Lune's Bridge', which was marginally north of it.

South Lune bridge — 61ft steel span between stone abutments — carries the railway over the Lune, which is not crossed again until north of Tebay. Renewed 2-3/4/1983, using steel box girders and steel deck sections.

32+ — *Tebay and its station*

The railway layout, around its peak in 1928, is shown on the line diagram and enlargement, further details of the signalboxes — two on the main line and one on the NER — being contained in the schedule, *ante*. NER aspects will be dealt with separately in some detail. The L&NWR engine shed and its duties also receive separate attention. The rundown of the station to final closure — effective 1/7/1968 — is discussed also in the account of passenger services. Today, the railway layout consists of the up and down main running roads, a long loop (extended 1970 over the platform site) on the down side, with siding, and facing and trailing crossovers, which render the loop accessible to both running lines. Of railway build-

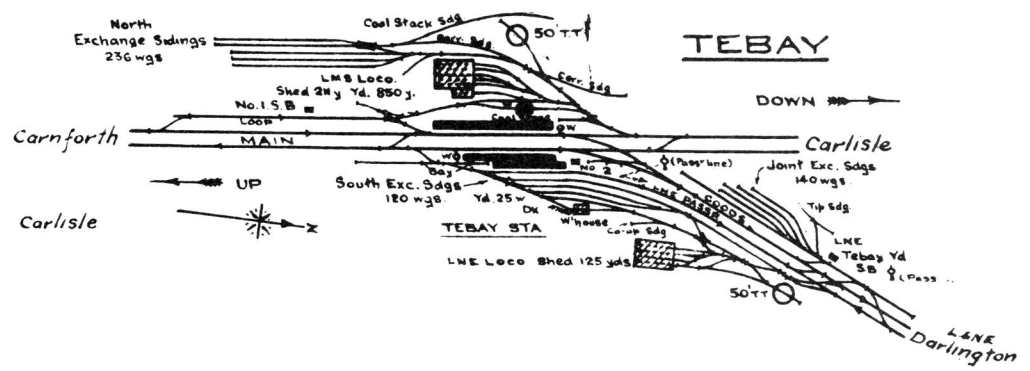

ings, there are scarcely any. The passenger station, which is illustrated, was of importance as a junction, normally calling for a change of train between L&NWR and NER. However, clients approaching from the village had to traverse a long footbridge over the up yard. This structure was exposed to all the winds which blow through Tebay gorge or down from the high fells; about a half century ago, Squire Goodwin of Orton Hall was making his usual dignified approach when, so legend has it, his trilby hat was whisked into the air and descended amidst the Durham-Furness coke wagons beneath, followed by strident representations which quickly reached Euston, or at least the Tebay Joint Station Committee (L&NWR and NER), with the result that the bridge was roofed and enclosed. Staff were employed by the committee and could seek promotion with either parent Company. The older members for long wore 'TJS' cap badges with some pride.

A feature of the working of NER passenger trains was the use of the passenger single line from No 3 signalbox to the gloomy NER back platform. This movement, and eventual departure by the same route, was authorised by possession of the 'one engine in steam' train staff, held at each end by the signalmen in No 3 (NER) and No 2 (L&NWR) boxes. The author's photograph of this battered object is reproduced. The inscription on the brass portion is deciphered as

TEBAY No 3   STATION PLATFORM

Its condition is partly accounted for by use when breaking coal for the fire in No 3 box, but also by other incidents in its long life. After the last NER passenger train of the day had left, the vacant NER platform road was used for making up a goods for Ince Moss (Wigan) in late evening. This goods was based on southbound traffic arriving by the slow 'road van goods' from Shap granite works and elsewhere. After the train was made up, the train staff was often placed in the ironwork of the leading wagon, by way of protection against admission of another train to the single line. In the early hours of next morning, the LMS engine would come off shed and take the train south. If the staff was forgotten and not surrendered to a night duty station inspector or No 2 signalman, it usually fell off somewhere on the descent of Grayrigg bank and was found well after break of day by the ganger. Meanwhile, the Tebay stationmaster's clerk was liable to be called out to serve as extempore train staff for a morning.

The general rule was that goods trains exceeding 19 wagons and van were to be banked to Shap Summit and many of the heavy night passenger trains also called for bank engine assistance; a driver requiring such aid was to give three 'crows' on his whistle when approaching No 1 box, then stop opposite the 'indicating post' on the down side

of the line, well north of No 2 box, and restart when the bank engine had come on and whistled up.

Tebay was one of the spots notorious to train crews during both world wars as a likely resting place 'in the loop'. On one wartime night, the signalman in No 2 box was providing shelter for the Carlisle guard off a down goods which was being held indefinitely and for which a relief crew would eventually be found. The guard was long over his official stint of duty, so our signalman thoughtfully stopped a down night passenger train to provide a lift to Carlisle. When the guard attempted to step aboard he was refused access, owing to 'security', as Winston Churchill was on the train — so the guard had to travel on the engine!

The village of Tebay is understood to have had Norse origins, the name signifying 'a dwelling place', but its development came with the L&NWR/NER joint arrangements as a junction station, with engine sheds, traffic marshalling, and much else, from 1860 onwards. All the railway houses stand today, generally in presentable condition. They comprise:

North Terrace, in stone — 12 houses of 1862
South Terrace, in stone — 14 houses (which were gas lit)
Whinfell Terrace, in brick — two blocks, each 15 houses, L&NWR 1898
NER houses in Church Street, in stone — 14 houses, of c1878

This makes 70 houses, plus a later detached one for the stationmaster. North, South and Whinfell Terraces represent the familiar line from north to south on the eastern (up side) cliff above the station, now above its site. It is thought that North Terrace were strictly joint houses and South Terrace not very different in date but L&NWR property. The NER houses came with their engine shed, hence the date and location in a street below the church. The larger end houses in Whinfell Terraces normally were let to locomotive foremen or other staff of superior grades. A house in the Whinfell group was allocated as enginemen's lodgings, chiefly for Edge Hill and Springs Branch men, and there was a matron in charge. All the houses have been sold out of railway stock and not all residents live in them throughout the year. A number of former 'railway' families remain faithful to Tebay village community but live nowadays in more modern houses built privately or by local authority. St James's parish church is one of the centres of village life. It is a worthy building and was built from funds subscribed by the L&NWR, the NER, James Cropper and other gentlemen of Westmorland, the granite for the building being given free by the Shap Granite Company. It was consecrated by the Bishop of Carlisle on 20/7/1880 and opened on 25/7/1880. A week-long centenary celebration took place in July 1980, a pleasant occasion with many mementos of Tebay's railway assocations placed on show by parishioners. Other public buildings include the Primitive Methodist church of 1865, rebuilt 1885; the institute, 1885; an assembly hall, 1902. The market hall above the station and railway houses was demolished in 1962. The nearby cooperative store is now the Barnaby Rudge Tavern, and bears the date 1888. A small building across the road is thought to have sold railway tickets in early days, before the station opened fully. There are several long-standing hostelries and no traveller need go on without sustenance. A speciality still remembered is 'OBJ', the Oh be Joyful Jubilee beer . . .

A number of notable railway photographers made Tebay their special place and came back again and again, being welcomed equally at the inn and by the signalmen and others on the job. The names of Will Whitworth, from the 1920s and 1930s, and after, and of Bishop Eric Treacy, are among those remembered. Others are still happily publishing pictures taken at Tebay and on the Shap incline.

North of Tebay station site one immediately reaches:

$32\frac{1}{4}$ — *North Lune bridge*, of three skew arches in brick and stone construction, carrying the main line over the Lune on to the start of the incline.

$32\frac{1}{2}+$ — *Loups Fell overline bridge*, skew span 56ft 3in, built 1968-69 to carry the M6 over the railway, from the west to east, as seen when travelling north by train.

33up — *Loups Fell cottages*, a pair of railway houses, taken down during 6/1965 (farm buildings immediately to their north remain).

$33\frac{1}{4}+$ — *Birkbeck viaduct*, with three arches of 44ft 6in span, in brick and stone, crosses the beck at about 45ft above the stream.

$33\frac{3}{4}+$ — *Orton Moor bridge ('Scotsman's bridge')* is an overline skew stone arch structure carrying the byroad from Orton to Greenholme over the railway.

34+up — *Lowmoor cottages (alt: Orton Moor cottages)* an early pair, in stone, facing right on to the line, remain occupied, 1981.

35+dn — *Scout Green signalbox site* follows the now-closed level crossing. The classic tall L&NWR up home signal was taken down on 9/6/1963 and a colour-light substituted. Many photographers took their shots hereabouts, many drivers blessed (polite euphemism) the down home signal here, bringing them to a stand on 1 in 75, in all weathers. In World War 2, signalman Joe had occasion to stop a down passenger train and then saw a man at the lineside. Thinking he had alighted by mistake, Joe called to him to climb in, which he did. It later turned out that this was a German officer prisoner-of-war, quartered at Shap Wells Hotel, in a hollow of the fell. The first and most enterprising escape was that of Harry Wappler and Heinz Schnabel, on

a Saturday in late November 1941. Having, with connivance, covered their tracks at the hotel, they clambered at dusk into an open wagon in a slowly ascending goods train, said to be double-headed, and descended when stopped by signals outside Carlisle. After a 'recce' on Sunday, they walked on Monday morning into the RAF station at Kingstown, located between the Caley line and main road just north of the city. With assistance from the ground staff, they took off in a Miles Magister training aircraft. Fuel was very low on reaching the East Anglian coast; a landing was made safely on a farm five miles north of Yarmouth. It proved too late in the day for the RAF station at Horsham St Faith (now Norwich airport) to send out a fuel tanker, so they were collected and offered accommodation overnight in the mess, with refuelling in prospect next morning — for the final hop to the Continent. Unfortunately for the intrepid airmen, a 'signal' reporting loss of an aircraft from Carlisle was associated with them — and before long they were back 'gricing' the traffic on Shap bank.

$36\frac{1}{4}+$**up** — *Salterwath cottages* — an early pair, akin to Lowmoor, also in stone, taken down in 3/1968. In early 20th century, these houses and those at Lowmoor, were occupied by pw staff. Coal was sent in two wagons, one for each site, twice a year from the Tebay coal agent to engineering department order, and shovelled out at each location.

$36\frac{1}{2}+$**dn** — *Shap Wells Hotel*, a quarter mile west of the line, beside Birkbeck, served by a minor road which extends to the A6 on Shap Fell.

$37\frac{1}{4}+$ — *Shap Summit cutting*, 60ft deep, in rock, and footbridge, this having a lofty 98ft span between brick abutments, and being built with wrought iron lattice girders.

$37\frac{1}{2}+$ — *Shap Summit*, with early pair of stone cottages surviving on down side.

up — Shap Summit box was between up main and up loop.

Many bank engines had to be crossed from down to up in steam days and sent back to Tebay as soon as possible.

Shap Granite Company's sidings have been on the down side since at least the late 1870s. Their standard gauge line ('tramway') ran about $2\frac{1}{2}$ miles south west to reach the main granite quarry near Wasdale Head and in the 1960s their 0-6-0ST locomotive could be seen out there at about 1,250ft od on Shap Fell, or making its way back to the granite works, which is by the main line. Outward traffic of stone for many purposes, especially granite setts for paving streets, and later concrete products, was transferred to the mainline system. Railway ballast is the sole output transferred today. The Company's private workmen's train from and to Shap station is later mentioned; its small platform was on the down side, at Summit.

Sidings north of the Granite Company's were put in for Manchester Corporation Waterworks Department. They do not appear on the 1928 line diagram but were installed when work began in 1929 on the Haweswater dam, which was reached from here by a private road. The 1927-29 plans differed from the original ones of 1919, when it had been intended to construct a private standard gauge railway of eight miles from the WCML just north of Shap Granite Works to the dam site, with a branch into Swindale, and the plans included use of electric power for traction. When the work was carried out, and after, a Corporation party made an annual visit to site, for some years, by special train, with motor coaches from the summit; portable steps were brought from Shap station to facilitate de-training in the Corporation sidings. Today, the sidings are used for BR purposes.

At Shap summit the railway reaches 916ft od. There have been serious thoughts of constructing a deviation line from the vicinity of Tebay to near Shap village, including a section in tunnel, with the object of reducing the northbound ascent from 1 in 75 to 1 in 135, but no serious work has been done on the ground. More significant have been the efforts of the L&NWR, and the LMS around 1937 too, in the direction of easing curvature at various points on the L&C route. Currently, the 'tilting train' is seen as a means of maintaining higher speeds over this winding main line.

Shap Summit (exc)-Penrith-Kitchen Hill (inc)

Signalboxes - 1928

Miles/yards	Name	Location and type	Functions	Historical
—	*Shap Quarry*	Up side, near MP 39, BR 'G'	BP; put in to control junction for new quarry at Hardendale.	*Box opened 9/4/1962* Box closed 2/4/1973*PB.*
2/48 (from Summit, in 1928)	Shap	Down side, at south end of station platform. L&NWR 'A'	BP, with limited sidings, up and down.	*Box closed 5/9/1966*.*
—	*Rosgill*	*Probably just south of the (later) Harrisons Sidings.*	BP	*Removed well before 1903.*
—	Harrisons Sidings	*Down side, 1/1265 from Shap station box. LMS 'E', plain brick base.*	BP; put in for down goods loop, giving access to private sidings of limestone works. Up IB signals could be controlled alternatively from here or Thrimby Grange.	*Plans for box dated c10/ 1943. It opened 9/4/1945* with dn goods loop and sidings. Box closed 19/3/ 1973*PB.*
3/423 (from Shap station box in 1928)	Thrimby Grange	Up side, midway along up loop. L&NWR 'D'	BP; put in to control new up loop, installed 1925-26.	Replaced box of same name on down side approx 900yd further north, in 1925-26. Loop shortened at south end wef 31/7/1967* taken out of use 5/7/1971*, and removed by 8/1972. Box closed 19/3/1973*PB.
—	*Bessy Gill*	*About two miles south of Clifton & Lowther.*	BP	*Removed well before 1903.*
4/18 (from Thrimby Grange in 1928)	Clifton and Lowther	South of station, between up main and up goods line. L&NWR 'C'	BP; controlled outlet from up goods line (opened 19/6/ 1905*) — entry was from Eden Valley Junction; also small down yard. **On closure of box, its functions were brought under control of Eden Valley Junction.*	Controlled up IB signals titled 'Bessie Ghyll' (spelling differed from old box). Box closed 10/6/1968*

Miles/Yards	Name	Location and type	Functions	Historical
1/30	Eden Valley Junction	Up side, at the precise junction with NER line. L&NWR 'C', lowbuilt.	BP; and controlled the NER junction with L&C; and access to up goods line opened 19/6/1905*, which was worked permissive but at times under absolute block. Also see previous entry.	Replaced (1903) tall early box of unusual design just to its north (of 1863). NER jn removed 16/5/1966*. Box closed 19/3/1973*PB.
2/317	Eamont Junction	Down side, just north of Eamont viaduct. L&NWR 'D'.	BP; and controlled the NER double track line to Red Hills Junction on CK&P, worked permissively; and the entry to two down goods loops.	Replaced (1906) a rather smaller box which was on same side and slightly farther north.
		The junction at Eamont dated from 1866 (and NER records show first box then opened). The loops dated from 1892; one was retained in the alterations preceding 1974 electrification and it runs through to north end of Penrith station. The NER line to Red Hills became unsafe and was condemned c1936-37, and was lifted in 1937. The box closed 11/7/1938* and was replaced by up IB colour light signals and on the down, unusually, by a down semaphore bracket signal installation, worked as IB signals from Keswick Junction (Penrith No 1) box: see further reference in following text.		
1290	Keswick Junction, No 1 (and variously titled — 'CK&P Junction, No 1' and 'Penrith, Keswick Junction, No 1')	Down side, at convergence of CK&P single line (Keswick line). L&NWR 'C', lengthy.	BP; controlled single track Keswick line*; exit from Nos 1 & 2 down goods loops on to down main; entry to loco shed; entry to two down loops (P&G); exit from goods yard and loop on up side. *Keswick line became entirely single and worked 'one engine in steam' wef 4/12/1967*	Keswick passenger service ceased wef 6/3/1972 and branch cut back to Blencow (Flusco quarry) but closed entirely 19/6/1972*, disconnected, and goods loop connected through from Eamont to Penrith No 3. Box closed 5/3/1973*PB.
463	Penrith Yard, No 2 (inscribed: 'Penrith No 2')	Down side, immediately south of station. L&NWR 'C'	BP; controlled south end of station and Eden Valley bay; also entry to up loop.	Rebuilt just to north, owing to subsidence: new box in L&NWR 'D' style but with lower portion in horizontal timbering, not brick: this box opened 24/8/1950 and closed 29/4/1968*.
360	Penrith North, No 3	Up side, immediately north of station. L&NWR 'A'. Tall brick box, carrying external Saxby & Farmer plate.	BP; controlled convergence of down Keswick platform road and down loops to plain double track northward.	Box closed 5/3/1973*PB.
2/915	Kitchen Hill	Up side, north of former Catterlen overline road bridge. Probably L&NWR 'A' of 1870s.	BP, but worked restricted hours and had periods 'temporarily closed' 'Closed at present' in 1905.	'Closed temporarily', at 7/1925 and 1/1927 — believed never reopened.

Other features, in sequence, northward from Shap Summit include:

39+up — *Shap Quarry*. The new plant and layout of 1962 were put in by Colvilles Ltd/British Steel to marshall and despatch block trains of limestone for Ravenscraig Works, near Motherwell; the traffic has continued ever since, with private diesel locomotive in the sidings but trains drawn out by BR power. For a few years, BR Class '9F' 2-10-0 steam locomotives worked the trains north, nowadays electric locomotives are employed.

39½+ — *Shap station*, closed (P/all) 1/7/1968.

dn — The L&C stone station building survives as a house, its neat canopy lost. A shunting rope — hazardous in use — was employed here, as witness the stabling for many years of the Shap Granite workers' train in a siding on the up side.

39¼-40½ dn — *Shap village* extends for over a mile, mainly along the parallel A6 main road. At the beginning of the century, it boasted three places of worship, a school, market place, market hall and three principal hotels.

40½+ — *'Main Road bridge'* — the A6 crosses the line by a 42ft skew span.

The falling grades from Shap to Penrith are retained from the LMS 1928 line diagram. A full gradient profile of the main line is presented elsewhere in the book.

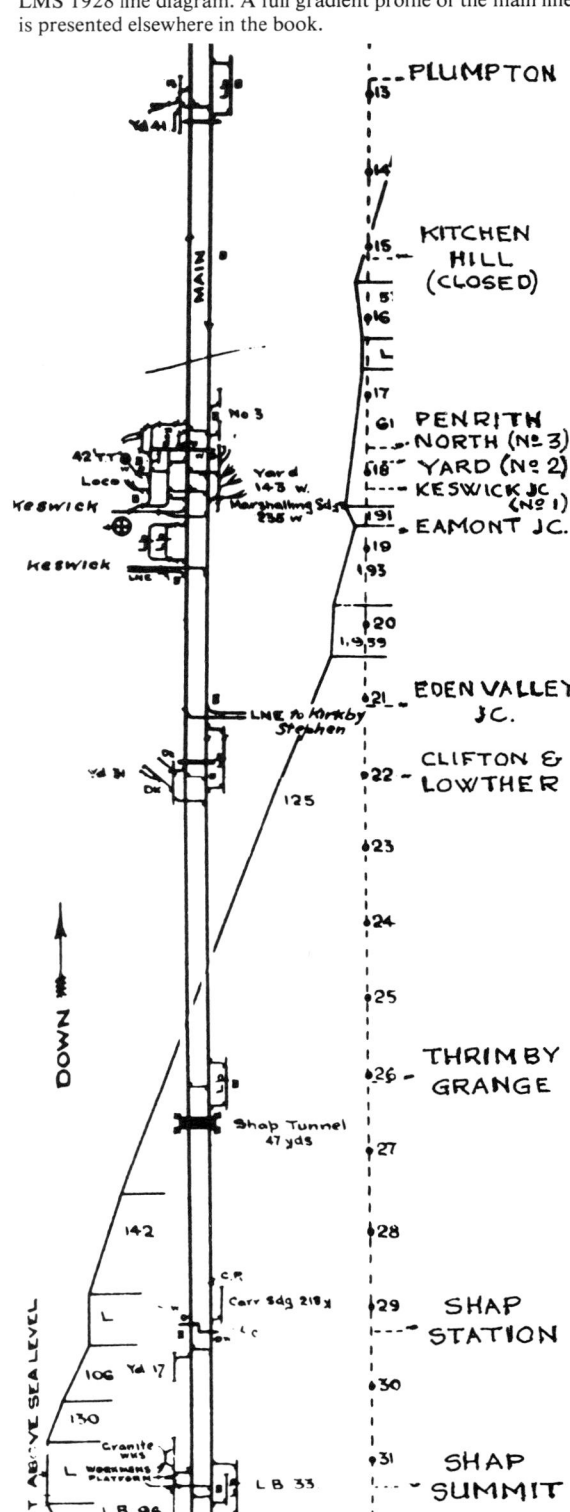

41½dn — *Harrisons Sidings.* The prominent limeworks dates from 1942 but its output was carted to Clifton & Lowther station for loading to rail until box, goods loop and sidings (all on dn side) opened in 4/1945 (see schedule). On up line protection was secured by control of Thrimby Grange up colour-light IB signals, when Harrisons was open, which in general was only during morning call of down road van goods or (as traffic developed) a trip working from/to Penrith. The box was operated for some years by a porter-signalman off the Shap workers' train. A modest traffic is brought out now by BR diesel loco.

42¼+ — *Shapbeck bridge,* the A6 crosses the railway by a 31ft 6in skew stone arch, known to the Railway as 'Shap Tunnel'.

The next 2½ miles embrace Thrimby curves, always a restriction on the running of down express trains; there have been adjustments in the alignments from time to time but with today's 'electric' speeds restriction extends to up (ascending) trains too.

42¾+ — *Harrowstead motorway overline bridge,* 44ft skew span, built 1968-69; going north, it takes the M6 from east to west of the railway.

42.9up — *Thrimby Grange box,* 1926-73, would be immediately north of the motorway bridge at this location.

43+ — *Thrimby bridge,* a single 25ft span on stone abutments, reconstructed 1966, carries the line over the river Leith.

dn — *Thrimby Grange itself (farm house)* is just across the parallel river.

dn — *Pre-1926 site* of Thrimby Grange box.

43½+ — *Little Strickland Road (Thrimby) overline bridge,* two 30ft stone arches. The railway crosses the river Leith, with Thrimby Mill below (up) and passes through woodlands — Thrimby Hall (farm) and the extensive

dn — Lowther estates to the west.

approx 44¾ — *Bessy Gill* is crossed; the early signalbox was probably to the north of this bridge.

45¼up — *Strickland Mill* below, by the River Leith.

47 — *Clifton & Lowther station* (originally: 'Clifton'), closed (P) 4/7/1938.

up — Stone buildings on up platform were demolished mid-1956.

dn — L&C stone station house happily survives but unfortunately, in 1980-81, it was disguised by external cement rendering.

A pair of standard L&NWR brick cottages stand immediately west of it.

up — The Eden Valley Railway (NER) from the direction of Kirkby Stephen (and thus from Darlington by Stainmore) and Appleby opened to here in 4/1862 (G) and 6/1862 (P). The NER used the title 'Clifton Old Junction' and paid for the L&NWR signalman until the end of 5/1875 — but the junction was effectively superseded soon after its completion, owing to the opening to Eden Valley Junction wef 1/8/1863. In 1875 the NER decided to lift the rails on the link to Clifton L&NWR; the site of the NER diverging curve by the trees was just visible from trains in the mid-1950s but has been increasingly obscure since then.

up — The up goods line (from Eden Valley Junction) is retained and converges into the up main, but its southern end was curtailed by 700yds wef 24/7/ 1967.

up — Fell View cottages, block of three neat L&NWR houses of 1914 — backing to line, beyond first bridge.

47-48 — 'Clifton widening works', part in cutting, were executed under Act of 1898 and tender of 12/1902, during 1903-05. They were on the down side, as can be judged from the two overline bridges, and the additional running road became the down main, but the operating improvement was provision of an up goods line, opened 18/6/1905, on the alignment of the previous up main.

up — The course of the Eden Valley Railway (NER), with white buildings of Clifton Moor station, is visible from the WCML, converging towards Eden Valley Junction.

ahead — The first full view of Penrith Beacon on its wooded hill can be secured from a northbound train.

48 — *Eden Valley Junction.*
The actual junction was, by 1906, maintained by the L&NWR at NER cost. The site is now only the junction for the start of the up goods line. The box had rotating permissive block instruments allowing up to four goods trains to be admitted and belled on to Clifton & Lowther; the diverging bracket signal had (until about 1968) a calling-on arm for use if there was traffic already on the goods line. However, absolute block working for passenger trains was in operation at times. In course of pre-electrification works, consternation resulted when an imprudent contractor suddenly brought down one of the ensuing byway overbridges on to the main line tracks, temporarily blocking them. The engineering occupation for demolition was not due until next day.

48+ — 'Clifton Main Road' overline bridge, with 46ft 6in skew stone arch, carries the A6 road over the railway; it was reconstructed in 1973.

48¼+ — Clifton motorway underline bridge, with two spans of 100ft and one of 190ft. Going north, it takes the road from west to east of the line.

48½+ — Hugh's Crag (alt: Lowther) viaduct, length 500ft, with six stone arches each of 59ft span and a height of 100ft above the river Lowther; a

dn — drive through Lowther Park to the former Castle is glimpsed below from passing trains. No doubt, in time past, the Earl's flamboyant yellow equipages, horse and motor, could be discerned by observant travellers.

49½+ — Yanwath overline bridge carries the A592 road, westward to Ullswater, over the railway.

dn — *Yanwath Hall*, with pele tower at its west end, commanded the (only) ford of the river Eamont into Westmorland, and is a fine example of the defensive farm, of which there were a significant number in the county. The river here marks the pre-1974 boundary between the counties of Westmorland and Cumberland.

50+ — *Eamont viaduct*, length rather over 300ft, with five stone arches of 51ft 6in span, bridges the river. Brougham Castle site is downstream, two miles eastward. Immediately north of the viaduct, the main line reaches:
Eamont Junction
The junction and curves beyond were protected by a large 60mph limit board, south of the viaduct and on the down side, at a time when only the LNER displayed speed restriction signs as a matter of policy (they have since been generally adopted by BR).

See the schedule of signalboxes, above, for basic information on the junction and the one-time NER curve, double track, to Redhills Junction — to be discussed in dealing with NER penetration of the L&C route and coke traffic from County Durham to West Cumberland by way of Keswick and Cockermouth.

The right hand curve (viewed northbound) which commences at Eamont Junction has long troubled operating and engineering staff. Under Act of 1889, a major realignment was completed in time for the 'twelfth August', 1892. The original main line became two down goods lines, commencing at Eamont Junction and re-emerging on to the main line at Keswick Junction. The new up and down main lines were on the inside of the curve, but nevertheless more fitted for fast running. In 1906-07 further realignment of the main line tracks was carried out, completed just in time to give better passage to summer traffic in 1907. A new signalbox was provided at this time. Further adjustments to the curves were made subsequently, believed to be about 1937. The loops were well used until the decline in general freight traffic of late years.

The configuration and operation of the signals for down trains heading for main, loops or Redhills curve were of considerable interest. When all the routes were available, the L&NWR bracket signal was located just *south* of the viaduct. The structure was carried on a pair of upright posts, topped by the arms for the loops (left to right) Nos 2 and 1, and the right hand post was very close to passing trains. A cross structure provided cantilever support for a left hand post ('doll') with higher arm for the branch — this outer doll called for strong nerves in an ascending lampman, as it was high above the valley. To the right, symmetrically cantilevered out, was a still taller doll carrying the down main home signal arm for Eamont Junction and the distant below it, worked from Keswick

Junction. This doll was just about over the centre of the down 'four foot', so here the lampman swayed in the breeze, felt the smoke and vibration of a fitted freight passing below and could glance down on to the swaying vans with the thought that, if one came off the road, the signal would be the first casualty to be hurled into the valley below. It was a notable signal installation.

Around the time when Eamont Junction box closed, in 1938, with Redhills curve abandoned, the loop entry points were electrified and brought under control of Keswick Junction box. The bracket signal was remodelled. It now had three dolls (for, left to right; No 2 loop arm; No 1 loop arm and calling-on arm below; main line home and distant) and, it is suggested but not corroborated, that the signal now had upper quadrant arms in place of L&NWR ones. The entire signal installation was worked from Keswick Junction box and regarded as an intermediate block signal; it was thus unusual both in being a *semaphore* IB signal and an IB signal *in rear* of the controlling box.

In 1945, 16 April*, the IB bracket signal was superseded, its replacement being 180 yards to the north, namely *north* of Eamont viaduct and close to the divergence of the loops; it had a lattice steel post and tubular dolls and the former calling-on arm for No 1 loop was not reproduced. The dismantlement of the old wooden bracket signal proved a delicate task and it is reputed that at one stage of the operation it threatened to topple into the valley near Yanwath Hall farm buildings, along with a supervising inspector.

No 1 loop had priority over No 2 and, in emergencies, it was permissible to use it for passenger trains, after absolute block working had been instituted in place of 'permissive' working. There were many safeguards attending the working of the rear section IB signals and the loops — and down main line. The distant at Eamont could not be pulled off by Keswick Junction (Penrith No 1 box) signalman until his colleague in No 2 box had 'line clear' from No 3. The down main line was track circuited throughout from Eden Valley Junction to Keswick Junction, so that the signalman could be certain that trains had cleared *complete* into the loops, and the facing points were locked by occupation of the track circuits. Keswick Junction also had an illuminated diagram and, when a train had cleared into one of the loops, a brief bell-note would call attention. During 1938-45, safe and speedy operation was further helped by the miniature calling-on arm below the signal arm (on the bracket signal, 1938 version) concerned with No 1 loop; this enabled an approaching driver to see at once that he was entering a vacant loop (top arm off) or a loop already partly occupied (lower miniature arm off). After the new signal of 1945, devoid of calling-on arm, was in operation, the entry of goods trains to the loop was slowed and clearance of the

down main for faster following trains was delayed. On occasion, however, drivers took the surviving loop signal arm as clearance for the full loop and collided, albeit not disastrously, with a train ahead. This, and a disaster in 1960 when an almighty crash occurred due to derailment at excessive speed, led to even more caution; some drivers made a point of stopping on the viaduct and telephoning to gain assurance that the loop ahead was clear. Between 17/6/1945 and 16/9/1945, all down traffic was diverted through Eamont No 1 loop, with a 15mph restriction, during repairs to an underline bridge.

50¾+ — *Penrith Motorway underline bridge* possesses two 100ft and one 158ft spans over the Penrith by-pass section of the M6 — which is carried from east to west of a northbound train. This bridge was built in 1965-67. A pre-existing railway bridge over the B5320 road was filled in and that road re-aligned.

dn — On the down side of the line and close beside the B5320 still stands Eamont Terrace, four standard L&NWR brick houses; their backs face towards the main line, in the angle of main and former Redhills curve, but they cannot be seen from the main line.

50¾+dn — *Keswick Junction, Penrith No 1 signalbox* was in the down side bank, just north of the M6 underline bridge. From 23/11/1964, the Keswick line lost its direct outlet here to the down main. In October-November 1965, the No 2 down loop, with its outlet at No 1 box, was eliminated. Until 5/6/1967, traffic from the loop(s) had always been obliged to emerge on to the down main, even if diverging almost at once to the station area loop lines — while trains off the Keswick single line could run independently to the down station loops or the back face of Penrith down island platform. Under the 1972-73 scheme, the retained Eamont-Penrith down goods loop was slued on to the Keswick branch alignment and continues independently of the main line, over the motorway bridge and right through to the north end of the station. There is now no CK&PR line, Cockermouth and Keswick to Penrith, nor NER traffic to accommodate.

up — *Southern approach to Penrith.* The large goods yard closed wef 7/1/1971. At 8/1972, a rail-served coal concentration depot was observed at its southerly end but this had gone before the time of electric working, May 1974.

up — *The castle ruins* are visible on a slight eminence between the station and town centre. The beacon stands on its hill behind the town.

51+ — *Penrith station* is on a left hand curve, northbound. Its design produces a rather austere and gloomy — but always clean and tidy — interior, but with a handsome L&C neo-Elizabethan exterior (up) facing towards castle and town.

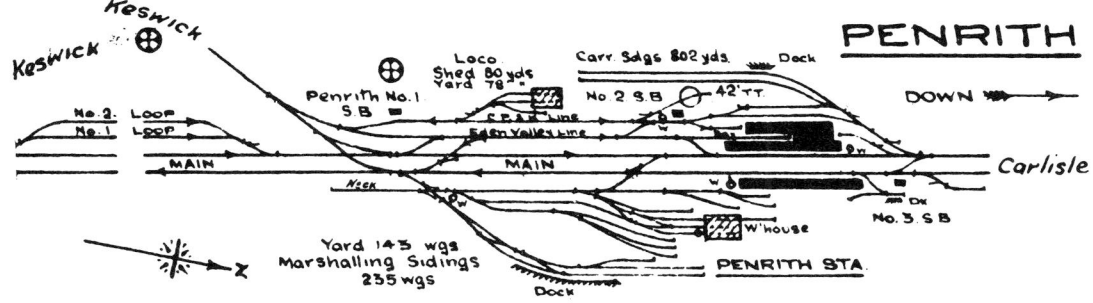

Under Act of 1862, the Penrith Joint Station Committee was formed; members were the L&NWR, the Stockton & Darlington Railway (becoming NER) and the CK&PR. The NER had running powers from Eden Valley Junction to the yard and station at Penrith; the 'Eden Valley bay' was for long a feature. The platforms were lengthened during pre-electrification works.

$51\frac{1}{4}$+ — *Greystoke Road overline bridge*, with a stone arch of 30ft span, carries the A594 over the line immediately north of Penrith station. The tall and ancient No 3 signalbox stood on the up side close against this bridge and the signalman could command a view northward over the top of it. The

box carried a Saxby and Farmer plate, presumably that box and equipment were originally by these familiar contractors to the L&NWR. Long Ash accommodation crossing is about 2 miles to the north.

$53\frac{3}{4}$ — *Kettleside viaduct*, overline bridge, with two spans of 55ft and two of 75ft, built 1967-68, carrying an M6 link road over the line.

$53\frac{3}{4}$+up — *Kitchen Hill box;* the site was immediately south of the river bridge (next entry): see schedule of boxes, above.

$53\frac{3}{4}$+ — *River Petterill underline bridge*, with three brick arches of 15ft span, and stone abutments, crossing the river.

Kitchen Hill (exc)-Carlisle Citadel

Signalboxes - 1928

Miles/yards	Name	Location and type	Functions	Historical
2/620 (from Kitchen Hill)	Plumpton	Up side, midway on up loop, which is north of station. L&NWR 'D'	BP; controlled up loop put in 1925-26, also small yard on down side. Controlled up IB signals, put in towards Kitchen Hill after its demise; also new IB signals wef 10/12/1962 (on down line).	Replaced (1925-26) box on same side but about 200 yards further south. Box closed 5/3/1973*PB, loop retained.
2/323	Calthwaite	Down side, north of station. L&NWR 'C'	BP, with crossover and two sidings on down side.	Replaced (probably around 1900) box on up side, north of station. Box closed 10/12/1962*.
3/1080	Southwaite	Down side, well north of station. L&NWR 'D'	BP; controlling up and down loops (which were converted 1925-26 from refuge sidings) also controlled new IB signal wef 10/12/1962 (on up line). Note reference below to Wreay tip. Up loop taken out of use from 5/4/1971* and down loop from 1/11/1971* Box closed 19/2/1973*PB.	Replaced (1925-26) box of L&NWR type 'A' also on downside but at north end of down platform, about 480yds south of 1926 box.
				Continued overleaf

Miles/Yards	Name	Location and type	Functions	Historical
2/191	Wreay	Down side, south of station and underline bridge.	BP; had one small coal siding on up side (this siding and its frame removed 7/1945).	Box closed 11/2/1935* and replaced by up and down IB sigs (later: two sets on up).
		Around 1914-18, ED sidings put in on down side, southward of station, for loco shed ash and were controlled (through medium of a ground frame). After the box closed, the ground frame was released electrically by Southwaite box, as was ground frame for coal siding.		
—	*Woodbank*	*Down side, south of underline bridge, on lane from Woodbank cottages.*	*BP; believed primarily to control private siding on up side.*	*Siding in use by 1879, although reference suggests new box (10 levers; dated 1884). Building survived 1899 but not listed by 1906.*
3/1116 (from Wreay)	Carlisle No 13 (Upperby Bridge Junction)	Down side L&NWR 'C', dating from 1877	BP; controlled southern access/outlet for Upperby Yard and goods lines.	Box closed 4/6/1973*PB
668	Carlisle No 12	Up side L&NWR 'C'	BP; with up direction connection to goods lines and down off goods lines.	Replaced 19/5/1946 by new box (LMS 'F') on down side. Box closed 4/6/1973*PB.
1320	Carlisle No 5, Crown Street	Up side, immediately south of Citadel station. L&NWR 'C', large and lofty, of 1880.	BP for all routes including L&C, at south end of station; and worked with 4A (Platform cabin, on upper floor on island).	Replaced 9/1951 by new No 5 (LMS 'F') on down, 120yd sth. Box closed 4/6/1973*PB.

Other features, in sequence, northward of Kitchen Hill include:

56 — *Plumpton station,* closed (P) 31/5/1948.

dn — The main building was on the down platform, single storey in sandstone but differing in style from the stations further south; it was empty in 9/1966 and razed by 7/1967.

up — The loop was put in 1925-26 and is retained today.

up — Petterill Terrace of eight houses, stands on the road which passes under the railway immediately south of the station site. The village is about three quarters of a mile further east, near the A6.

dn — other L&NWR cottages survive, to west of the site.

dn — Hutton Hall, residence of Sir H. R. Vane in 1859, is at Hutton-in-the-Forest, two miles to the west, and the station was sited to serve it.

58¼+ — *Calthwaite station,* closed (P) 7/4/1952.
There were small buildings on each platform and sloping footways down from each platform to reach the road passing beneath the line at the north end. A shunting rope was used for wagons; the yard was on the downside.

up — A terrace of five L&NWR brick cottages, the westerly one much the largest and clearly for the stationmaster, stands on the roadside.

dn — The village is a third of a mile to the west.

up — There was at one time an up siding in section, to the north of Calthwaite.

61½+ — *Southwaite station* — closed (P) 7/4/1952

up — The main station building survives, on the up side, and is in the 'L&C Keeper's cottage' style, in stone.

up — The village adjoins, to east.
Note that loops were adapted, north of the station, but both abandoned prior to electrification.

approx 64dn — *Wreay engineer's ash tip* was south of Wreay station, with ground frame and small fan of sidings. The tip was built up, from a start round about 1914, using ashes from Upperby (Carlisle) engine shed, and reached main line level by the late 1930s, there being probably four or five sidings by then. It existed in 1939-45 but the ash was later recovered and the ground lowered and grassed; the site is difficult to identify without guidance.

64+ — *Wreay station* — pronounced 'Reeah' — closed (P) 16/8/1943.

dn — The substantial sandstone station building of two storeys, but not in the L&C cottage tradition, stands as a residence. Small timber buildings on the up platform have long been demolished.

dn — The village is a quarter mile to the west.

65¼ — *Low Hurst underline bridge* has four spans: 58ft, 95ft, 95ft, 58ft — built 1968-69, it carries the railway across the motorway. From a northbound train, the road passes west to east, obliquely and somewhat concealed in cutting; it is heading to by-pass Carlisle well to the east of the city.

65¾ — *Brisco overline bridge,* with one skew span of 34ft 4in, was built 1968-69, carrying an M6 link road; it replaces the bridge which carried a road from the A6 to Durdar and which previously crossed the line just south of Brisco station, but has been demolished.

65¾+ — *Brisco station,* closed after about six years, in early L&C days. A typical L&C sandstone

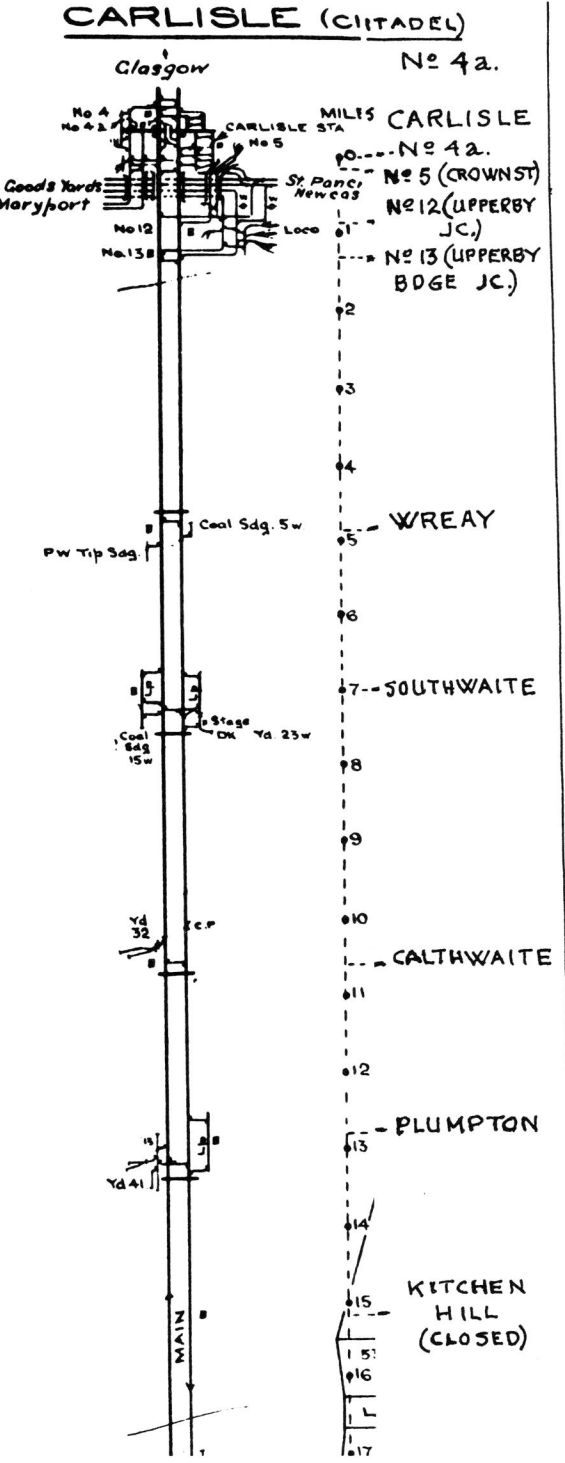

CARLISLE (CITADEL)

Glasgow   № 4a.

MILES CARLISLE
    № 4a.
  № 5 (CROWN ST)
  № 12 (UPPERBY JC.)
  № 13 (UPPERBY BDGE JC.)

WREAY

SOUTHWAITE

CALTHWAITE

PLUMPTON

KITCHEN HILL (CLOSED)

building survives on the up side, as a well-kept residence.

approx 67 — *Woodbank*. This site is approximately $1\frac{1}{2}$ miles north of Brisco old station house and just over a half mile south of Upperby Bridge Junction; it is immediately north of MP67. An insignificant lane comes down from Woodbank cottages, one third mile south-west, to pass Woodbank House and squeeze muddily under the main line to end near the river Petterill, a few hundred yards east of the line. Woodbank Works was at the end of the lane (east-up side of railway), near the river; only its nearer wing remains, as a house.

Cowans Sheldon & Company established Woodbank Works in 1846, year of opening of the L&C. By 1858, Mr John Cowans resided at Woodbank and the Company were 'ironfounders and forged iron manufacturers and manufacturers of malleable iron wheels and axles for railway and other purposes, and railway waggon and truck builders.' From 1857, the Company also developed St Nicholas Works, London Road, Carlisle. About 1870, all work became concentrated at St Nicholas, beside the NER leaving Citadel station, where the Company is today so well known as makers of rail-mounted breakdown and other cranes, also having constructed railway turntables and, for example, an early mechanical coaling plant for Upperby engine sheds.

A blockpost was established at Woodbank in the 1870s, with a siding; on site, it is clear that this would be a short one, immediately south of the underline bridge, and trailing off the up main line. It is believed that the siding dates from the early days of Cowans, Sheldon & Company. In 7/1879, it figured as a private siding of C. Vynne & Company. Previously (1873), John Jackson, manure merchant, had occupied Woodbank and, until at least 1897, the Woodbank Chemical Manure Company occupied the works, so probably C. Vynne was an intermediate proprietor of the manure business. By 1899, the works was 'disused' and the siding was certainly not listed in 1904. The box was closed by then. The siding may have been worked in early days by ground frame, as the box is believed to have dated from 7/1884, with 10 levers in use. The site and foundations of the tiny box can be located on the ground, in the *down* side banking beside the line, opposite to where the siding points were probably located in the *up* road.

$67\frac{1}{2}$+ — *Upperby Bridge Junction, site of Carlisle No 13 box (on down side)*. A byroad is crossed with its 'Upperby Bridge' over the Petterill below railway level, to east. The goods lines diverge and run initially parallel on up side.

See the enlarged layout diagram of 1928 and the schedule of boxes, above — but note that the schedule has been curtailed to show only the boxes controlling L&C passenger trains until they reach Carlisle Citadel station. Many of the other signal

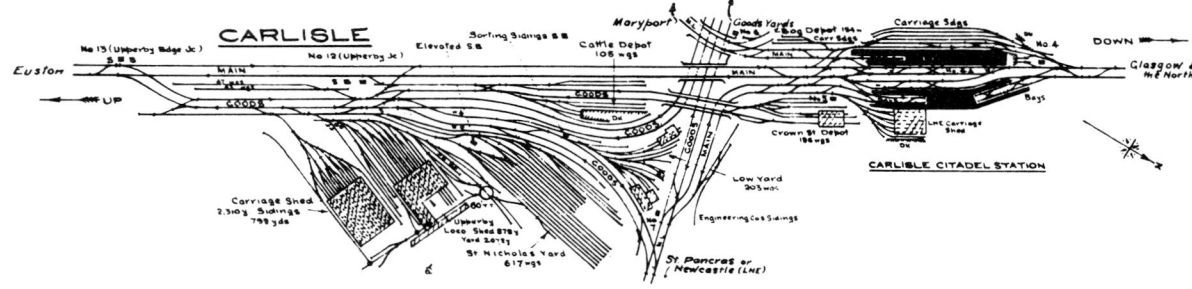

boxes in the Carlisle area were of L&NWR design. The accounts of Carlisle Upperby yard working and of Upperby engine sheds, which follow, are relevant to the scene from Upperby Bridge to Citadel.

A new cement plant for receiving traffic by rail has been under construction during late 1981 into 1982 on a site beyond the former Upperby engine sheds — it is seen over to the up side near the Upperby to London Road curve.

69+ — *Carlisle Citadel station*

The original station was greatly enlarged in 1880. The massive island platform, with its magnificent range of buildings, dates from then and is used by down trains, and its east face also by some up trains. More up main line trains use the platform on the original, eastern, side of the station, near the entrance in the Citadel square.

From 1880, maintenance of the station was shared by the Caledonian Railway and the L&NWR, until they merged in 1923 in the LMS. The former L&NWR Crown Street goods depot, which closed 1/2/1966, was over to east of the entry by rail to Citadel station and the buildings

gave place during 1980-81 to new commerical structures, a warehouse and showrooms development.

The L&NWR 'railway community' mostly centred on the Upperby district; a long footbridge crossed directly from the engine sheds to the neighbourhood west of the railway where Company houses were situated; it was removed in the alterations prior to electrification.

Oxenholme-Kendal-Windermere

Schedule of stations and signalboxes

also referring to level crossings which are not blockposts

The schedule seeks to present the branch line as it was during most of the 20th century until conversion to single track and elimination of almost all signalling was effected in April-May 1973. The stations are shown with official cumulative mileages from Oxenholme, the signalboxes with individual mileages culled from appendices between 1905 and 1954.

Mileages		Title of station, box or crossing	Location, type and further remarks
from O'holme	*Individual*		
2⅛		*Kendal station*	
	2/404	Kendal box	Down side, well north of station, with back to goods yard; mileage quoted from Oxenholme No 3 box, also revised (longer) mileage from Oxenholme No 2 new box, as applicable 1943-55. L&NWR 'C' type. Replaced by new box (LMS 'F') on same side but 22yd further north: opened 25/7/1955*, closed 30/4/1973* (or 14/5/1973*).
	2/647 from 16/7/1943		
		Burneside Higher Crossing	Just south of yard and station, located down side, to north of crossing: small timber cabin, open frame, stone cottage. See later notes.
4		*Burneside station*	
	1/1378	' Burneside '. 'Burneside Station Frame'	Up side, south end of platform: it was an open frame, instruments believed in station office; small hut erected over frame and reduced mileage implies transfer of instruments to this structure, which closed 14/5/1973*
	later 1/1357		
		Burneside Lower Crossing	Just north of station: frame in small wooden cabin on up side, stone cottage opposite on down side. See later notes.

Mileages		Title of Station, box or crossing	Location, type and further remarks
from O'holme	Individual		
		Staveley level Crossing	Approx $\frac{3}{4}$-mile south of Staveley station: small timber cabin, frame, stone cottage, all on up side, just north of the crossing, on main Kendal-Keswick road A591. See later notes.
$6\frac{5}{8}$		*Staveley station*	
	2/811 later 2/827	Staveley box	Up side, significantly south of station. Believed L&NWR 'C'. Upper portion of box rebuilt in LMS style after fire of 1948, but L&NWR brick base and L&NWR frame retained. Box closed 1 June 1964*.
		Droomer's Crossing	About $\frac{1}{2}$-mile south of Windermere station, with cottage. Crossing closed to road traffic at or by 1973.
$10\frac{1}{4}$		*Windermere station*	
	3/987	Windermere box	Down side, before underline bridge at entry. L&NWR 'C'. Box closed 14/5/1973*.

Access to the Windermere Line and conversion (1973) to single track

The northern double-line junction at Oxenholme was controlled by No 3 signalbox, and from 1943 by No 2 box; this junction was taken out of use wef 13/5/1968*. From then on, the double track on the branch was only connected with the main line through the single outer platform road. The branch itself was converted to single track, with 'one engine' working throughout its length, from 30/4/1973*. From 14/5/1973*, control of this access was transferred from Oxenholme No 2 box to Carlisle power box. An authority to enter the branch is secured at Oxenholme platform and an approach-controlled colour-light signal admits a train from the branch to the platform. The 5/1973 layout at Oxenholme appears on the 1974 line and signalling diagram reproduced. In general, the track retained on the Windermere line was the pre-1973 up road, except through Kendal station, where the old down track and platform are the ones in use.

Gradients, Oxenholme to Windermere

miles

0-2	Oxenholme to Kendal	falling 1 in 80 throughout		
2-2$\frac{1}{8}$	Kendal station	level		
2$\frac{1}{8}$-4	Kendal to Burneside	2$\frac{1}{8}$-2$\frac{1}{4}$	:	falling 1 in 165
		2$\frac{1}{4}$-3$\frac{3}{8}$	:	rising 1 in 146
		3$\frac{3}{8}$-3$\frac{5}{8}$	:	falling 1 in 116
		3$\frac{5}{8}$-4	:	rising 1 in 120
4-6$\frac{5}{8}$	Burneside to Staveley	4-5$\frac{5}{8}$	:	rising 1 in 80
		5$\frac{5}{8}$-6$\frac{5}{8}$	:	rising 1 in 147
6$\frac{5}{8}$-10$\frac{1}{4}$	Staveley to Windermere	6$\frac{5}{8}$-7$\frac{3}{8}$	:	rising 1 in 80
		7$\frac{3}{8}$-8$\frac{7}{8}$	:	rising 1 in 89
		8$\frac{7}{8}$-9$\frac{1}{8}$	:	level
		9$\frac{1}{8}$-10$\frac{1}{4}$	:	falling 1 in 75
		10$\frac{1}{4}$-end	:	level

The frequent, and ruling, gradients are steeper than anything in the 90 miles between Preston and Carlisle, except the four northbound miles of 1 in 75 on Shap incline.

Further, the ascents are from standing starts, for most trains: going down, from Burneside station and again from Staveley station; coming up, from Windermere station and the culminating two miles of 1 in 80 from Kendal to Oxenholme platforms. It is not surprising that, from time to time, heavy trains had problems with unfavourable weather when combined with these re-starts. Piloting of the heavier up trains was a feature in the days of 2-4-0 'Jumbo' locomotives, while banking of freights from Kendal yard to Oxenholme took place until close on the end of steam days.

Other features of the route, Oxenholme to Windermere

dn — *Kendal castle* (ruins).

dn — *Kendal engine shed.* The site remains vacant, approaching the town; it is preceded by Castlepark Terrace (backs of eight houses of mid-19th century, seen on up side), then (down side) early villas in gardens face the vacant site across an intervening road.

1$\frac{3}{4}$+ — *Handsome underline bridge* crosses onetime Peat Lane, now for long called Castle Street, A684, immediately following the old shed site.

2+ — *Kendal station*

Entering, the underline bridge over Longpool, the A6 road for Shap and Carlisle, carries on oval plate reading: 'Cochrane & Co, Woodside Iron Works, Dudley, Worcestershire, 1859'.

The station had up and down platforms and subway, also a trailing 'dock' road on the down side at down end. The surviving track uses the down platform, with (externally) quite interesting stone buildings facing a courtyard and the County Hotel; the station buildings, sadly decayed and unstaffed, are to be curtailed in extent.

up — *Kendal carriage shed* had three roads and was beyond (north of) the station; it was eventually demolished but the sidings survived, chiefly for bogie parcels vans, until final rundown and closure of facilities.

dn — *Kendal goods and coal yard*

Access trailed off beyond the box (and surviving

footbridge) and before the river. For much of its life there were 14 principal roads in this yard, viewed from those nearest the running lines and looking westward:

Two good roads on which trains could be made up
Two roads entering the large goods shed
Two shorter roads for stabling and assembling vehicles
Two long roads, primarily for livestock traffic ('Super D' 0-8-0 engine No 9151 had an aversion to the cattle dock and came off here repeatedly)
Three short roads, each allocated at one time to a coal merchant for his traffic (but indeed there were more merchants who used the yard)
Two roads into the huge, old-world bonded warehouse, a building in the 'canal tradition'
One more outside road liable to be used for oil traffic ('Shell' storage adjoining) and at one time a track left the yard via a wagon turntable, crossed Station Road and entered the wool warehouse of Whitwell, Hargreaves & Company — a substantial stone building which is one of the town's museums.

On a typical day, there was Windermere and Burneside traffic to despatch and receive by local goods workings, plus the express goods train for Liverpool and the coal empties for Wigan to assemble and despatch. Horse and cattle sales and — in time past — touring fairs produced exceptionally busy days for the staff in what was, until the 1960s, a traditionally busy yard. Much coal was handled but there was a great amount of varied merchandise, both in and outward. Final rundown was rapid and formal closure took effect on 1/5/1972.

2¼+ — *Kent viaduct* of five skew spans, varying from 37ft 3in to 40ft 6in, with stone abutments and piers, carries the line across the Kent. This is a short river from high fells to the sea and thus subject to rapid changes in flow and level, a situation much improved by control works in recent years. Dockray Hall bridge, four spans of 16ft 10in, over a former mill race, is immediately north of the viaduct.

around 4 — *Burneside station* had staggered platforms, with a timber structure on each, and the gabled stone station house is on the up side; the up platform is the one in use, unstaffed.

The paper mills and their railways
The mills have had a long and close association with the Windermere line, at Burneside. The proprietors are James Cropper & Company Ltd, a private limited company. At the time of his interest in the promotion of the Kendal & Windermere and Lancaster & Carlisle Railways, Cornelius Nicholson was partner in the active business of paper making at Burneside and nearby Cowan Head (alt: Cowen Head). These mills were taken

over by James Cropper in 1845, when he moved, aged 22 years, from Dingle Bank, Liverpool. He married a daughter of the Wakefield family; note the lengthy Wakefield interests in Westmorland gunpowder and the present-day interest of Lord Wakefield of Kendal in the Ravenglass & Eskdale Railway. A third paper mill was established at Bowston and horse-worked tramways were developed from Cowan Head via Bowston to Burneside station yard (1¼ miles) and from Burneside mill to the station yard (about ¼-mile), with interlaced tramway and L&NWR tracks for transhipment purposes. Croppers were directors of the L&NWR; from 1914 to 1934, a 'Claughton' class four-cylinder 4-6-0 locomotive carried the name *Charles J. Cropper*. During his chairmanship, the private tramway system was converted to a standard gauge railway, using rails captured from the Turks, in the Palestine campaign, by General Allenby. Physical connection was made with the L&NWR in Burneside yard, up side, south of the station. Petrol locomotive *Rachel*, Motor Rail and Tramcar Company No 2096, was acquired new (or virtually new) on 22 September 1924 to work the line. Initially, it was driven by Derek E. Willink, who came down that year from university to join the business and, as a first assignment, to see the new railway satisfactorily commissioned. Later, Mr Willink was a chairman of the Company and is happily an active figure today. The original locomotive — now preserved on the Lakeside & Haverthwaite Railway — was supplemented in 1951 by another, a product of Ruston & Hornsby Ltd, their No 294266/1951, itself preserved since 1973 at Steamtown, Carnforth. The longer private branch closed wef 8/11/1965. Croppers decided late in 5/1971 to lift their remaining tracks, namely at Burneside, but in fact continued to exchange traffic with BR and to use their own locomotive until at least January 1972, indeed closure to rail traffic took place on 9 June 1972, nominal last day of working. *Public* goods and mineral traffic at Burneside had ended in 1964 and the exchange with Croppers had in latter years been limited to inwards coal and outward empty wagons.

Burneside and Staveley level crossings
The crossings were all gated and all except the one at Burneside station were manned by resident crossing keepers, who had a stone cottage adjoining. At Burneside station, away back in 1913, the junior porter would open the level crossing gates at 9.00 each morning, for Mr Charles James Cropper to cycle down from his home, bound for the mills. Under the arrangements of 1973 onwards, there are no crossing keepers but a qualified signalman is on duty during the working hours of the line, at 'Higher Crossing'; he is provided with a small timber cabin and open lever frame beside it. Going down, the present arrangements are as follows:

Burneside Higher:
   manual gates — signalman — semaphore home
   and distant signals in each direction — a buzzer
   warns when a down train is leaving Kendal.
Burneside Station:
   occupation crossing — gates padlocked.
Burneside Lower
   ungated crossing — trains operate yellow and
   red lights for road traffic and the driver of the
   train is given a white signal aspect for 'proceed',
   at severely restricted speed; there is no red aspect
   for the driver.
Staveley
   auto half-barriers, with usual lights, on the main
   road, operating since 16/10/1967; on the
   railway, up colour light home and distant signals
   are maintained at green but can be put to red by
   the signalman at Higher Crossing; he would do
   this in the event of emergency or failure of the
   barriers.

$6\frac{1}{2}+$ — *Staveley station* had a gabled stone building,
which survives, on the up side, with house at the
lower level and, formerly, offices on the upper (platform) level. There was a small brick building on the
down platform, which was lengthened in timber to
facilitate collection of tickets (for Windermere). The
up platform is in use, unstaffed. The yard, with
three roads, was on the down side.

$10\frac{1}{4}$ — *Windermere station*

The plan on p48 conveys a good idea of the layout
during 1900-70. Central to this are four passenger
platform roads. To the westerly side were five roads
of modest, some short, lengths, available for stabling
stock, also one turntable road, which also led to the
engine shed until that closed, c1917-19. A plan
made in 1910 shows a 'gunpowder shed' in the
extreme west — for traffic from the Elterwater
factory in the Langdale valley. To the east
was a useful road terminating in the handsome,
double-gabled goods shed (a building which just
about stands today), two roads serving the cattle
dock and three more tracks for goods or coal, but
which could be cleared and pressed into service for
stabling carriages. This summary tallies with a
statement that in pre-1914 days there were eight
roads, as maximum, for holding carriages. On a
peak summer day, at that period, there would be 16
or 17 excursions into Windermere; thus a
'Cauliflower' 0-6-0 goods engine was kept busy
working stock to Staveley and Oxenholme for-
stabling, and bringing it back towards evening.

The two most westerly sidings, near the
boundary of the railway site, were lengthened (over
reclaimed ground) and the third track from the
boundary on that side was cleared of structures;
thus three fairly useful carriage stabling roads were
created — in, it is believed, 1911, to supplement
four platform roads and 'middle road' (and any
tracks temporarily 'requisitioned' from the goods
department).

The 'town' end of the passenger station is stone
built, with a well-proportioned 'train shed' and a
shapely entrance portico over the original
carriageway, at the side. The train shed is about to
be converted to a food store, scarcely ideal use for
part of potentially the principal railhead for Lake
District residents and visitors. In 1910, a partially
glazed 'cab awning' was provided on the main platform, adjoining the goods shed, in order to protect
travellers and luggage using road conveyances to
and from the trains; it has recently been
demolished.

There was a 'middle road' between the two
principal platform tracks but there were no convenient engine runround facilities and an arriving
train had either to be drawn out by an engine on the
rear or, more often, propelled out by the engine
which had brought the train in. The rule in 1905
was that an engine must be *attached* to lower the
stock of an empty train safely back into the same,
or another, platform; if the train was too long, it
was permissible to lower it on the handbrake sufficiently to *attach* a locomotive, which would then
complete the process of lowering it down the
gradient into platform or siding. In later years, the
rule was relaxed and, after propelling, train brakes
were released and the handbrake used to control
the lowering of the stock; this had an unfortunate
outcome on more than one occasion, notably in
August 1962! In 1971, it was possible, after partial
propelling, to run round five coaches but longer
trains were dealt with by 'gravitating'. During that
year, the layout was pruned of all but four roads, of
which three had platform faces, with box and basic
signalling retained.

At that stage, there were plans in being, with
target May 1973, for building a new box at
Burneside and reducing that at Windermere to
ground frame status. By 1973, the 'single track and
one unit of motive power on the branch' school predominated. Various responsible bodies represented
that the layout should not be curtailed further at
Windermere and a thoughtful article in *The
Guardian* made the point with clarity. However,
the Beeching-promoted management of the day
insisted on destroying the remaining 'operating'
assets at Windermere, apart from a single platform
road, along with 'singling' of the whole branch line.
Since 1973, it has not been possible even to provide
connections for Windermere with all down and up
express trains; a diesel set which connects out of a
down express at Oxenholme often cannot complete
the round trip in time to connect into the next up
(or down) main line train and, with frequent late
running on the main line, the restriction becomes
even more significant. Again, express trains which
in L&NWR/LMS days ran from London and
Manchester to Windermere now have to make 100
miles round trip Oxenholme-Carlisle and back over
the empty fells. There are occasional stirrings

which suggest that realisation has dawned that economical working and expansion of inwards and outwards traffic could result from restoring certain features of the layout and, one hopes, effecting 10 mainly single-track miles of electrification; ample power is available at Natland feeder station close by Oxenholme.

Hours of operation

In general, the last trains were the 5.50pm (approx) from Crewe, reaching Windermere just after 9.30pm, and the 'Kendal Whip', which terminated at Kendal around 11.30pm; in each case, the engine returned to Oxenholme. The line was then closed until service resumed with the down 'Mail', into Windermere about 5.30am (1982 time: 05.41). For years, the last train or engine at night between Kendal and Windermere was required to carry a 'target' — an additional tail lamp painted white and showing a white light — the respective station-masters being responsible. Gatekeepers were not to close for the night until the 'targeted' workings had passed. Kendal and Windermere boxes used to close accordingly; those at Burneside and Staveley worked shorter, or more intermittent, hours.

The Windermere Hotel

The hotel on the Orrest Head slope, above Windermere station and the main road, was opened 12/5/1847, the railway company having one third share in the project. The hotel, which exists today, was noted for its proprietor Mr Rigg and his enterprising provision of coaches for guests and other tourists.

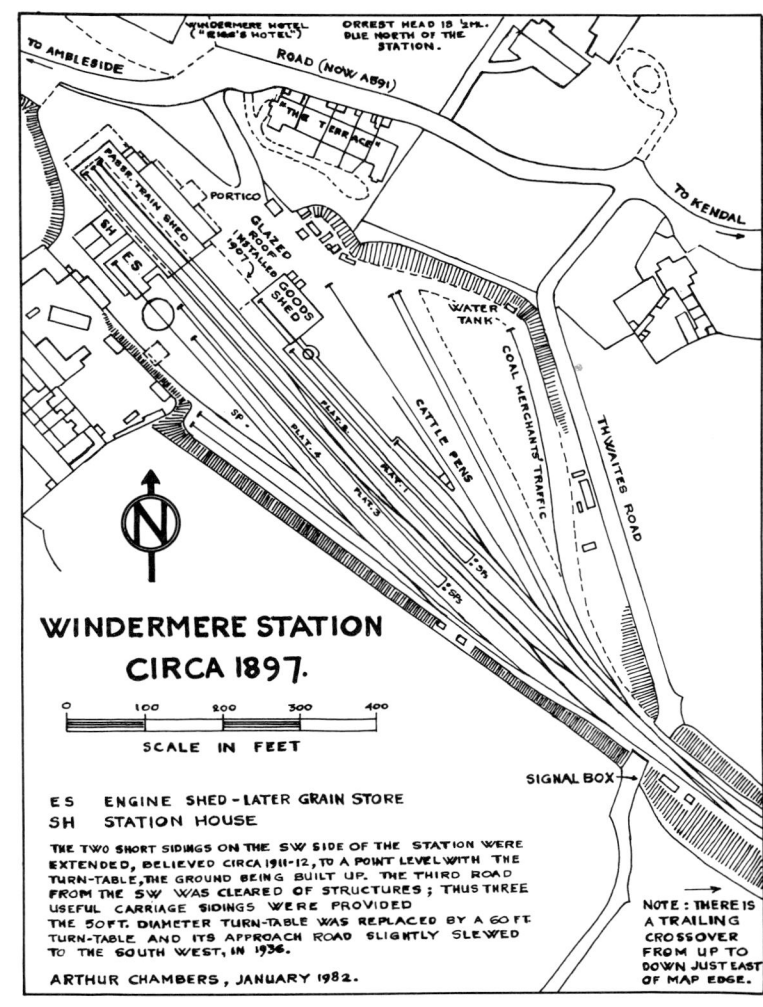

WINDERMERE STATION
CIRCA 1897.

SCALE IN FEET

ES ENGINE SHED - LATER GRAIN STORE
SH STATION HOUSE

THE TWO SHORT SIDINGS ON THE SW SIDE OF THE STATION WERE
EXTENDED, BELIEVED CIRCA 1911-12, TO A POINT LEVEL WITH THE
TURN-TABLE, THE GROUND BEING BUILT UP. THE THIRD ROAD
FROM THE SW WAS CLEARED OF STRUCTURES; THUS THREE
USEFUL CARRIAGE SIDINGS WERE PROVIDED
THE 50 FT. DIAMETER TURN-TABLE WAS REPLACED BY A 60 FT.
TURN-TABLE AND ITS APPROACH ROAD SLIGHTLY SLEWED
TO THE SOUTH WEST, IN 1936.

ARTHUR CHAMBERS, JANUARY 1982.

NOTE: THERE IS A TRAILING CROSSOVER FROM UP TO DOWN JUST EAST OF MAP EDGE.

Permanent way over Shap

The L&NWR claimed 'the finest permanent way in the world'. In the north, it was the responsibility of the engineer of the L&C, based at Lancaster Castle station. In early 20th century, the incumbent was styled divisional engineer, northern division, L&NWR, still based in the 1858 offices, but his successors in LMS days occupied premises near the Castle. His chief permanent way inspector was also based on Lancaster, with five district inspectors, of whom one looked after the Whitehaven Junction lines in the west. Permanent way depots were at Leyland (for the NU line), Kendal (central to the L&C) and Workington (in the west).

The most exposed and steepest parts of the division fell in the Penrith district, Tebay to Carlisle (inclusive). The Penrith inspector supervised 24 gangs, Nos 74-97 in the divisional list. Each basic gang comprised four men — a ganger, sub-ganger and platelayers. Such a gang took two miles of double-track main line, often including a wayside station layout. The route mileage was reduced slightly if it included an extra road, while on complex sections the strength of the gang was increased to five or six and their pay scaled up. In 1904, a ganger's pay in this district was between 25/6d and 28s weekly. A gang's tools embraced 108 different categories — lever skid, spirit level, flags, shovel, beesom, gauges, snow shovels, lamps, and so on. Precise instructions, with diagram, were given for laying out the tools on the railway bank, for inspection; the precision was akin to a rigorous military kit inspection. It will be apparent why so many railway houses were allocated to pw staff and that the intensive use of manpower, quartered locally, permitted rapid attention to problems such as flooding, snow, ice, damaged rails, or the call to stand by for a Royal train.

The standard rails for the main line were of bullhead section, 90lb/yd, in 60ft lengths, 24 sleepers per length (23 before 1903). Around 1900-06, 55ft lengths existed on Carlisle through goods lines, 60ft and 45ft on 'second class' lines, which category included various platform roads and the Windermere line.

The northern division became Lancaster district. This merged in 1966 with Barrow and Blackburn districts; then, from June 1969, the combined divisional headquarters was concentrated at Preston. From around the same date, mobile gangs were organised by the divisional civil engineer, grouped (in L&C territory) under four pw supervisors. Typically, outside the complex layouts of Preston and Carlisle, they are 11-12 men strong and look after 12-14 miles of route. The division employs six Plasser '07' multi-purpose mobile machines for maintenance of track, plus a crane fleet, and the majority of work is mechanised, but related also to systematic inspection and checking on the state of the road.

It should be appreciated that the engineer, down the years, has always had bridges and buildings under his charge, and specialised support and staff concerned with these and other structures. Principal bridges and stations have been listed earlier.

Part of the layout controlled by Preston signalbox from 1972-3.

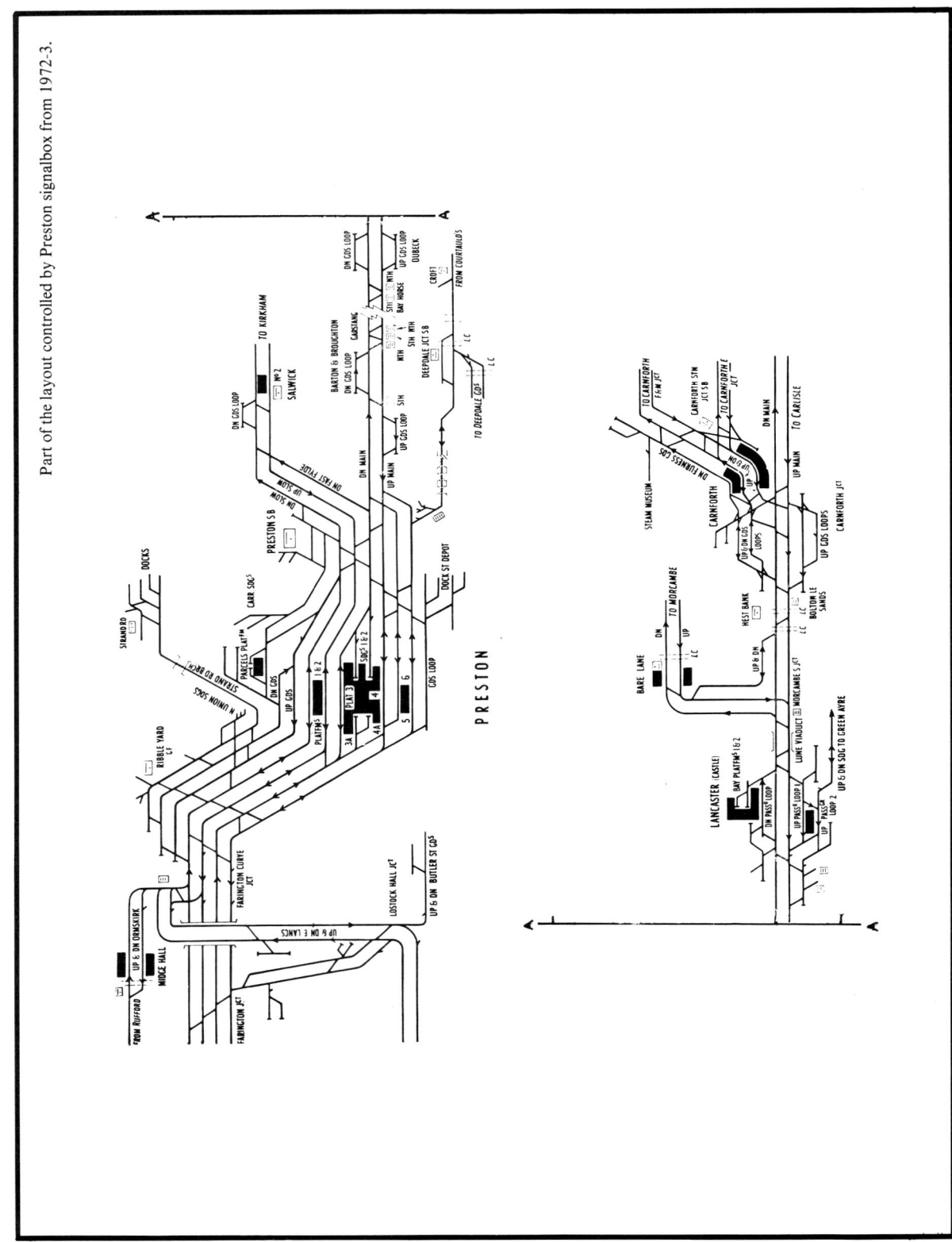

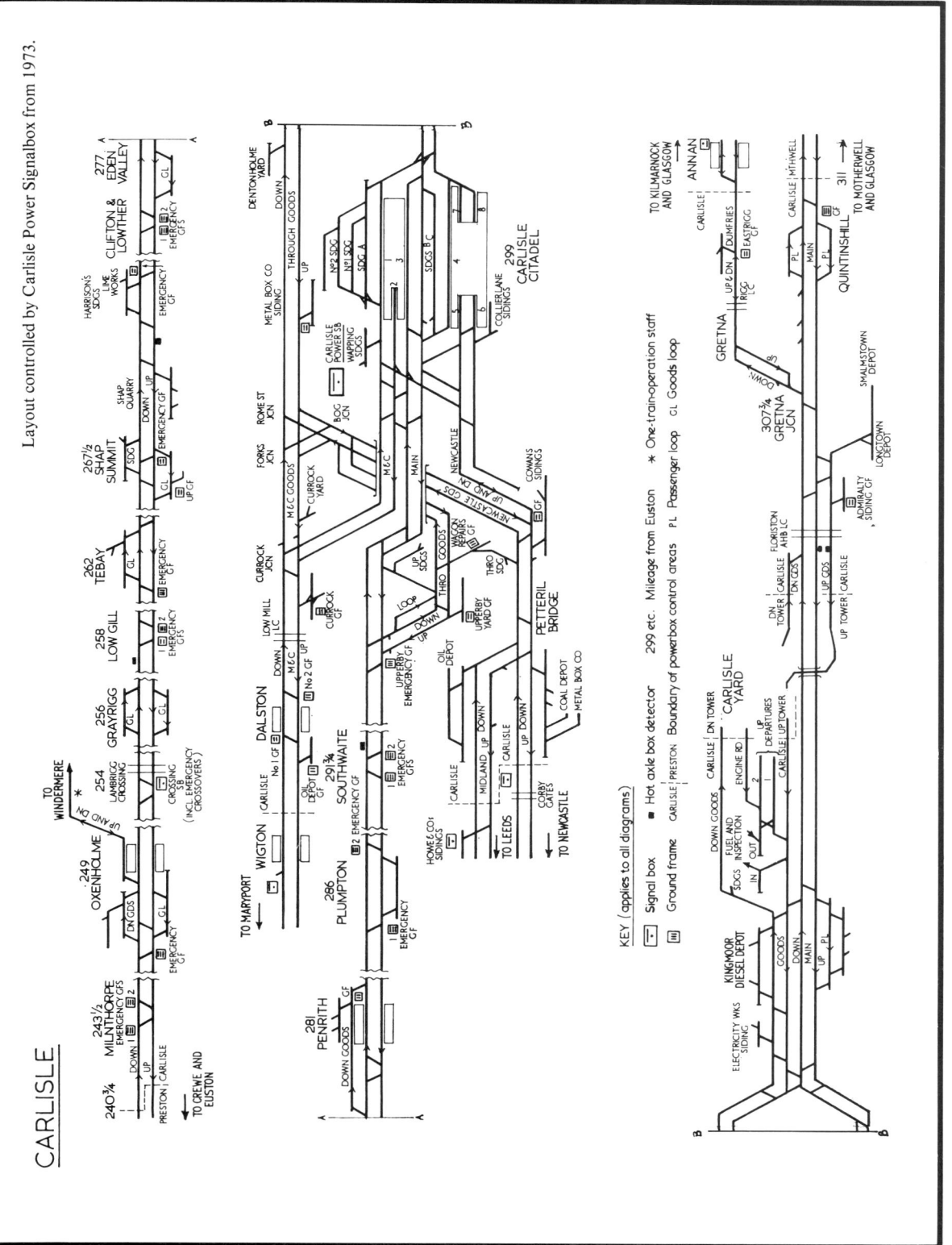

Layout controlled by Carlisle Power Signalbox from 1973.

CARLISLE

KEY (applies to all diagrams)

- Signal box
- Ground frame
- Hot axle box detector
- 299 etc. Mileage from Euston
- * One-train-operation staff
- Boundary of powerbox control areas   PL Passenger loop   GL Goods loops

Accidents in the 20th century

On Saturday 5 December 1903, in the early hours, the 8.10pm express goods, Liverpool-Carlisle, comprising (north of Tebay) almost new four-cylinder compound 0-8-0 No 1226, 31 vehicles and brake (32 and two brakes has been quoted) became divided at speed, after passing Eden Valley Junction intact. The signalman at Eamont Junction was observant in the darkness, saw the engine and two wagons go by, with the rest of the train in hot pursuit. A violent collision occurred just north of Penrith station, wagons being hurled on to the up line. Signals were thrown on but the driver of 2-4-0 No 1668 *Dagmar* on the 1.00am up express from Carlisle had scarcely time to check his speed before crashing into the wreckage; all vehicles, including a composite and sleeping saloon, were derailed but only the driver suffered injury, by burns.

An alarming mechanical failure occurred in daytime, on 30 August 1930. A connecting rod broke on the engine of a goods train while descending Shap incline; the firebox was pierced, with consequent escape of steam. The enginemen climbed on to the tender and the driver jumped to the lineside but was seen by the guard, who stopped the train. The down 'Royal Scot' was brought to a stand short of the site by display of a red flag.

Just before midnight, believed to be in September 1943, the down Euston-Stranraer Harbour train was, as usual in those days, made up to about 500 tons, plus a full complement of servicemen and kit. A 'Baby Scot' 4-6-0 was working the train from Crewe to Carlisle but piloted by a 'Black 5' in 'ex-shops' condition. Restarting from a signal stop on the 1 in 106 at Lambrigg, the '5' slipped so violently as to damage the rails beyond repair; they assumed a sinuous shape, the engine heeled over and was derailed. Train and train engine were eventually hauled back on the wrong road to Oxenholme, involving a delay of eight hours to traffic and a reprimand for the young Preston driver of the '5'. The catchpoints south of Hay Fell were evidently properly clipped to permit the rescue but it was different on 10 September 1971. An authorised spell of single line working took place on the down line between Oxenholme, Hay Fell site (where the box had been done away with in the meantime) and Lambrigg. Towards the end of the occupation, a shouted instruction was misunderstood and catchpoints a little south of Hay Fell site were unclipped; a diesel locomotive with the 11.45 Motorail train from Stirling to Sutton Coldfield came down the bank running 'wrong road', was derailed and went over the bankside — and was there for some time owing to the problems of organising recovery. No passengers were hurt.

A broken rail brought the last seven vehicles of a Carlisle-Euston passenger train off the road between Brock and Barton & Broughton, at 11.05am on 22 November 1946. The fireman jumped down and ran to warn a down Liverpool-Glasgow express, whose driver braked but could not stop in time. His train was scraped from end to end and 10 passengers injured, five seriously.

Again, at 02.20 (new timings now) on 20 May 1965, rail breakage had alarming results. The 22.10 Glasgow Central-Kensington Olympia sleeping car express was passing over Hest Bank water troughs, north of the station and level crossing, at 70mph. The diesel locomotive and first three coaches passed unharmed and ran ahead for 746yd but the next four coaches came off and ran up the station platform ramp, overturning between the platforms. The last five coaches remained upright and in line, derailed beside the track but restrained by the heavy water troughs. Only 11 out of 114 passengers sustained injuries, all minor. Sadly, the signalman, who was in the present box, was severely shocked and his early death may have been a direct result. The cause of derailment was interesting. The line is beside the sea. Salt spray and overspill from the water troughs were conductive to wheelslip and burning of railheads. A transverse crack through the head of the cess rail (a fb steel rail rolled in 1964 and metallurgically satisfactory) was found to be underneath an old wheelburn. An unusually cold night increased stress and accelerated fracture. A piece of railhead no less than 4ft 7in long became detached and a further 9ft 0in of the head was broken into several pieces, this last probably by the derailment. The track had been examined the previous day but no defect was apparent.

Docker Garths viaduct is to the south of Lambrigg box, where the descent southwards eases slightly from 1 in 106 to 1 in 131. 'Wrong line' working was in force for engineering reasons on Sunday 18 May 1947. The facing crossover at Lambrigg did not then exist, so up trains ran past the box under hand signal and set back 'across the road', then continuing south, but on the *down* line. To assist heavy trains, 4-4-0 No 565 of '2P' type was waiting on the up road facing north, but prudently 440yds south of the home signal and just on the northern end of the viaduct. The Carlisle driver of the up 'Royal Scot', with 4-6-2 No 6235 *City of Birmingham* on 13 coaches, had read the notice of diversion but overlooked it, also failing to see the well-sited semaphore distant signal for Lambrigg and only braking on seeing the home at danger. The driver of the '2P', standing on a lofty viaduct, saw the express approaching at speed about 400yd distant. He wound his engine into back gear and his mate unscrewed the tender brake; they retreated, but were struck at about 25mph and pushed some 77yd across the viaduct. The 'Pacific' and three coaches were derailed but kept in line, near the parapet. 37 people were injured, but none seriously. At some stage, a buffer of *City of Birmingham* fell to the valley. It remained there for a long time but was eventually recovered by an enterprising engine driver and friends and reposes in a garden to this day, while the locomotive stands resplendent, floodlit, in the Museum of Science and Industry, Birmingham.

This does not pretend to be a full inventory of mishaps on the L&C route.

The scene at Preston

Above: Southward on platform 2 (a few years after its opening in 1902, with island 3-4 (now 1-2) to left and buildings seen on 5 (now 3). *F. Moore*

Left: Southward, still pre-1914, on 5 (now 3), west side of main island. The entrance to the subway, still in use, is seen beyond the clock. *J. D. Darby collection*

Below left: And the northward view on 6 (now 4), main island, around the end of L&NWR days, with No 3 box and East Lancashire (EL) platforms to the right. Note signals on the platform, near the intermediate crossover. The locomotive is No 856 *E. Tootal Broadhurst* of the 'Claughton' class. *Ian Allan Library*

OMO
adds brightness
PASSENGERS MUST
CROSS THE LINE
BY THE BRIDGE

Left: The EL side of the station, looking north from East Cliff in July 1964. No 3 box is seen to the left and Butler Street warehouse to right. A northbound train is running into platform 8 (now 6). No 44767, a 'Black 5' with link motion, is leaving from bay 13. The through platform 10 is next to the warehouse. *HDB*

Below left: Back to the NU (North Union) side of the station, with L&NWR mechanical starting signals and fixed distant arms, in July 1955. Departure northward is under Fishergate bridge. The County offices at Fishergate/Pitt Street junction are visible above the bridge. *J. D. Darby*

Right: Immediately north of Fishergate bridge: interior of No 4 (Dock Street Junction) signalbox, containing L&NWR frame of 184 levers, seen in June 1946 but in service until 1973. The diagram and inscriptions emphasise the track circuits. *Ian Allan Library*

Below: Up and away: No 45653 *Barham* leaving Preston curve, northbound for the Lancaster & Preston Junction route, which became Lancaster & Carlisle Railway, L&NWR and West Coast Main Line (WCML). Four tracks to the Fylde bear westward, short of St Walburge's magnificent church. A corner of the engine shed is glimpsed (left). *D. Ian Wood*

Between Preston and Lancaster

Above: Substantial early buildings on the down side at Barton & Broughton, seen in July 1971 and still surviving. The platforms are cut away. *HDB*

Left: Badger bridge: a replica badger, set in artificial stone on the overline bridge, looking north in May 1978, with the M6 to the right and pipelaying to the left. *HDB*

Below left: The underline badger bridge, from the down side, in May 1967, with four original badgers (since replaced) in the capitals, also the delicate railings (lost in subsequent reconstruction for new permanent way). *HDB*

Above: Garstang & Catterall, northward, in October 1947, with Knott End branch line and loop (by then available to main line trains) on down side. LMS No 9255, 'Super D', is southbound, past the creamery siding. *Wilfred Cooper*

Left: A well-proportioned Saxby & Farmer signalbox of c1870, at Bay Horse, with L&NWR frame (13 levers), in August 1971. *HDB*

Below left: L&NWR signalbox of the later Crewe pattern (Brock and Oubeck boxes were latterly very similar) at Lancaster No 1, looking north in August 1971. The 1840 course to Lancaster Old lies half right. The engine shed was in the angle between this and the curving main line. *HDB*

Lancaster Castle Station

Right: The Lancaster arms, with inscription 'Luck of Loyne', on the 1858 battlements of Castle station, August 1979. *HDB*

Below: A fuller view of the down side, Castle station: the 1858 extensions, with tower ('turret', with spiral stair) and, beyond, the symmetrical double-gabled 1846 building, seen August 1979, with the Priory Church tower on the wooded hill. The L&CR's engineer enjoyed the bay window and their board room was under the far gable. *HDB*

Above: A typical 1905-built Manchester-Windermere train set, headed by L&NWR No 1400 *Felicia Hemans*, a 'Prince' of 1914, coming into Lancaster Castle station. No 2 box is on the down side and a shunt is in progress to the down goods depot.
H. Gordon Tidey/Ian Allan Library

Left: An experimental 25kV electric train is leaving Castle station for the Midland line to Green Ayre and (with reversal) to Morecambe Promenade, August 1963.
Preston Whiteley

Below left: Northward view, c1902, on completion of widening and reconstruction, with the new and resited No 4 box (earlier Crewe pattern, 1901): two 'Jumbos' are entering the platform road with an up express, a 'Cauliflower' is in the Morecambe bay.
R. E. Charlewood, per Brian Reed

From Lancaster northward

Right: The windswept farm remains a sturdy landmark above Morecambe Bay. A 'Renown' and a 'Prince' on, maybe, a summer Keswick train recall early LMS days. *G. W. Smith, per G. D. Whitworth*

Right: The 'Caledonian' up express from Glasgow to Euston passing Hest Bank station in July 1958, with No 46231 *Duchess of Atholl*. This signalbox, of earlier Crewe pattern, was replaced in December 1958 by the new box to the north. Note Morecambe line bay and very early crossing house. *Wilfred Cooper*

Right: The old crossing house is seen southward from the 1958 box, which contains a 'back-to-front' frame, 1981. The Morecambe line has been extended north to converge by the crossing, platforms swept away. *HDB*

Right: This interior of the 1958 box shows both Hest Bank and Bolton-le-Sands level crossings on a foreshortened diagram; Bolton-le-Sands crossing is observed on the t/v screen, with handy telephone facilities for reprimanding kids swinging on the barrier during school holidays. *HDB*

Below: A L&NWR steam railmotor carriage (engine leading) is on a Carnforth-Lancaster run, probably just north of Hest Bank station, around 1923. *J. M. Dunn collection*

Bottom: Bolton-le-Sands, with the low up platform near its early L&CR buildings; probably Oxenholme men with superheated 4-6-2T engine on a Windermere set coming carefully to a stand at the raised platform, about 1923. *G. W. Smith, per G. D. Whitworth*

Carnforth and environs

Above: LMS No 5909 *Charles N. Lawrence* is leaving
Carnforth on an up express, in August 1931, showing (left) the
two-roads engine shed adapted as a coaling shed. The wagon
shop (above L&YR carriage at the front of the train) is
recognisable today, but the tall L&NWR signals of No 2 box
and the ironworks blastfurnaces are no more. *W. J. Young*

Below: The long footbridge connected the railway houses in
Grosvenor Place (seen) with the L&NWR engine shed. Here, on
shed in the 1930s, is 'Super D' No 9197, for long of Springs
Branch, with a 'G3' 0-8-0, probably on the Rose Grove duty,
and a spotless Carnforth 4-4-0 compound. Wagons of all four
grouped railways are represented. *Howard Vogt*

Below: The new motive power depot of 1944, at Carnforth, seen in July 1964, with ash-handling tubs in and beside the pits. *HDB*

Bottom: The notable south end of Carnforth joint station in close-up, early 20th century, with stock at the single FR line platform face and L&NWR 1824 of Webb's three-cylinder 'A' class engaged in shunting. *J. H. Wright*

Above: For a few months, the new 'Royal Scot' express train called at Carnforth to change engines and crews; the up train, with 'Super Precursor' and 'Claughton', is leaving for London, non-stop, in August 1927. *John Dearden*

Below: The L&CR station building of 1846, with typical gables, dormers and leaded lights, is disguised and almost lost among the 1880-period buildings of the joint station at Carnforth, April 1981. *HDB*

From Lancashire into Westmorland

Left: Yealand Box, of Saxby & Farmer type, is seen on the down side, with signalman George Hird and Doreen Hunter, and cat. The box was replaced in 1943 by IB signals and the two L&NWR cottages have disappeared in widening of the A6 road. *Courtesy J. E. Roberts*

Below: Burton & Holme up platform, with L&CR buildings, in L&NWR days; the main building, cleaned, is today a residence. *D. J. W. Brough collection*

Bottom: Milnthorpe station, looking north, around 1900, with L&CR buildings on down side; the down starting signal and up home share a post, with their arms probably in slots. *R. E. Charlewood, per Brian Reed*

Above: The road bridge at Milnthorpe was typical of the handsome structures on the L&CR route. BR No 42319 is calling, with the 3.23pm Windermere to Liverpool Exchange, in September 1963.
Preston Whiteley

Right: A southward view from the spartan interior of Milnthorpe's early signalbox, in July 1971. From the window towards the camera, the farther group of levers controlled: colour-light distant; semaphore home; semaphore starter; colour-light distant and home IB signals at Hincaster; colour-light distant and home IB signals at Sedgwick — all on the down road. *HDB*

Below : Hincaster Junction, and signalbox of 1914 vintage: Arnside single line trails (left) into the down main; L&NWR houses are in the lane (right); No D374 is on the up 'Mid-day Scot' — in August 1962. *Preston Whiteley*

Focus on Oxenholme

Below: The northward approach to Oxenholme is through a deep cutting, climbing 1 in 111. No 1 box is glimpsed over the A65 road bridge, likewise the L&NWR starting signals for the up main and up loop. LMS No 6222 *Queen Mary* is on an up express, probably soon after the removal, in 1946, of streamlining and the fitting of smoke deflectors. *Howard Vogt*

Bottom: Oxenholme engine shed, on the down side, with its small turntable nestling below sheltering trees, and the tall No 2 signalbox. Locomotives are LMS No 2393 2-6-4T, and Nos 6790 and 6784 4-4-2 'Precursor' tanks, in March 1937. *W. A. Camwell*

Above: A southerly view of Oxenholme shed and approaches, c1933, shows a 'Prince' with Belpaire firebox, probably 5765, just returned from Grayrigg or Shap Summit after assisting a down train. In the down loop is a 'Crab' on freight. Beyond the L&NWR bracket signals of No 2 box is a 'Precursor' tank and the typical L&NWR coal stage. No 3 box worked the distant signal. The 'Crab' may want the 'Prince's' help. *Howard Vogt*

Below: The south end of Oxenholme station, then with short platforms but full roofing; No 2 box's up starter and No 1's distant are off on the L&NWR bracket for LMS No 5684 *Jutland* (which had a Kylchap double blastpipe during 1937-38). The tall down starters at No 3 box (itself glimpsed over the canopies) had no need of banner repeaters. *Howard Vogt*

Above: By February 1968, No 2 box (actually LMS, 1943, build) is on the up side, the layout has been pruned, No 3 box has long been done away with, the down starters are underhung and have banner repeaters (close to the canopy). The double line junction at the north end was abandoned three months later. *HDB*

Left: Back in 1932, a Kendal-Grange train is in Oxenholme up main line platform, with LMS No 11083, shapely 4-4-2T, built for the Furness Railway; its Vulcan Foundry Ltd building plate of 1916 is on the smokebox saddle. *Howard Vogt*

Below left: LMS No 6147 *Courier*, of the 'Royal Scot' class, is picking up the Windermere-Euston carriages in Oxenholme's back platform, for attachment in front of the 8.30am (approx) working from Carlisle to London, in 1932. *Howard Vogt*

Below: A Saturday seaside train, returning from Southport in 1932 summer, is calling at Oxenholme on its way to Tebay, Stainmore summit and Newcastle upon Tyne. *Howard Vogt*

Bottom: A Sunday in August 1962: the diesel multiple units were in top form and ventured far at weekends, this one bound presumably from the West Riding to Windermere, in the back platform at Oxenholme. *Preston Whiteley*

Top left: The 2.0pm Glasgow Central to Manchester with LMS No 5547, new three-cylinder 'Baby Scot' of Newton Heath (C1) shed, on the through engine working of 1934, passing through the Windermere line junction at Oxenholme No 3 box. Note also the Caledonian Railway route indicator set for the Beattock main line and the tall signals, with repeating arms below. *Gordon Tidey*

Centre left: At 'the Tidey spot', a down local is climbing away from Oxenholme in early LMS days, with No 3 box just visible. The superheater tank engine from Oxenholme or Tebay shed heads two L&NWR non-corridor carriages, one still in L&NWR colours, and seemingly a L&YR six-wheeled brake third. *Gordon Tidey*

Below: Oxenholme, once Kendal Junction, was named after the farm, below. In February 1981, the L&CR buildings of c1850 are glimpsed beneath the bare branches; an up electric express train glides into the lengthy platforms, rather bare of roofing. The order goes: 'Will passengers requiring second class accommodation on the train to London please proceed to the north end of the platform, beyond the station canopy!' *HDB*

Grayrigg bank

Above: Coke empties, both wooden and steel-bodied wagons, returning from Furness to County Durham, with BR No 44594 ('4F', with high-sided tender), seen about a mile north of Oxenholme; the locomotive will hand over to a NER loco at Tebay (date: believed c1950).
Howard Vogt

Right: The L&CR bridge near the site of Peat Lane signalbox, in August 1950; No 46245 *City of London*, with the down 'Mid-day Scot' is making a fast climb of the 1 in 124 on the fellside above Kendal.
HDB

Below right: Hay Fell, June 1935: LMS No 8793, '19-inch Goods' 4-6-0, is descending with empty stock, the two railway houses (nowadays a single modernised white house) are on the down side and box is obscured by steam.
H. C. Casserley

Far right: Here is the box, said to be taken c1900-1910. *Percy Duff collection*

Above: Docker viaduct, of six arches: the 09.10 Glasgow-Euston is coming down the bank, with a Class '87' electric locomotive. *HDB*

Right: Lambrigg Crossing, June 1963: the magnificent L&NWR down home signal, the stone house which probably derived from the station of 1848-49 at this location, the minor crossing and the Saxby & Farmer signalbox all appear; of these, only the box remains today. *Preston Whiteley*

Above left: 'Mosedale Hall Xing' was all the title that the quaint little down-side box could accommodate. It was of indeterminate design, with brick base, timber frame and infill plaster work, seen in July 1964. *HDB*

Above right: Grayrigg station, the down side being seen with stationmaster's house, entry to loop and short sidings — and the box of 1926 — in May 1951. *H. C. Casserley*

Below: A broader vista at Grayrigg, after closing to passengers, shows on the up side the L&NWR starter for the loop, with Mosedale Hall's distant below it. The main line signals are off for No 42449, which has piloted an express from Oxenholme to Shap Summit and is returning home light, July 1964. *HDB*

The Lune gorge

Below: At Low Gill, c1901, 'Jumbo' No 1486 *Dalton*, with up express from Keswick, is calling at the main platform. *R. E. Charlewood, per J. D. Darby*

Bottom: At Low Gill, in May 1950, No 42601 2-6-4T, with the 1.51pm Carlisle-Oxenholme slow, is entering that same main platform; note the NE Region Gresley corridor stock (see text), the sunken garden with lily pond, the Ingleton tracks to the right of the platform and the signalbox (at the actual junction) distantly beyond the train. *HDB*

Below: A 'Royal train', on the down line near the site of the onetime tiny Dillicar signalbox: 'Black 5' locomotives Nos 45236 and 45141 are in fact working empty stock from Barrow-in-Furness to Scotland, while the Royal party proceeds by sea. The composition of the train is interesting. *W. J. V. Anderson*

Bottom: A dramatic entry to the gorge from the north: a 4-6-0 of the 'Scot' class, on mainly contemporary stock, is southbound over Dillicar troughs, c1930. *J. W. B. Hext collection*

The Tebay scene

Top left: Tebay station is seen, looking north, in June 1935, complete with glazed footbridge and (right, over up yard) glazed approach walkway: LMS No 6784, an Oxenholme 'Precursor' tank, is leaving with an up slow of Midland stock. The old No 2 box is just visible under the footbridge. *H. C. Casserley*

Centre left: Tebay L&NWR engine shed, with early pattern of roof, and glazing, c1930. The 'Cauliflower' may well be LMS No 8368. LMS Nos 12513 (left) and 12514 (right) were built by Yorkshire Engine Company in 1922, for the Maryport & Carlisle Railway, and resembled Great Central Railway 'Pom-Poms' (LNER 'J11' type); they were at Tebay for coke traffic to Furness.
W. H. Whitworth

Below: The Tebay scene changes; the rebuilt engine shed is to the left, with mechanical coaler; the signals are upper quadrant; the bridge is roofless; No 45512 *Bunsen* is a rebuilt 'Baby Scot' on a Glasgow-Blackpool train, in July 1963. *Derek Cross*

Above: Tebay North Terrace: 12 stone houses of 1862, in July 1980. *HDB*

Above right: The southern end of South Terrace, 14 rather later houses, and the two brick blocks comprising Whinfell Terrace, 30 houses of 1898, with gables provided selectively, as symbols of status in the service, also seen in July 1980. *HDB*

Centre right: St James's Church, Tebay, built by the subscription of the L&NWR and the NER and local people, consecrated in July 1880 and seen in February 1981. *HDB*

Bottom right: The interior of the new Tebay No 2 box, opened in December 1952 and photographed in May 1953; signalman Jack Lord is working the frame, with his back to the main line. There are glimpses of coke wagons in the up yard, railway houses, station buildings (up side). *Brian Lord collection*

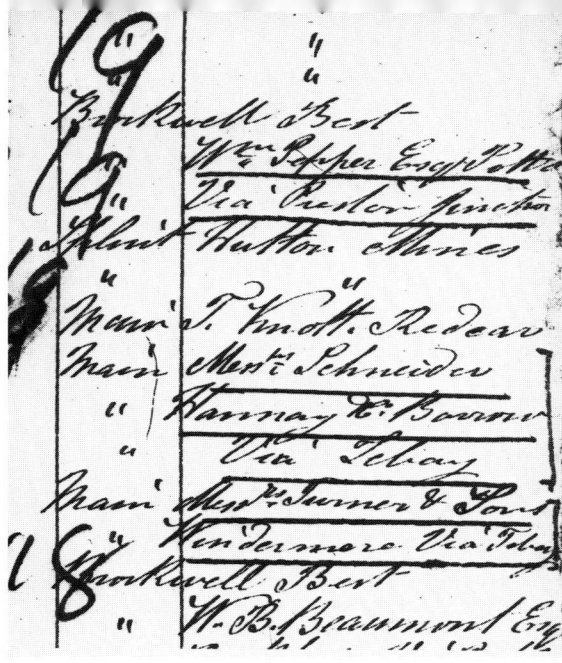

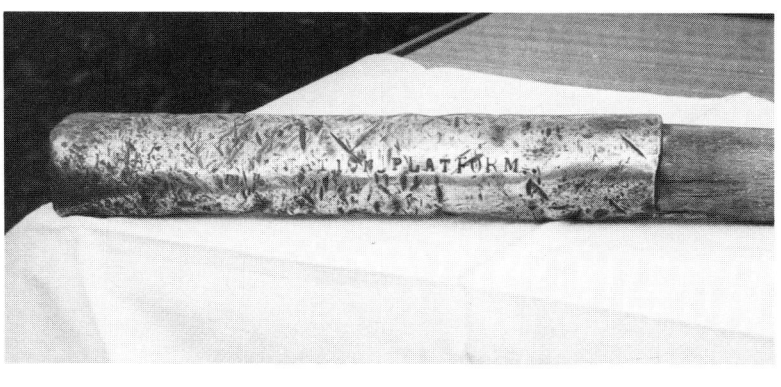

Above: Backbone of the Stainmore route: coke and coals. Here is an extract from Stockton & Darlington Railway weighbill, dated '18 day of 2 mo 1862', for despatches from Adelaide's colliery. Observe Schneider Hannay's traffic for Barrow Iron Works and that for Turner & Sons, Windermere, both 'Via Tebay'. *Harold D. Bowtell collection*

Above left: Emerging from 'the grim cavern', the Geordie platform at Tebay: No E5098, 'J21' 0-6-0, of Darlington, is on a passenger train to the NER line, probably c1948. The covered approach to the footbridge, and coke wagons, are to the left. *Harold D. Bowtell collection*

Centre left: The wayward train staff, discussed in the text, authority to proceed from the Geordie platform to No 3 box. *HDB*

Bottom left: Tebay No 3 box and 50ft table, beside the NER route; BR No 76048 was built in 1955 and withdrawn in 1967 and would probably be engaged in North East to Blackpool Saturday holiday workings, prior to 1962 (when the Stainmore route closed). *Howard Vogt*

Shap Incline

Above right: Starting away from Tebay with a down freight, c1929: No 5834 (a 'Prince') and No 10455 (a 'Lanky Claughton') are both believed to have been of Upperby shed, Carlisle. The long-closed NER engine shed is clearly seen and there are plenty of coke wagons.
W. H. Whitworth, per J. D. Darby

Right: Midpoint, Scout Green, seen with the long-lived box of about 1870 and its lofty up line signal; a 'Super D' is in full blast, with a Tebay bank engine in rear of its freight, c1930.
J. W. B. Hext collection

Below: And, peaceably, on a Sunday in May 1962, No D115 slips by Scout Green on the 1 in 75 descent with the diverted up 'Thames-Clyde Express'. *HDB*

Top: My favourite picture: 'Aberdeen express', with No 2189 *Avon* on typical 'Highland Tourist' stock, at Shap Wells, July 1899. *L&NWR 1905/HDB collection*

Above: Two years later, much the same place but a very different train is seen: the 10.00am Scots express from Euston, made up of 13 bogies, including two 12-wheeled cars, with engines Nos 90 *Luck of Edenhall* (a magic goblet, and L&CR name) and 1536 *Hugh Myddleton* (a John Hick three-cylinder compound of 1898), taken by R. E. Charlewood. *L&GRP, courtesy David & Charles*

Left: Shap Wells again: a 'Swami' four-cylinder compound 0-8-0 raises the echoes on a huge coal train, with 'DX' 0-6-0 in rear — presumed to be a 'Jellicoe' special from South Wales to the far north, in 1914-18. *J. D. Darby collection*

Below left: Evening of their days: 7.29pm on 29 August 1964 — No 46240 *City of Coventry* makes the fastest climb of the afternoon (diesels, *et al*) with the 1.30pm Euston-Perth, at Shap Wells, Salterwath cottages in shadow to the rear. *HDB*

The Summit

Above: A northbound freight tops Shap Summit, behind
No 70028 *Royal Star,* in April 1963, and No 42110 drops off,
just by the pair of L&CR houses. The 1926 signalbox, on its
rather narrow base, is seen. The up loop is nearest to the
camera. *Wilfred Cooper*

Right: George Grayland in Summit box, in early 1950s.
Arthur Grayland collection

Far right, top: The Summit box of pre-1926, with down refuge
siding below the wall, and main lines.
Arthur Grayland collection

Far right, bottom: Southbound at Shap Summit, in 1930,
No 8907 with freight. The granite workers' private train (see
text), then of L&NWR six-wheeled stock, is stabled on the up
side, while on the down an Atkinson-Walker upright-boiler
locomotive of the Shap Granite Company is standing by their
workers' platform. *Locomotive Publishing Co collection*

82

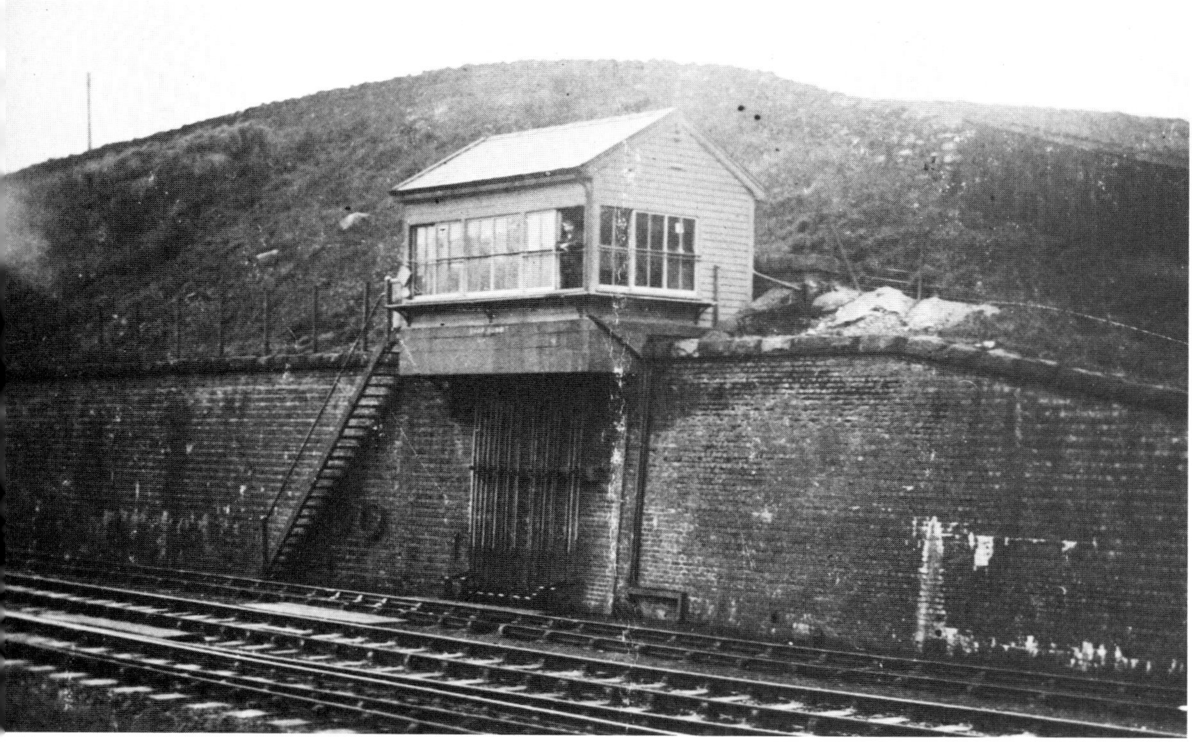

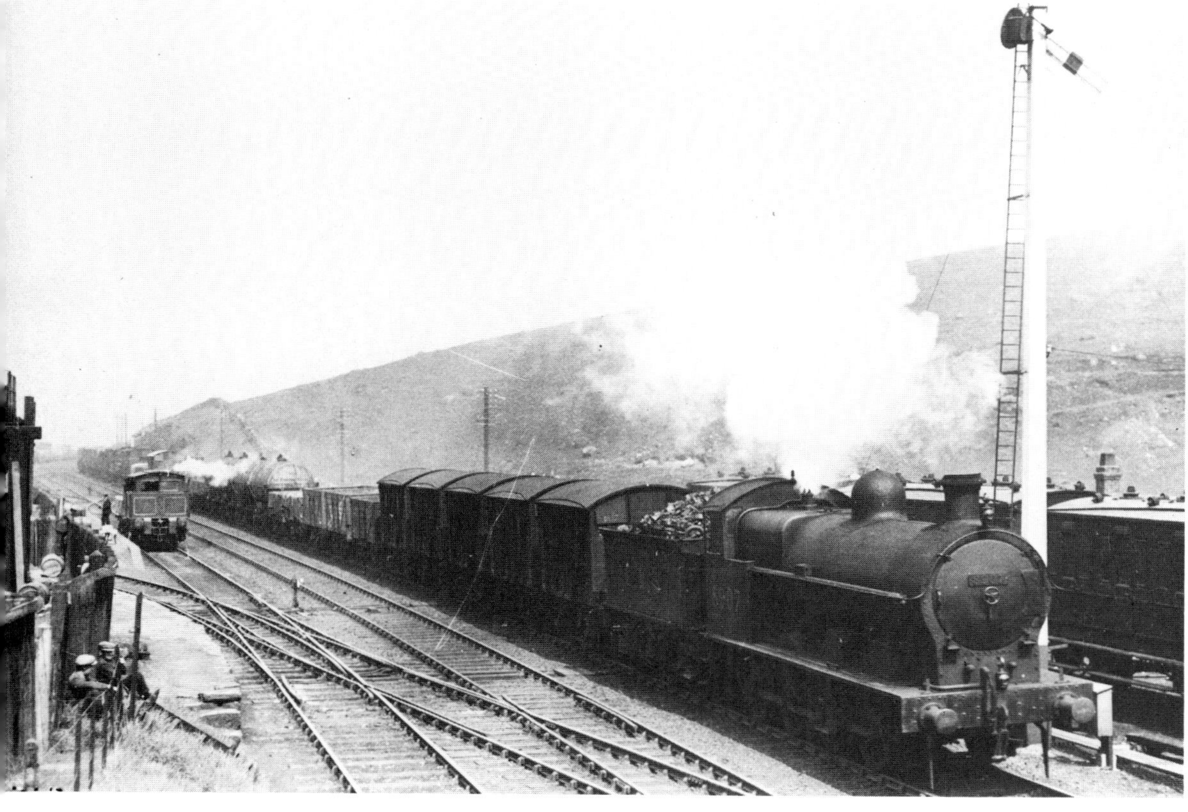

North of the Summit

Above: Shap Quarry box of 1962 is visible distantly in this northward scene recorded in 1964: No 72007 *Clan Mackintosh* 4-6-2 is on limestone traffic in the lengthy headshunt and No 92022 ('9F' 2-10-0) is passing on an up freight.   *Derek Cross*

Right: Shap station, looking south, c1900. The lead by which the granite workers' stock was rope-shunted, with some risk to life and limb, is in the foreground.
R. E. Charlewood, per Brian Reed

Below : Thrimby Grange box of 1926, beside the up loop of that date: No 40629 '2P' and No 70051 *Firth of Forth* are on a Glasgow-Manchester, July 1958. *R. H. Leslie*

Above: Clifton & Lowther station site, looking south, in August 1963; empties wait to leave the up goods line, which dates from 1905, and 45531 *Sir Frederick Harrison* is working a Wigan-Edinburgh excursion, passing the L&CR station house and L&NWR cottages. *Derek Cross*

Below: At Eden Valley Junction, the box of 1903, a late example of the earlier Crewe type, replaced a tall and ancient one for the opening in 1905 of the up goods line to Clifton & Lowther and it also controlled access to the NER's Eden Valley branch for Appleby and Kirkby Stephen. No 42343 is on the 1.53pm Carlisle-Oxenholme slow; in August 1956, this train is no longer formed of NE Region stock. *R. H.Leslie*

Above: Hugh's Crag viaduct, in Lowther Park, six stone arches of 59ft span, 100ft above the river Lowther; No 45475 is on a down goods, in July 1963. *Derek Cross*

Left: Eamont viaduct, with unique down bracket signal (see text) and 'Claughton' on short express train, viewed from Eamont Junction signalbox, in 1934. Some $2\frac{1}{2}$ miles upstream is Dalemain, handsome home of the Hasell McCosh family and onetime of Edward Hasell (1796-1872), chairman of the Lancaster & Carlisle Railway Company. *Sid Ridley*

Below left: Eamont Junction signalbox, built 1906 and closed 1938, seen in 1934. *Sid Ridley*

Penrith

Above: No 46103 *Royal Scots Fusilier*, a 'Rebuilt Scot', stands in Eamont No 1 down loop, with a trip working from Harrisons Siding, and No 78018 — tender first as Penrith table was always too short to turn a '2MT' engine — climbs the single line, bound for Keswick and Workington, in July 1962. Down signals for Keswick Junction (Penrith No 1) and distants for No 2 box are seen. *Derek Cross*

Left: In the first summer of electric working, August 1974, this southward view is from just south of the site of Keswick Junction box. No 87014, not yet named, is crossing the M6 motorway by a bridge built 1965-67. Observe that the one surviving down loop from Eamont has assumed its present form, running independently to Penrith — and the Keswick line has lost its connection and is ready for lifting. *HDB*

Below left: Keswick Junction (No 1) box, south of Penrith: No 42594 is heading for Oxenholme with the 'Lakes Express', Keswick-Euston portion, in July 1963. *Derek Cross*

Top right: Approaching Penrith station, with the engine shed on the down side and No 2 box just visible below the signal which is pulled off: in Penrith yard, LMS 'Cauliflowers' Nos 28422 and 28423 prepare for action, as train engine and banker of the Keswick goods, in May 1946. *HDB*

Centre right: A dramatic passage of the up 'Coronation Scot', with Penrith No 2 box and its signals, and Penrith Beacon in silhouette, in February 1938.
Percy Duff collection

Below: Penrith station is seen from the south, in March 1950: 'J21' No 65047 is in the CK&P platform, the EVR bay platform road is empty, No 42964 2-6-0 with a freight train is on the up main, beside the water tower and the imposing L&CR station buildings. A banner repeater is provided for the down starting signal of No 3 box. *HDB*

Below right: 'Ting-a-ling-a-ling . . .' The shrilling bells were for long a feature of Penrith (here), Tebay and Oxenholme stations — seen in October 1956.
R. B. Parr

North of Penrith

Above: The 'Caledonian', 8.30am Glasgow-Euston, seen this time on its inaugural up run, 17 June 1957, with No 46229 *Duchess of Hamilton* (which engine sojourned in the USA, 1939-42, as No 6220 *Coronation*), passing Plumpton box and loop. *R. E. Gee*

Left: Calthwaite box, with 'Crab' No 42940 and down freight, slipping gently past, in February 1957. The station was south of the box. *R. H. Leslie*

Below: Southwaite box, of the later type from Crewe, with No 45526 *Morecambe and Heysham* facing *south*, on a ballast train in the down (*northbound*) loop, May 1964. *R. H. Leslie*

Above: The up West Coast Postal Special, with No 46224 *Princess Alexandra*, climbing between Carlisle (Upperby) and Wreay, in July 1957, at sundown. *R. H. Leslie*

Below: The last main line pick-up apparatus in use in Britain, on the up line north of Penrith, shortly before its final use in 1971. *Courtesy The Post Office*

Carlisle Upperby

Top: Upperby Bridge Junction, Carlisle No 13 signalbox, in April 1962: No 46221 *Queen Elizabeth* is working our old friend the 8.40am up, Carlisle to Euston. The goods lines diverge/converge right. *R. H. Leslie*

Above: Turning back the clock to c1900, this southward view is from near Carlisle No 12 box: a three-cylinder compound 0-8-0 and train are on the down goods lines, entered at No 13. Reception sidings are seen to right and the main lines to right again, while on the far left is the approach road to the carriage shed. Early slotted-post signals, including a bracket signal with slow line rings, are nearing the end of their era.
Doctor Tice F. Budden/Ian Allan Library

Above: Upperby (St Nicholas) yard, looking northward, June 1962: No 47614 0-6-0 Side Tank is shunting and 'Black 5' No 45284 is on an up freight. The early mechanical coaling plant for Upperby engine shed is to the right. *D. F. Tee*

Right: Upperby engine shed, with the middle section almost devoid of roof, c1939; LMS Nos 5439, 5534 *E. Tootal Broadhurst* and 5139 are in evidence; Harrowby Hill House, 'the barracks', is up behind the sheds. *Howard Vogt*

Below right: Upperby sheds, the end section and the workshops: LMS No 10456, a Horwich four-cylinder 4-6-0 ('Lanky Claughton') of 1924, was rebuilt in 1926 as a four-cylinder compound and is seen here c1932, as such, along with 'Crab' No 13110 of 1929, also stationed at Upperby. *Harold D. Bowtell collection*

Citadel station, Carlisle

Below: Citadel station interior: a view from the 1880 island platform towards the earlier up side of the station, believed to be around 1922. 'Jumbo' No 1531 *Cromwell* is piloting unnamed 'Prince' No 261 on a train for the south. *Gordon Tidey*

Bottom: The southern end glazed screen, Citadel station, as drawn and signed by the architects, in Edinburgh, May 1878. At rail and platform level can be seen, left to right, provision for carriage sidings, a running road, the island platform with M&C bay, a running road, middle roads, up main platform road and platform, with bays for Midland and North Eastern Railways.

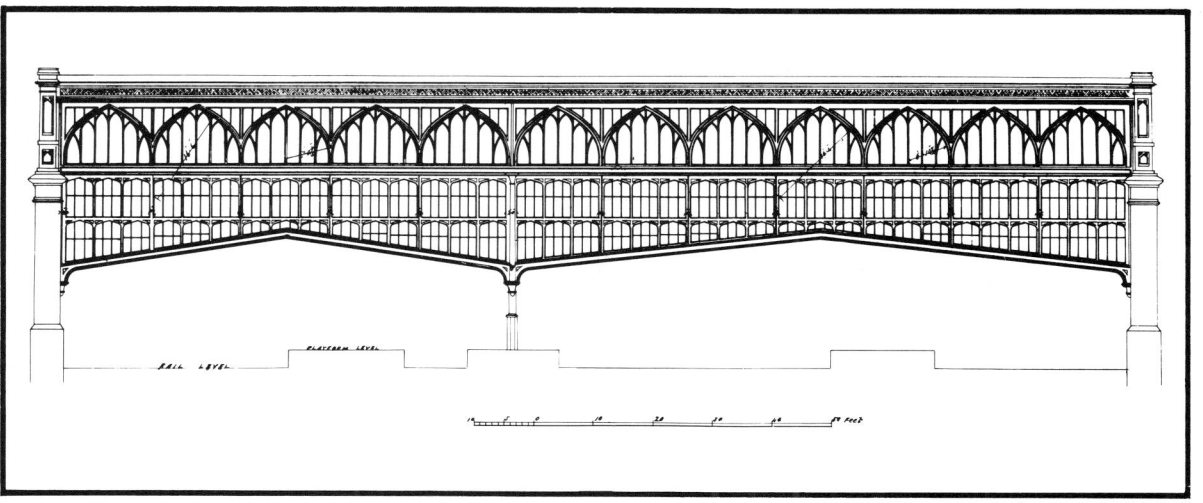

The Windermere line

Top: Climbing the 1 in 80 from Kendal to Oxenholme:
No 49449, with the nucleus of the fast freight train to Liverpool,
July 1961. *Preston Whiteley*

Above: The 4.55pm Windermere-Oxenholme passenger, leaving
Kendal, August 1963, with engine No 42322. *Preston Whiteley*

Top right: Up express from Windermere entering Kendal
station, c1900; the large goods yard is below (left), the box and
footbridge are seen, and (right) the carriage shed.
E. Pouteau/D. J. W. Brough collection

Bottom right: Kendal yard in the 1950s: main running lines to
left, with station; parcels traffic is on the site of the former
carriage shed. *Howard Vogt*

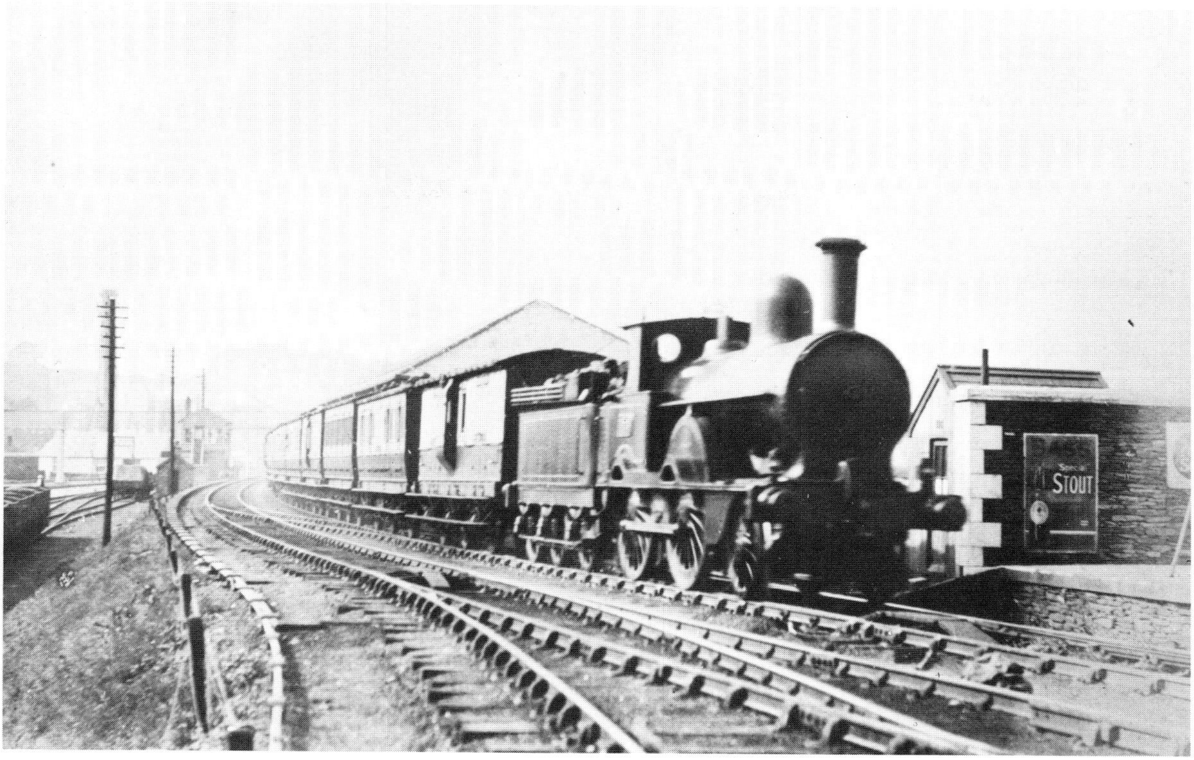
STOUT

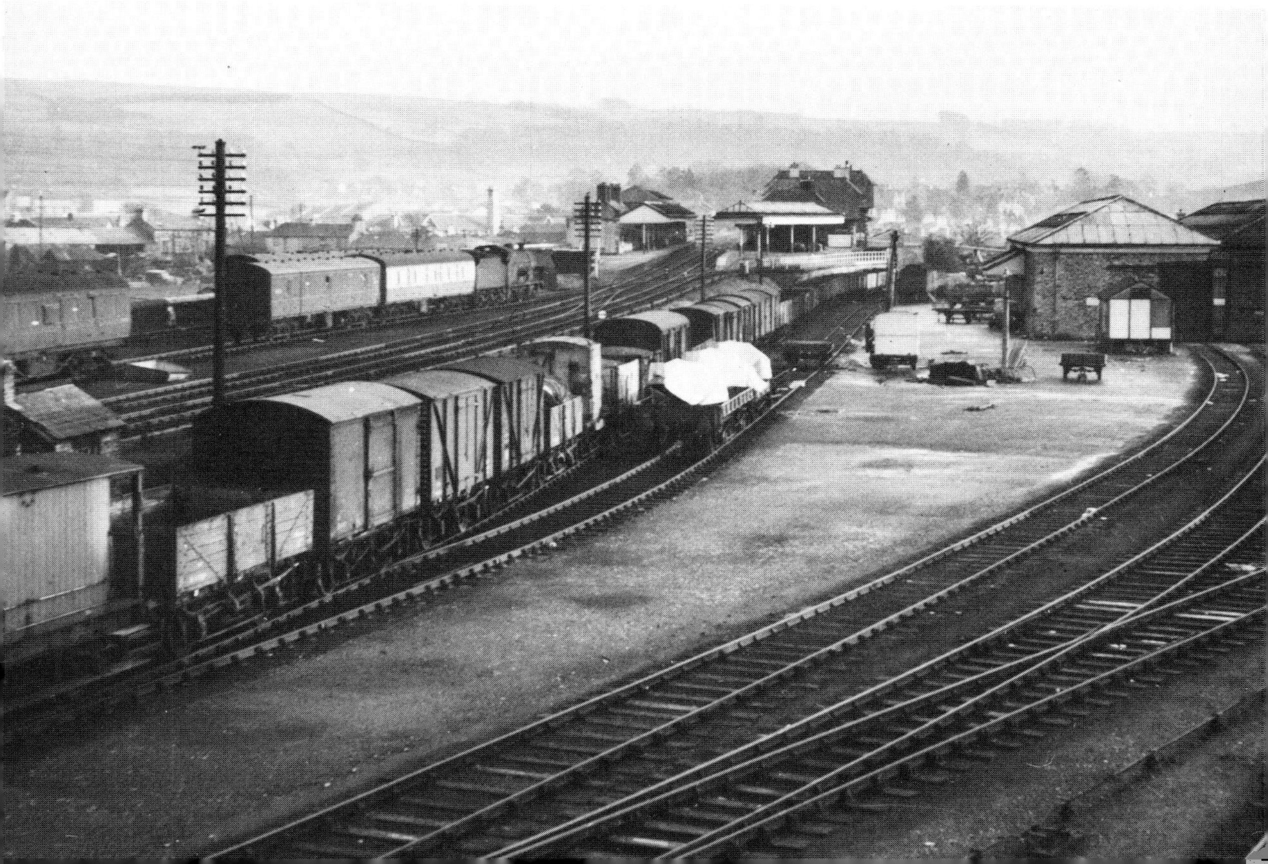

Above: Burneside Higher crossing, March 1980: the open frame is concealed by the hut, the signalman is Edgar Corless, with long experience on the L&CR route. *HDB*

Below: Burneside station, looking towards Windermere, when the buildings were ivy-clad and the frame (extreme right) was not boxed in, probably taken before 1914.
Courtesy Lens of Sutton

Below: From much the same period: Burneside station and village, with 2-4-2T locomotive on six-wheeled stock of an up train. *Percy Duff collection*

Bottom: Staveley station, August 1962: No 44709 of Carnforth shed is arriving with the 1.30pm Crewe-Windermere express. *Preston Whiteley*

Top: NER No 1450 of '174' class, built in 1876, on that company's old four-wheeled stock — believed to be a NER excursion train in No 4 platform at Windermere, with a train of L&NWR vehicles in No 3, probably in the 1890s. *Kendal collection, courtesy Percy Duff*

Above: L&YR No 455, with 7ft 3in coupled wheels, on 4.15pm express to Manchester Victoria, in Windermere No 2 platform, c1914. *Eric Mason/Harold D. Bowtell collection*

Top right: Return excursions at Windermere, in the late 1930s. The onetime engine shed building, gabled, is visible. Prominent are the starting signals for platform roads 4 and 3, which are vacant. The 'Crab' and train are in the middle road, the 'Black 5' and train are at platform 2 and 'Baby Scot' No 5537 *Private E. Sykes, VC* is at platform 1. A train is stabled (right) in the goods yard. *C. M. Doncaster/courtesy Gordon Biddle*

Right: Windermere train shed, exterior (side), with portico, November 1971. *HDB*

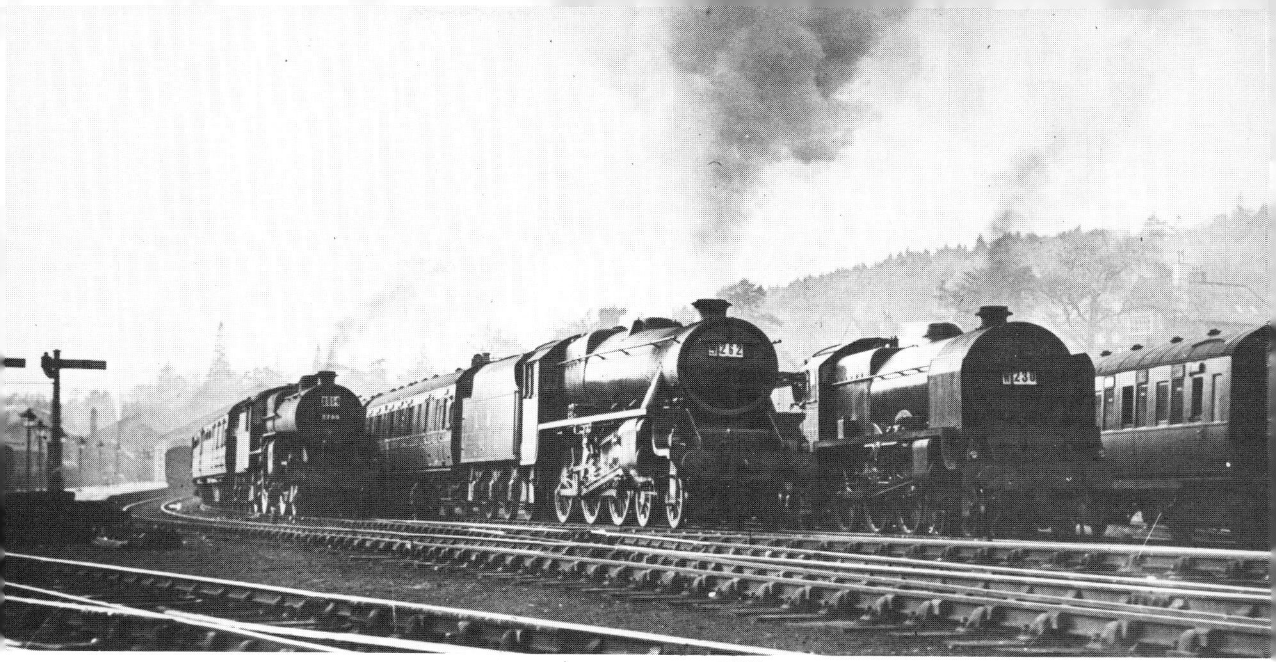

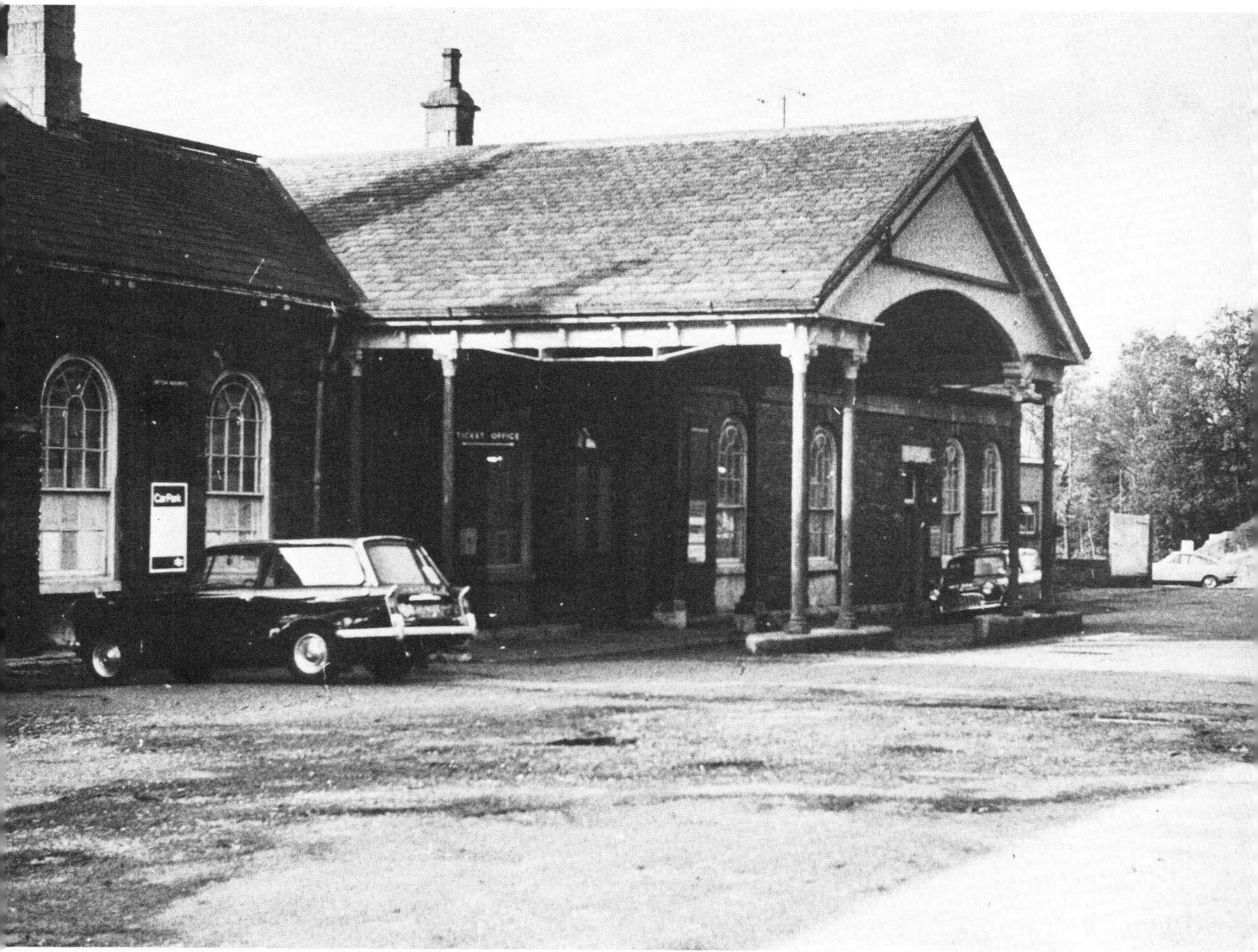
Car Park
TICKET OFFICE

Express Trains over Shap

Above: Tackling Shap! No 163 *Holland Hibbert*, fifth of the classic 'Claughtons' when built in 1913 at Crewe, is fondly recalled by the author as the engine which headed the train south after his first serious visit to Carlisle. As illustrated, the train is typical of period 1913-23, engine being in gleaming lined black and 11 carriages in L&NWR 'plum and spilt milk', some 370 tons tare; there are three 12-wheeled vehicles, the third and seventh from engine being early restaurant cars. Tebay railway village, the North Lune bridge, the old No 2 signalbox and stopping train coaching stock (below the station 'tower') are seen to right. *J. D. Darby collection*

Below: 'The Caledonian' express train of 1957-64 is entering upon the northbound ascent of Grayrigg bank, above Oxenholme, with engine No 46242 *City of Glasgow*. This locomotive lost its streamlining in 1947 and was directly involved in the disastrous collision at Harrow & Wealdstone in October 1952, returning to service in October 1953 and being hard at work until 1963. It had been built, at Crewe, in 1939. *Howard Vogt*

Express Trains over Shap - their appearance, composition and weight

During the latter half of the 19th century, the West Coast route between England and Scotland, by the London & North Western and Caledonian Railways, achieved the supreme hallmark of respectability. Since 1861, the Queen had travelled this way annually, on her end of summer pilgrimage to Balmoral, where quietude and autumn tints awaited and the faithful Brown was on hand.

Rather earlier in each season, as 12 August — the 'Glorious Twelfth' — approached, the more wealthy exiles from Scotland and southern connoisseurs of a grouse moor joined in making the journey to the Highlands. Increasingly, in late Victorian and Edwardian times, family parties also set off from Euston, during school holidays, to enjoy a month's domicile in Scotland. The management at Euston probably expected this traffic to come their way as by right. However, they were business men and aware of competition from Kings Cross for Inverness, also seeing that their newer and prospective clients might be tempted down the road to St Pancras, to travel north in Pullman cars or in 'thirds' gleaming internally with polished mahogany; the Midland Railway's 'Johnny come lately' route by Settle, Ribblehead, Ais Gill and Appleby was just over the fells from Shap. Accordingly, the appearance of the L&NWR express trains changed out of recognition between 1890 and 1910. The length and weight of a typical express increased enormously in the same period, and with it the demands for locomotive power.

My favourite picture is one passed to me during schooldays by my father. The back of the card indicates 'L&NWR series, March 1905' and its face depicts a 'Jumbo' 2-4-0 express locomotive in full cry on the bank near Shap Wells, with no motorway on the background fell. No 2189 *Avon* is the engine and the train is described as an Aberdeen express; as it is broad daylight, this *may* indicate that it is a posed scene. The original photograph is understood to have been taken on 18 July 1899, on Shap, and a print was autographed by Francis William Webb, the Railway's chief mechanical engineer. The train of nine non-corridor vehicles comprises five passenger carriages interspersd by four vans. Three of the passenger carriages are of the semi-rigid eight-wheeled radial-axled type, each about 42ft long with lavatories and a luggage compartment. Two are six-wheelers and they likewise have central luggage compartments. Gas lamp-tops and torpedo ventilators adorn the roofs. This type of stock enabled each family to have their trunks and other baggage close to their compartments. The carriages were often composites (multi-class), so nannies, governesses and servants could be accommodated in adjoining compartments for the long overnight journey. The train was typical of the 1890s. Its weight, tare, could be around 150 tons.

A great step was taken on 6 June 1891, with the introduction by the L&NWR of a dining car in the 2.00pm down from Euston to Glasgow/Edinburgh and the 2.00pm up from those cities, eliminating the meal stop of 20min at Preston. The September 1892 timetable styles these trains 'Express' and the column (for the down train) proudly states 'Dining Saloon Euston to Glasgow'. The same table shows dining saloons on the 4.10pm Euston-Liverpool and the 5.30pm Euston-Manchester. At this date, passengers had to walk along the platform at Rugby, Crewe, Preston or Carlisle to reach the car for tea or dinner or return from it to their compartments — akin to the long-time custom on Indian railways. From May 1893, second class was abolished on West Coast Anglo-Scottish trains and on 1 July 1893 the 2.00pm trains became 'Corridor Expresses', with new rolling stock to complement the dining vehicles. The L&NWR introduced imposing 12-wheeled bogie dining saloon carriages with clerestory roofs and entry only by end vestibules, where the handsome doors were inset and flanked by brass handrails. However, a smaller dining carriage with central kitchen between small saloon compartments, one with nine first class seats and the other with 12 third class seats, appeared on the Euston-Edinburgh service from August 1893 and it later moved to the evening Manchester-Glasgow service. The bogie coaches of 1893 (apart from the diners) had conventional compartments, with individual doors externally as well as to side corridors, and there were gangways between the coaches. Their outline was severe, with the rather flat sides and low roofs so familiar in the rolling stock of the Company, right back to the days of four-wheeled carriages and likewise the six-wheelers and eight-wheeled 'radial' carriages. The contrast with the diners is clear to see in photographs, such as the one of 'Luck of Edenhall' and 'Hugh Myddelton' (the latter built in 1898) at Shap Wells with the all-corridor 10.00am Euston-Glasgow/Edinburgh; there are two diners in a train of 13 vehicles, weighing in all about 350-360 tons. This 10.00am service became all-corridor in 1900, but it was well into the new century before all the West Coast Scottish trains were made up of corridor carriages, usually with diners too by day and 'sleeping saloons' by night. A well-known view of 'Liver' and 'Renown' (this last built in 1899), stated to be on the 11.25am Birmingham-Glasgow train, shows 12 assorted vehicles, only two corridors among them, and no diners. Three Great Western clerestory coaches are well dispersed in the train, portions of which have evidently come from the west country: weight some 275 tons behind the engines. The principal trains weighed 225-375 tons between Peston and Carlisle in the period 1900-1910, except when — chiefly in summer — Edinburgh and Glasgow portions ran separately and that for Edinburgh could be in the 125-175 tons range.

The night trains often conveyed varied stock, which could include private or family saloons, invalid saloons, carriage trucks, horseboxes, and the like. A contemporary observation, around the turn of the century, records a summer evening at Wigan when trains came in from Manchester and Liverpool and vehicles were on hand for a late evening departure to Scotland. Their destinations were Perth, Dundee and Aberdeen, the Caledonian Railway's Callander & Oban line, also Blacksboat (on the Great North of Scotland Railway's Speyside line), Nairn (Highland Railway, between Forres and Inverness), Garve (HR Skye line), Golspie and Forsinard (HR 'Farther North' section). The only map available to help the staff was said to be in the L&NWR's penny timetable.

In autumn 1892, the 8.50pm 'Scotch Mail' from Euston to Glasgow was a 'Sleeping Saloon Express' — and so were the 'Irish Mail' and a midnight service — the 'sleepers' being heavy 12-wheeled vehicles with styling akin to the 'diners' but with separate sleeping compartments and side corridors; this basic layout was found acceptable and adopted right through to the present time. By 1908-09 sleeping cars ran all through the winter to Stranraer, Perth and Aberdeen (in the formation of the 8.00pm 'Tourist' express from Euston), also to Glasgow (in the 8.50pm) and to both Edinburgh and Glasgow (in the 11.50pm). By 1 May 1922: the 'Tourist' was at 7.30pm down, sleepers as in the prewar 8.00pm; the 9.20pm down carried sleepers to Glasgow; the 11.00pm had sleepers to Edinburgh and Dundee; and the 11.40pm was a Glasgow sleeping car train; while in summer services expanded in the direction of the Highlands.

In early days of the LMS Railway, April 1923, one found: 7.30pm down (for many years the traditional time for the 'Tourist') with sleepers for Dundee, Aberdeen and Inverness; 7.50pm down with sleepers to Stranraer; and 11.00pm down with sleepers for Edinburgh, Glasgow and Aberdeen.

The continued expansion of night services is clear from the timetable for 1981-82, advertising sleeping car services from Euston to (inter alia):

20.50 Inverness
20.55 Stranraer
21.50 Inverness, also Fort William
22.15 Glasgow
22.35 Perth

23.30 Glasgow (the entire train made up of sleeping carriages)
23.45 Barrow-in-Furness

Note that, from June 1965, British Railways trains have been identified with the 24-hr clock.

Including the Euston-Barrow and the 21.25 Bristol-Glasgow/Edinburgh, there are thus eight down services north of Preston with sleeping accommodation, ignoring any height-of-season additions to Inverness.

Looking backward to pick up the story of the daytime trains, the '2.00pm corridor' was provided in 1908 with two sets of fine new carriages, dual fitted (with vacuum and westinghouse brakes), each train being made up of:

Four for Glasgow, including a 12-wheeled diner	Eight coaches, each 65ft 6in long and of 9ft overall width — length 556ft
Three for Edinburgh, including a 12-wheeled diner	
One for Aberdeen (detached at Preston)	

Two conventional side-corridor coaches in rear from Euston to Crewe, one bound for Whitehaven and the other for the Cheshire Lines via Knutsford.

The diners, believed actually to be built in 1905, were 12-wheeled, with clerestory roofs, following essentially the external style of those of the 1890s; each had a central kitchen and butler's pantry, flanked by separate first and third class open-plan saloons, furnished with independent dining chairs and tables. The 'first' saloon was panelled internally in mahogany on walnut framing, decorated in ebony and tulip-wood. The mahogany tables were covered in red leather. The ceilings were decorated with white lincrusta — the stiff, embossed paper with floral devices, much favoured in *art nouveau* decoration and particularly popular with the Midland Railway's carriage department. The 'third' saloon was panelled in light oak on teak framing, with tables in teak, leather covered. The six passenger coaches were the real innovation, approximately 65ft long and 9ft wide like the diners, with elliptical roofs, side corridors and external access only through end vestibules; each compartment had a pair of windows but no external door, thus reducing draughts when travelling and the chill and disturbance of open doors at stations.

From 1 January 1912, second class accommodation was withdrawn by the L&NWR except for local services south of Harrow; also by the North Staffordshire Railway, the Cambrian Railways, the L&YR, the Cockermouth, Keswick & Penrith and Maryport & Carlisle Railways. New trains were built by the L&NWR at Wolverton in 1913 for West Coast Joint Stock account (L&NWR and Caledonian Railway). These were for the 10.00am expresses between Euston and Glasgow/Edinburgh and at least one other day service, but, although the 12-wheeled dining cars followed the style of existing cars, the remaining passenger carriages (side corridor) were conventional, with individual external doors to each compartment — but elliptical roofs — and austere interiors, especially in the third class compartments and corridors. Apart from special L&NWR vehicles for ocean liner trains, built initially in 1907, the advanced layout of the '2.00pm' coaches of 1908 was not widely adopted for about another 20 years. It became standard LMS practice, after a transition in 1927-30, leading to that Company being far in advance of all others as concerned interior design and comfort of coaching stock, with the seclusion of compartments but wide visibility from every seat. The layout pioneered by the 'Corridor' indeed pointed the way adopted by British Railways until the move of recent years to open saloons and badly placed windows, features influenced by costs of construction and carrying capacity rather than the preferences of travellers.

The 10.00am Euston-Glasgow/Edinburgh varied around 1911-12 from 7 to 12 coaches, about 205-340 tons, north of Crewe and Preston; it was divided from Crewe northwards, or throughout, according to seasonal demand, and strengthened too as necessary on busy days. These 10.00am trains were titled 'The Royal Scot' from July 1927 and received new LMS stock, the Glasgow and Edinburgh portions combining to make up a summer maximum of 15 vehicles in each train, weight about 475 tons. Further new train sets were introduced to these trains in July 1930. By about 1938, the basic formation was eight for Glasgow and five for Edinburgh, 13 coaches, say 420 tons — the load having been curtailed to facilitate acceleration and the number of trains expanding at peaks.

The 2.00pm load had been typically 10 vehicles, 370-380 tons, but in the 1930s its 1908 stock became dispersed and post-1923 coaches predominated in the Anglo-Scottish trains, although pre-1923 diners were often included. With the rapid carriage-building of the era from 1933, the later LMS flush-panelled coaches became almost universal, apart from strengthening and relief trains. The normal set for the 'Mid-day Scot', successor to the 'Corridor', in the later 1930s was about 13, plus a GWR Plymouth-Glasgow coach, making some 450 tons northbound over the Crewe-Preston and Carlisle sections. Southbound, in summer, the load could reach about 500 tons.

The 'Coronation Scot' ran between Euston and Glasgow in 1937-39, with 1.30pm departure each way. The train sets of nine coaches looked externally very like other Stanier stock but with roof profile adjusted to accommodate pressure ventilation and a deep blue livery, plastered in poor taste with 'silver bands'. Train weight was about 300 tons. Externally, the crisp styling and delicate blue of the LNER streamline trains would have been hard to surpass, although the more conservative internal *decor* of the 'Coronation Scot' might be found preferable to the furnishing of the LNER streamliners. The pattern of Euston for Glasgow and Kings Cross for Edinburgh, implicit in the 'Coronation Scot', became settled in the 1939 wartime services and in the practice of 1946 onwards. When British Railways introduced a daily high-speed train, 'The Caledonian' of 1957-64, between Euston and Glasgow, there were many of the beautifully proportioned Mark 1 standard coaches, constructed 1951 *et seq*, available; even so, two LMS coaches ran in the train for its first years, but standard coaches made up the set after that. The set was of eight vehicles, 263 tons initially (and little changed later). BR Mark 2 stock, built 1963 onwards, will be familiar and indeed today one complains if the vehicles are not of air-conditioned Mark 2/3 vintage (built from 1970 onwards). Externally, the writer holds that the side profile, with 'tumble-home' in the upper part of the sides, and the roof profile too, also the crisper corners, are more attractive in the trains of Mark 1 era than the more rounded features of the newer stock. The high carriage waist-line, abandoned by the LMS in their big advance around 1930, came back to the WCML in the 1970s, with air-conditioning and fixed double glazing. Riding of bogie rolling stock of L&NWR design — as coming into service in the late 1890s — was excellent on their superbly maintained track at the speeds of up to about 80mph which prevailed during 1900-30, and the same was true of the LMS coaches. The 'Mark 1' riding was rather inferior but that of today's coaches is even better, up to fully 100mph.

The basic colours of the trains over Shap were chocolate and cream (or 'spilt milk') all through our L&NWR period, then 'Midland red', gradually darkening, for the whole LMS era (1923-47), soon bright red with 'spilt milk' above the waist in BR days — rather brash at close quarters but making an attractive spectacle in the landscape. A near-LMS maroon red livery returned to the Region from 1956 onwards but, by the time this was established, 'electric blue', normally with light grey above the waist, was introduced (from 1965); it is another attractive livery, except when stock is coupled with restored steam locomotives which are painted in LMS red or shades of green.

Express Trains over Shap - their timings

It is intended to concentrate attention on the 'down', namely northbound, express train services but at all the periods to be touched upon there have been broadly corresponding 'up' trains to serve the Glaswegians or bring home the Londoners, Mancunians and others.

Away back in 1848, soon after the West Coast route, London-Scotland, was established, it took all day to travel from London Euston to Glasgow. One train was run daily, departing at 9.00am and arriving 13hr later, at 10.00pm — with the same times in each direction. The time allowance from Preston to Carlisle, 90 miles by way of Lancaster, Carnforth, Oxenholme, Grayrigg bank, Shap incline and Penrith, was 158 minutes. From June 1862, the start was at 10.00am, a time which became familiar down the years, and by March 1863 this train was calling at Preston, for the passengers to dine, from 3.23 to 3.43pm and running from there to Carlisle non-stop in 147 minutes. In September 1892, the time from Euston was about one hour less and the halt from 2.20 to 2.40pm was styled a lunch stop. The allowance onwards to Carlisle was 105min; this time is worth noting as a basis for comparison throughout the following 80 years. Glasgow was reached at 6.45pm and the Edinburgh portion of the train reached its destination at 6.30pm. The 10.00am train conveyed dining cars from 1899 and the Preston stop was eliminated.

From early days of railways in Britain, the night has been the time for mails. The 'Limited Mail' train of 1859 left Euston at 8.30pm and reached Glasgow at 7.12am, booked non-stop between Preston and Carlisle in 146min; it is understood to have included only three passenger carriages, no doubt four-wheelers, one each for Edinburgh, Glasgow and Perth. To this day, one may experience this tradition of night mail trains with an odd passenger carriage, in Ireland. The separate provision, from 1885 to the present time, of an all-mail train will be discussed later, but it is interesting to observe the passenger-carrying 'Scotch Mail' still in evidence in October 1892; 8.50 pm from Euston, calling after Crewe at Wigan, Carlisle and Glasgow (6.30am). Development of night sleeping-car services over the route has already been mentioned. It is not proposed to trace the precise timings of the sleeper services; after all, when once the passenger settles in his berth for the night, he is not concerned with progress, only with arrival in time for breakfast, or shortly after taking that meal on the train.

Many travellers start their journeys from the widespread south of England, or the Channel ports, or they may require to put in a morning's work in the City. Thus, as journey times from Euston to Glasgow/Edinburgh were curtailed, an afternoon departure (2.00pm — dating from 1889) became possible and — as explained in dealing with its advanced rolling stock — this became the '2.00pm Corridor Express' of 1893. After World War 1, a time of 1.30pm predominated. It was pleasing, from June 1981, again to have a 2.00pm (now 14.00hrs) down; it made useful calls on the Lancaster and Carlisle line, but failed to survive the ensuing winter as a Scots train.

The service thus settled down to 10.00am, 2.00pm (or 1.30pm) and a steadily increasing number of overnight expresses, most of these last composed partly or wholly of sleeping cars. Extra day trains, notably separate Euston-Perth and Aberdeen workings, closely followed the 10.00am and 1.30pm down, and ran principally in high summer or at other holiday times until the coming of the later afternoon 'Caledonian' and the more liberal provisions since electrification throughout (1974).

Having already sketched in the picture of the trains themselves, their accommodation and weight, let us consider briefly the intermediate timing, Preston to Carlisle, of the morning and afternoon Scots expresses of Euston, also of the Manchester/Liverpool-Glasgow/Edinburgh expresses. When this has been done, the demands on motive power can be appreciated.

Timings of 103 and 105min for 90 miles Preston to Carlisle, start to stop, existed in the early 1890s. At the time of the disastrous Preston derailment, July 1896, the 8.00pm night 'Tourist' express from Euston was booked over $105\frac{1}{4}$ miles, Wigan to Carlisle start to stop, in 112min — very tight indeed and calculated to inspire over-fast approach to the curve at Preston. In summer 1901, the fastest booking was the up Scots train leaving Carlisle 12.40pm, 102min start to stop to Preston, but it was noted for its light load. At the same date, the 2.00pm down 'Corridor' had 106min start to stop, reduced to 103min from October 1904. When, from that autumn of 1904, the 10.00am down was accelerated from $8\frac{1}{2}$ to $8\frac{1}{4}$hrs overall, the time Preston (pass) to Carlisle was cut to 100min but this was adjusted to 104min from 21 November 1904. In summer 1906, the 10.00am down was allowed 102min, pass to stop, and the 2.00pm down still 103min start to stop. During the ensuing years to 1914,

Preston to Carlisle start to stop timings varied from 104 to 102min, with an example in 1913-14 of 101min pass to stop. The expresses — chiefly on Manchester-Scotland service — which made intermediate stops could be relatively harder to operate. Northbound starts from Lancaster, Carnforth or Penrith offer no problem but it has always been a different story if a heavy train has to be re-started from Oxenholme, right on the Grayrigg bank; in a driver's recollections, it is always autumn, with wet leaves in plenty on the rails of this bank. On Shap fell, the mists are down and a fine, slippery film covers the rail heads. Even electric locomotives are not immune from these hazards to the timetable!

The 1913-14 timings of 100min pass to stop for the 10.00am down and 103min start to stop for the 2.00pm down included, respectively, 39min and 42min from passing Carnforth to passing Shap summit, a stretch of $31\frac{1}{2}$ miles which includes ascent of the Sedgwick, Grayrigg and Shap banks, some 900ft of elevation. In 1906, Carnforth to summit had been given 40min in both cases.

In the 1890s there were plenty of through carriage workings from Manchester and Liverpool to Glasgow and Edinburgh. Surprisingly, the 5.40pm through carriage from Manchester to Glasgow left from Victoria, the L&YR's station, and it was conveyed from Preston (dep 6.42pm) by the '2.00pm Corridor'. The other departures were, as might be expected, from Manchester Exchange (L&NWR station) and they started at 1.00am, 10.00am and 2.30pm. The first of these connected at Wigan with the 'Scotch Mail' (dep 1.44am, next stop Carlisle) and with the slower 10.00pm ex-Euston, but it is not too clear by which train it was conveyed. Liverpool Lime Street (L&NWR station) despatched through carriages at 12.45am, 9.35am, 11.10am and 2.30pm. Liverpool

Exchange (L&YR station) offered through carriages at 10.10am, 2.50pm and 5.55pm, so once again the L&YR had the monopoly of the evening through carriages. The early years of the 20th century saw a pattern of through trains established from Manchester and Merseyside to Scotland. By 1900, the L&NWR had an evening service of their own: 5.45pm Manchester Exchange/Liverpool 'Corridor and Dining Saloon Express', calling inter alia at Preston, Carnforth, Penrith and Carlisle, reaching Glasgow 11.05pm/Edinburgh 10.55pm but at that time and for a few more years the 'Corridor' was divided from Preston northwards and this Manchester/Liverpool train merged with the 'Second Corridor'. By 1906, the Manchester/Liverpool had achieved emancipation. The old-established 5.15am 'Newspaper Express' from Euston — leaving at a time peculiar equally for newspapers or people — was accelerated in summer 1903, to reach Glasgow at 3.00pm and Edinburgh at 3.15pm, including a 103min booking between Preston and Carlisle; its special significance was its joining with the 9.50am from Manchester Exchange and 9.50am from Liverpool, for the benefit of whose travellers a luncheon car was provided. An afternoon train, dating from summer 1902, was running from Manchester Exchange and Liverpool Lime Street by winter 1903-04: non-stop Wigan 3.45pm to Penrith and into Glasgow 8.35pm/Edinburgh 8.30pm.

Effective in January 1905 was an agreement between the L&NWR and L&YR which brought the companies closer together. Among heads of agreement were the greater use of Manchester Victoria for through trains to or from the north and the transfer of the morning Manchester-Glasgow working, by the 9.50am, to run from Victoria. By winter 1908-09, there were four through day trains, namely:

Manchester Exchange dep	—	—	—	5.45pm
Manchester Victoria dep	9.50am	12.40pm	3.00pm	—
Preston dep	10.51am	1.37pm	4.00pm	6.40pm
Carlisle arr	12.33pm	3.22pm	5.55pm	8.37pm
(time from Preston)	(102min)	(105min*)	(115min†)	(117min‡)
Glasgow Central arr	3.00pm	5.55pm	8.35pm	11.00pm

* includes Oxenholme stop (SO)
† includes 3min standing at Lancaster and 4min at Penrith
‡ inclusive of 2min each at Carnforth, Oxenholme and Penrith

The tight bookings of these trains on the Preston-Carlisle road will be noted. All conveyed Liverpool portions, likewise carriages for Edinburgh. The corresponding up trains were 10.00am, 2.00pm, 4.30pm and 10.55pm from Glasgow due, respectively, into Victoria 3.24pm, Exchange 7.30pm, Exchange 9.45pm and Exchange 4.50am. By 1913, the 4.30pm up was considerably slowed, owing to lengthening of its three stops between Carlisle and Preston. A sleeping car on the Manchester-Glasgow night trains (which in LMS days included the 1.10am Manchester Exchange-Glasgow) came much

later. The evening train, 5.45pm from Exchange, ran much as in 1900, *ante*, in the years to World War 1, following the 'Corridor' by about 15min on leaving Preston.

By 1922, the 'Corridor', now 1.30pm down, missing Preston but calling at Lancaster, was followed by the 5.05pm SX Manchester-Windermere express and this in turn by the Manchester-Glasgow: 5.00pm from Exchange, calling at Wigan (the Windermere residential train slipped past on the Whelley avoiding line), Preston, Carnforth, Oxenholme, Penrith and Carlisle — including through carriages Liverpool Exchange-Glasgow and — interesting! — Euston to Whitehaven and Windermere. In 1923, the evening pattern was the same but the 5.00pm Manchester-Glasgow also conveyed through carriages Euston to Aberdeen: more remarshalling! In 1934, the Manchester-Glasgow service was still at 5.00pm, but during the later 1930s it was provided by a new and faster train, leaving Exchange 4.45pm and calling at Wigan and Lancaster to Carlisle, en route Glasgow. At the same period, the up evening service was accelerated to become 4.30pm Glasgow-Manchester Exchange (9.47pm), almost as speedy as in 1908. As to speed generally, Preston-Carlisle (start to stop) by the evening train was allowed 102min in 1913 but 110min in 1922 and through the earlier years of the LMS. There was general speeding-up in the late 1930s and this train had 101min in 1939. During the years from 1946, the departure was from Victoria and varied between 4.15pm and 4.20pm, with a reversion to 5.45pm in the 'diesel' era which preceded the electrification of 1974. The morning train was back to 101min by 1961, as 9.30am Manchester Victoria-Glasgow and in 1969 (diesel-operated period) had 99min Preston-Carlisle (start to stop), including standing at Lancaster for one minute. With a start at 9.00am, Glasgow was reached by 2.00pm — progress. Electric days brought an extra and earlier train from 6 May 1974: Victoria 07.53 (24hr clock now in vogue) to Glasgow 11.27, advertised in 80min Preston to Carlisle (start to stop), including a call at Lancaster; now at last there was real advance.

It was not until the mid-1920s that a through day train — as distinct from through carriages — from Birmingham to Glasgow, with Edinburgh portion, became a normal feature. In 1927 it left at 11.45am (6hr 55min to Glasgow), in 1939 at the same time (6hr 40min), in autumn 1946 at 11.00am (7hr 3min), in 1956 at 11.25am (6hr 55min); the rather nondescript starting times in late morning, necessitating putting virtually a whole day aside for the journey, were presumably dictated by the large catchment area, from the West Country to South Wales. One of the successes of the electric service, right from May 1974, has been the running of well-used expresses from Birmingham to Scotland, five by day in that first year, six in 1981-82: 08.10, 10.05 (originating in Bristol at 08.11), 11.16 ('Clansman' 09.35 Euston to Inverness), 12.05, 14.05 and 18.00, with a night service too; overall times have improved to $4\frac{1}{2}$-5hr.

Reverting to the daytime Euston-Glasgow trains, the LMS, in 1927, named the 10.00am the 'Royal Scot'; interesting changes in its operation took place in 1927 and 1928. The 2.00pm (by then 1.30pm) became the 'Mid-Day Scot'. Taking winter 1929-30, the 'Royal Scot' was allowed 104min (pass to stop), Preston-Carlisle, including 43min Carnforth (pass) to Shap summit (pass). The 'Mid-Day Scot' had 112min, Preston (pass) to Carlisle (stop); this includes a stop and restart at Lancaster (but omits the standing time). It was allowed 44min Carnforth (pass) to summit (pass). Acceleration came gradually from 1932 onwards, notably in May 1936, and lasted only until September 1939. From summer 1937, the 'Coronation

Scot' of nine coaches, 297 tons, with large streamlined 'Pacific' locomotive, ran 1.30pm Euston-Glasgow in $6\frac{1}{2}$hr, and likewise 1.30pm Glasgow-Euston. One intermediate stop, Carlisle station, was made. Euston to Carlisle was booked in 283min and Carlisle-Glasgow in 105min. Preston (pass) to Carlisle (stop) was given 89min, including 35min for Carnforth (pass) to summit (pass). The 'Royal Scot' was accelerated in spring and summer 1938, the earlier 'Pacifics' being used that year on a train allowed 420 tons, with seven hours end-to-end and stops at Carlisle and Symington. Preston (pass) to Carlisle (stop) was timed in 95min with 39min from Carnforth to summit, pass to pass.

Sadly extended schedules were introduced in September 1939 and these were soon matched, in the prevailing wartime conditions, by very heavy loadings. Members of the armed forces often made more lengthy journeys than the typical peacetime passenger. Owing to naval activity in the far north, the 10.05am Euston-Thurso became a daily feature, following the 10.00am over the Lancaster and Carlisle line in mid-afternoon. It stood in Perth from about 8.30 to 10.30pm to allow a supper interval and was due in Thurso about 7.20am. Digressing from the L&C, I recall a lightning trip on leave from my unit in Surrey, to view the Southern Railway's Stroudley 0-4-2 tank engines at the Mound and Wick when, coming south over the Farther North section of the Highland line, the previous morning's 10.05am down was passed at 9.50am at Scotscalder; Class 5 4-6-0 No 5083 of Inverness on 12 bogies, including two vans — set against the incredible autumn colours of the moorland in brilliant sunshine, 4 November 1941: a scene worthy of Shap! In 1941-43, non-stop runs were made by such trains as the 'Night Scot' between Crewe and Glasgow or Crewe and Motherwell and Crewe-Carlisle non-stops were numerous.

War ended in August 1945 and in October 1946 the LMS operating department nobly introduced a timetable which owed much to those of 1937-39, but timekeeping was at once atrocious; locomotives and their crews were, in general, not yet fit or attuned to smart running and the winter ended also with exceptionally severe weather, followed by a drastic shortage of coal. It was not until around 1956 that improved schedules figured again.

A landmark was introduction from 17 June 1957 of the 'Caledonian', 4.15pm Euston-Glasgow and 8.30am Glasgow Central-Euston, which ran until Friday 4 September 1964. For the period 9 June 1958 to 14 September 1958, there was a second 'Caledonian', at 7.45am from Euston and 4.00pm from Glasgow, but subsequently only 3.55pm down and 8.30am up applied. The set of eight coaches (263 tons initially) was much the same weight as the nine coaches of the 'Coronation Scot' of 1937-39 and its timings of 89min Preston-Carlisle (pass to stop), including 35min Carnforth to summit (pass to pass), were identical with the WCML's high speed train of 20 years earlier.

By June 1961 there were four day trains from Euston booked at commendable speeds, namely:

Euston dep	9.15am	10.00am	1.00pm	3.55pm
Preston pass	12.59pm	2.06pm	5.02pm	7.39pm
Carlisle arr	2.28pm	3.43pm	6.38pm	9.08pm
	('The Royal Scot' to Glasgow)	(to Aberdeen)	('Mid-day Scot' to Glasgow)	('Caledonian' to Glasgow)
with Preston to Carlisle in	89min	97min	97min	89min
incl Carnforth (p) to summit (p) in	35min	41min	39min	35min
and loadings	XL limit	Special limit	XL limit	XL limit
	max 290 tons		max 420 tons	max 290 tons

In the all-diesel era of 1969-70, the pattern was Euston depart 10.05 (the 'Royal Scot' to Glasgow), 12.05 to Glasgow and Perth (97min Preston-Carlisle including Penrith stop), 14.05 to Glasgow (98min Preston-Carlisle including Oxenholme stop), 16.05 to Glasgow and 17.05 to Carlisle. For one year 1970-71, the advertised Preston-Carlisle timing came down to 76min, relaxed to 91min from May 1971.

With electric timetables, 6 May 1974 onwards, Preston has been a 'key' stopping point for all regular express trains, a number of which are non-stop between Euston or Watford Junction and Preston (and *vice versa*).

Advertised times from Preston to Carlisle (start to stop) were initially 68 or 69min, in general. By 1981-82, this has been extended to 73-74min, with, usually, a working time of 69min, including 4min for out of course delays. There are less Preston-Carlisle non-stop runs than in 1974, as the traffic potential of Lancaster and Oxenholme (and their hinterlands) has been better appreciated. Overall time Euston-Glasgow was five hours by the 10.45 down 'Royal Scot' in 1974, calling Preston only, with the other trains in 5hr 7min to 5hr 10min. By 1981, the best time advertised is 5hr 14min by the 07.35 SX from Euston, calling only at Preston.

Passengers for Windermere, Whitehaven out in the west, and Morecambe

Origins of Windermere as a railhead

Away back in the 1840s, the site of Windermere station was selected to minimise opposition by landowners — and Wordsworth. A line through to the lake shore at Ambleside, with perhaps two intermediate stations, would better have served the demand for access and eliminated much of the need for connecting omnibuses, horse and motor. However, the attractions of Lake Windermere and its superb setting, along with the enterprise of Rigg, the coach proprietor, overcame the disadvantages and the Railway Company built up its inwards passenger traffic; much of this originated in London and the Home Counties, also in and about Manchester and Liverpool. It started as inwards tourist traffic but during the period c1880-1914 many attractive houses were built, with vistas over the lake to the mountains at its head; the well-to-do residents looked for fast and comfortable travel southward, even for daily journeys to and from Manchester, some 80 miles distant. Today, the peak travel demands are those of June-September inwards to South Lakeland but, with vast further expansion of Windermere, Bowness and Ambleside as a residential district, there is a significant all-year call for outward travel, to which the old town of Kendal and its wide, prosperous hinterland also contribute. The L&NWR clearly appreciated the value of a railhead at Windermere where trains could terminate or originate.

Long-range travel to Windermere

The first down train of the day has traditionally arrived very early indeed, bringing mail and newspapers for Kendal and Windermere — and a few bleary-eyed travellers. In the 1890s, the 10.00pm Euston-Carlisle called at Oxenholme around 4.40am and the connecting train was into Windermere around 5.10am. This pattern continued. Around 1906, the 10.00pm was held for 45min at Oxenholme; the Windermere vehicles were detached and sent promptly on their way but northbound mails and a handful of passengers transferred to the 11.35pm down, to reach Carlisle 5.30am (rather than 6.00am) and to be in time for an onwards service to Scotland. By 1909, the Carlisle train ran non-stop Preston to Oxenholme and called for 6min to detach. In 1910, the Euston-Carlisle portion comprised four carriages, two being WCJS Post Office vehicles, and there were two London-Windermere carriages, a tri-composite passenger coach (scheduled to

return to London by day on the 9.15am up) and a brake van, while Wigan attached vans for both Carlisle and Windermere; at this time, all the Windermere vehicles were detached at Carnforth and proceeded from there as the 4.12am Carnforth-Windermere. In winter 1913-14, detaching at Oxenholme seems again to have been in vogue. Through the 1920s and 1930s, there was a 1.40am (and thereabouts — it was 1.25am by 1939) Crewe-Windermere, which conveyed London and other vehicles, typically reaching Oxenholme 4.52am, Kendal 5.02am and Windermere 5.30am; at Carnforth connection was given into the early mail train for the Furness line, which departed at 4.30am for Barrow and Whitehaven. The LMS (in its latter days) and BR developed a sleeping car service between London and the Furness line and this reconciled with the running of the main train Crewe-Barrow. The pattern was seen at its full development in the mid-1950s. The 10.50pm from Euston had become a Perth sleeper. The 11.05pm (Crewe dep 2.18am) divided at Lancaster, the Windermere portion leaving first, at 4.11am. The second portion called at Carnforth 4.29-4.37am and went on its traditional 'Furness Mail' path, while the sleeping carriage was held back and conveyed by the 5.40am Carnforth-Workington — presumably so as to eject the men from the Ministry at Barrow at the relatively civilised time of 6.44am — and the carriage was detached at Whitehaven Corkickle, as it was not allowed through the tunnel to Whitehaven Bransty. By early 1960s the Whitehaven was 1.56am from Crewe and the 11.05pm from Euston followed, calling inter alia at Carnforth, Milnthorpe (newspapers put down), Oxenholme, Kendal and Windermere. Around this period the Windermere passenger facility was a single brake composite carriage and wakeful passengers could (early on Sundays) observe the curiosity of a 2-6-4 tank locomotive on a goods brake van, which vehicle was being loaded in Oxenholme's down main line platform with the newspapers for Tebay. In 1981-82, the 02.14 from Crewe called Lancaster 04.33 and reached Barrow 05.55, the sleeper terminating its journey here. A connecting DMU train ran from Lancaster at 04.50 to Kendal (5min to unload mails) and Windermere.

The 7.15am (alternatively, 7.10am) 'North Mail' Euston-Carlisle called at Oxenholme through the years to 1914, with prompt connection to Windermere (arrival around 2.20-2.25pm). A reasonable connection was maintained in the depths of World War 1. By 1922, the old 'North Mail' had become 6.45am Euston-Windermere (arr 2.18pm), with no Carlisle portion. In the 1930s it was 7.00am Euston-Windermere, 6.50am in summer 1939 with arrival 1.55pm, and through carriages conveyed for Whitehaven. The honorary title of tne 'Mail' remained with this train into BR days and the service only succumbed with West Coast electrification; in the early 1960s it was 6.40am ex-Euston, 2.48pm into Windermere, and detached coaches for Workington via Barrow.

Commencing in winter 1902-03, Windermere had a through carriage working from London on the 10.15am down and this was maintained, first on the 10.15am and later on the 10.10am (overtaken by the 10.15am Liverpool/Manchester express) until 1914. By that time, Whitehaven had a through carriage, via Carnforth, on the same train. In LMS days the usual departure was 10.40am to Carlisle, with through carriages for Blackpool, Whitehaven and Windermere, broken by a period of conveyance on the 10.30am down Manchester to Crewe, thence by a Crewe-Carlisle train. The 10.40am down Carlisle restaurant car express, with Barrow and Windermere carriages, was a feature of the late LMS and much of BR era; it became known to staff at Carlisle as the 'All-change'!

The foregoing are basic winter services. In *summer*, 1901-14, the pattern was to run:

1. 10.25am from Euston, alternatively 10.15am or 10.10am, primarily Windermere.
2. 11.30am from Euston, to Scotland, but with through carriages for Whitehaven, Windermere and Keswick; as early as 1903, the restaurant car worked to Windermere for most of the summer. Towards the end of this era, the Euston-Windermere/Keswick portions, supplemented by Manchester Exchange-Windermere, Manchester Victoria-Keswick and Liverpool-Keswick coaches, formed an independent train from Preston northward.

With the naming of trains by the LMS, in 1927, came the 'Lakes Express', 11.35am Euston to Blackpool/Whitehaven/Windermere/Keswick, with the restaurant car usually to Windermere. Typically, in 1934, from May the 'Lakes' (as it became known colloquially) ran at 12 noon on Fridays and Saturdays, Euston-Windermere, with a portion for Keswick and Workington. On Saturdays from 19 May that year, the train called at Rugby and Wigan to Oxenholme (4.41pm), thence first portion to Windermere (arr 5.15pm) and second portion leaving Oxenholme at 4.55pm, calling Shap, Penrith and stations to Keswick and Workington. In summer 1939 there was a Lancaster call and Windermere was reached at 5.25pm. The Workington arrival was 7.26pm SX by the portion serving Keswick but a through carriage was detached at Lancaster for the Furness line and worked right through to Maryport (calling at Workington at 8.04pm SX). On Saturdays, in that prewar summer, one train ran at 11.35am Euston to Maryport (via Furness line, with two vehicles penetrating beyond Barrow, where nine, including the restaurant car, were detached). The second train was at 11.50am Euston-Windermere (arr 5.15pm) with restaurant car, non-stop Wigan-Oxenholme, and with rear portion as usual for Workington via Keswick. In preceding summers there had also been a Saturdays 9.30am restaurant car express, Euston-Windermere, rostered for 14 coaches between Stafford (where four from Birmingham were attached for Windermere) and Oxenholme; the last four coaches were Euston-Barrow and detached *at Oxenholme* to be worked back southward via Hincaster Junction, Sandside and the Furness line. This method of working on busy Saturdays was employed on one or two trains, back to at least 1936.

An all-year working of very long standing provided an afternoon service from London to Windermere. In the 1890s, it was 5.40pm Crewe-Windermere, soon becoming 5.50pm Crewe-Windermere, a timing which prevailed until 1939. Connection (commonly with through carriages) was variously on the 2.15pm 2.35pm or 2.40pm Euston-Crewe. (In 1936-37 there was also a faster 1.30pm Euston-Windermere, with a successor on Saturdays). In 1946, the connection was 2.40pm ex-Euston but the northbound semi-fast train left Crewe at 6.05pm, bound for Carlisle and calling at Oxenholme 8.59-9.03pm, while 10 years later connection was 2.30pm from Euston into 6.00pm Crewe-Carlisle (Oxenholme 9.10-9.16pm). In these years, a Lancaster-Windermere 'slow' followed, reaching Windermere just before 10.00pm. Before the working ended in the 1960s, it had become 6.10pm from Crewe and ran SX to Windermere, not Carlisle, being overtaken SX by the down 'Caledonian', 3.55pm Euston-Carlisle-Glasgow express.

There was one more down train within the compass of this review of long-range services or connections to the Windermere line and that was the 'Kendal Whip', which ran from 1888 until the 1960s, but never bore its name on roofboards or timetables. Presumably it was acquired by the need for late and last comers to be whipped in. Commencing as 9.35pm Preston-Kendal, it was 10.03pm and 10.05pm in the period 1906-14, with connections via Crewe off the 5.30pm from Euston and arrival Kendal around 11.10pm (usually a little later on Saturdays owing to extra calls). In 1923, the times were 5.20pm (connection) from Euston, 8.30pm from Crewe, reaching Kendal 11.28pm SX (11.36pm SO); in 1934, Preston 10.30pm SX (10.15pm SO) to Kendal 11.38pm; in 1939, Preston 10.45pm SX (10.25pm SO) to Kendal 11.52pm (SO 11.43pm and extended to Windermere due 12.05am in that summer). In the latter part of World War 2 the 'Whip' terminated for a time at Carnforth but the 2-6-4 tank locomotive had to run light to Oxenholme, so often conveyed Kendal lads on service leave, who would otherwise have been stranded overnight; it was found prudent for the locomotive to take water and be fired up before inviting the passengers aboard, as the footplate could become severely overcrowded. The 1946 pattern differed, with the 'Barrow Whip' leaving Preston at 10.30pm, a portion (detached at Carnforth) going on at 11.37pm to Kendal, due 12.05am. In course of 1947-48, it became 10.10pm Preston-Barrow, with through carriage to Kendal, arr 11.45pm. In summer 1948, the

'Kendal Whip' *started* at Carnforth 11.17pm for Kendal (11.45pm) *and Windermere (midnight)*, connecting out of the 'Barrow Whip'. In 1956, 10.23pm Preston-Barrow connected into the 11.17pm Carnforth-Kendal. By 1961 summer, there were signs of the imminent demise of the 'Whip'. It ran SO, connecting out of the 10.40pm Preston-Barrow 'Whip'; Carnforth 11.30pm, due Kendal 11.59pm — echoes of Cinderella on those summer Saturday nights. However, there were strange goings-on SX; the connection was 10.02pm FSX from Preston but 9.39pm (trap for unwary late-comers) on FO. The 'Whip' itself left Carnforth 10.50pm SX and ran non-stop to Oxenholme, due 11.00pm in WTT, $12\frac{3}{4}$ mainly uphill miles in 10min start to stop, which compared favourably with the 12min allowed the 'Caledonian' in the same time-table! The Kendalians were then left, exhilarated, to walk from Oxenholme. One might say, tradition was ending in a blaze of glory.

It was said that the first class accommodation in the 'Barrow Whip' was patronised by senior Admiralty folk and executives of Vickers, on the final stage of the trek from Whitehall to business at the Shipyard. As late as 1969-70, that working survived; connections 19.05 from Euston and 21.55 from Manchester Victoria into 23.02 Preston-Barrow, due 00.36. In 1981, the last train to the Furness line is incredibly early. On the main line, 19.15 Euston-Carlisle is due Oxenholme 22.48, with connection FO to Windermere.

In general, the train services on the Lancaster and Carlisle route reached rock-bottom around 1969-70, worse than conditions in either world war. The Anglo-Scottish situation has been mentioned earlier. Only three trains bound for the north called at Oxenholme: at 11.56 (Birmingham-Carlisle); at 18.05 SX (14.05 Euston-Glasgow, no connection to Windermere); at 21.30 (17.05 Euston-Carlisle, no connection to Windermere).

There was the usual very early arrival with mails; 05.00 Carnforth-Windermere, connecting out of 02.15 Crewe-Preston, which had brought the Barrow sleeping car. The 06.00 from Warrington ran to the Furness line and had connection Carnforth 08.00 to Windermere 08.43. The only real bright spot was the 09.05 Euston-Windermere restaurant car train, due 13.53, which ran all year, its relative speed-up being due to electric working Euston-Crewe, introduced three years earlier. An 11.05 Euston-Barrow had connection 15.35 Carnforth-Windermere (16.19). The 17.05 Warrington-Windermere (19.36) was the sorry successor to the Windermere 'Club train' — of which more anon. Passenger stations had been decimated progressively; from Preston, there only remained Garstang & Catterall, Lancaster, Hest Bank, Bolton-le-Sands, Carnforth, Oxenholme and Penrith to Carlisle. The Windermere line was double track, but not for much longer, and had access/egress only through Oxenholme back platform. Keswick-Penrith, cut off from Working-ton, lost most of its southerly links from 18 April 1966.

The up services from Windermere

These were generally in balance with those in the down direction, and likewise expanded during the summer.

Basic all-year departures were:

7.00am approximately, Kendal to Crewe, gradually curtailed, but always with London connection.

9.15am approximately, Windermere-Euston, attached at Oxenholme in front of the (usually) 8.30am Carlisle-Euston.

11.25am Windermere-Crewe, from which derived seasonally, 1927-39, the 'Lakes Express', with restaurant car from Windermere.

9.00pm approximately from Windermere into the up overnight 'Scotch Mail' to Euston, with through carriages from Windermere for much of its long career.

Morecambe passengers

Little mention has been made of Morecambe as a desti-nation or originating point for long-distance traffic over the Preston-Carlisle route. It is a pleasantly sited town with vistas seaward and also northwards to the Furness shore and Lakes mountains. It has never seemed to decide whether primarily to compete with brash Blackpool for the trippers or with dignified Grange-over-Sands for sedate holiday visitors and retired residents. Further, the Midland Railway made it almost their preserve, stimulat-ing holiday traffic from Leeds and Bradford, also some high-class residential traffic inwards to the West Riding of Yorkshire. Accordingly, the L&NWR at Euston Road station was the 'junior partner' and most of their train ser-vices were of branch line character, supplemented by odd inwards summer Saturday trains from Manchester and Liverpool and in LMS days numerous Sunday excursion trains from all over the north of England. Summer-time through trains from Morecambe via Bare Lane-Hest Bank northward to Windermere, also to Lake Side, became a feature in LMS days, enabling visitors to Morecambe to make day outings to the Lakes. In BR times, a summer Saturday train from Glasgow to Morecambe figured, even worked through by a 'Duchess' Pacific locomotive. This working would not have been practicable until the provision of a facing connection from the up main line to the Morecambe single line in the 1930s; in summer 1939 there was a passenger train into Morecambe from the north, which originated at Carlisle, but not Glasgow.

In 1904, the L&NWR introduced an 8.15am from Morecambe Euston Road to Manchester Exchange, due 9.47am. It made several calls between Lancaster and Preston, then ran non-stop from Preston via Standish, Whelley line, the GCR link and Tyldesley — 92min overall for the 57 miles; it was angled at potential daily business travellers; however, it was only a summer train and did not become established as an all-year service until after World War 1, when it combined each morning with the 7.00am Windermere-Manchester Victoria. It later combined with a train from Barrow; for example in 1934, Barrow 7.10am/Morecambe Euston Road 8.15am, calling Lancaster, Bay Horse, Garstang, Preston, Leyland, Chorley and Bolton to Victoria (10.01am). At the same period there was a 5.45pm Manchester Victoria/ 5.48pm Liverpool Exchange-Morecambe Euston Road (7.29pm). The 4.10pm Manchester Exchange-Barrow/

Windermere provided a connection, due Morecambe 5.59pm.

The Windermere and Manchester residential train services

The 'Windermere club train' and the magic hour of 5.05 (or 5.10)pm at Manchester Exchange station became synonymous with the lakes and mountains — but how did this come to pass? Windermere in late 19th century, and after, was associated with Manchester and Liverpool by through carriages and through trains, but mainly in the holiday season and especially on Saturdays, the times varying so much over the years as to defy convenient summary.

However, there was another factor at work; this was the influence of the shipowners from Merseyside and the business and professional folk from Manchester, who came to live around the shores of the lake, many in this community sailing their own yachts or commissioning steam launches with some of the beauty and character of steam yachts in miniature. The demand was first for weekend travel — out to Windermere on Friday afternoon and back to town on Monday morning, then for summer residence with daily travel to town; and finally, also for permanent residence and all-year daily travel — some of the textile directors coming in mainly on Tuesdays and Fridays, when the business men met on the floor of the Royal Exchange ('on change'). The residential train service can be traced back to 1875 and by 1890 it was at 8.10am up, due Manchester Exchange 10.30am, and 4.15pm down, due 6.50pm, and there was significant first class season ticket travel by these trains. Pressure upon the L&NWR management produced an *additional* express train, from July 1895. By 1899-1900, the new express had settled down to run Monday-Friday in summer, FO down and MO up in winter: 8.30am up, due 10.35am, and 5.02pm down, due 7.10pm — calling only at Kendal and Wigan, but also at Lancaster from summer 1900 onwards. From October 1905, the *down* train always bypassed Wigan but called at Preston and the up train called at both Preston and Wigan until the 1960s. Continued pressure led to all-year running, Monday-Friday, from winter 1911-12, with departures at 8.30am up and 5.07pm down. This achieved, a group of regular travellers, well aware of the L&YR's travelling clubs (Fylde coast to Manchester since 1896) and the L&NWR's popular club carriages on the Llandudno and Colwyn Bay to Manchester business train, quickly secured use of a coach which incorporated a private saloon compartment and accommodation for an attendant; this institution of 1912 was rebuilt internally in 1923, with a more spacious saloon, and replaced in 1928 by a vehicle with still larger saloon, the whole coach now reserved to club members. The train itself was suspended from March 1915 and reinstated in Ocotber 1921 at 8.30am up and from February 1922 at 5.05pm down (5.10pm from 30 April 1934); with slight variations, the timing was 2hr each way, until slowed in autumn 1939. The 8.30am up became 8.00am during the 1939-45 war, subsequently 8.20am and finally 8.10am. The 5.10pm down departure applied right through from 1934 to 1964, changed to 5.22pm from *Victoria* wef 15 June 1964. The last double journeys were accomplished on Friday 15 April 1966, the weekend of all-electric services Crewe-Euston but of sadly curtailed services in the north. The club carriage ran until a date in 1941-42.

'Locals' in the north

Introductory

It has been seen that, north of Oxenholme and its deviation for Windermere, the main stopping points for express trains have always been Penrith, then Carlisle. The junction with the North Eastern Railway at Tebay and the village's resident community — mainly comprising railway folk and their families — led to calls there by all the semi-fast passenger trains, as well as by the longer distance 'slow' or 'parliamentary' workings. Between Penrith and Carlisle, the four rural stations usually enjoyed a reasonable service, provided by the Penrith-Carlisle local passenger trains as well as calls by longer-distance slow trains. Of special interest, however, is the story of those 'locals' which operated over the Grayrigg and Shap banks, through the fell country. Some were long-lived.

On the down road

In the 1890s, there was a 10.00am from Preston, calling Oxenholme around 11.20am and terminating at Tebay, with onward connection into the 5.15am Euston-Carlisle (the 'Newspaper Express'), similarly a 3.10pm from Lancaster, providing a service at 4.05pm Oxenholme-Tebay and into a down express, while in between ran a true 'parliamentary': 12.45pm Preston-Carlisle calling all stations (it was at Oxenholme about 2.30pm). By the late Edwardian period, the 5.15am and 7.10am from Euston provided the real middle-day links north of Oxenholme, but the first of these was followed by the 12.15pm Oxenholme-Penrith slow and there was also a 3.10pm Oxenholme-Penrith slow on Saturdays, presumably a homeward shoppers' train from Kendal market. Strangely, by 1913-14, the 12.15pm was running as empty stock, still to Penrith. There were virtually no local workings in the depths of the first world war, when line capacity was at a premium. Subsequently, a 1.15pm MFSO Oxenholme-Carlisle slow of 1922-23 soon became a daily train in LMS days — variously 1.05pm, 12.59pm, 12.55pm (1939), 12.50pm (1946) but 12.50pm SO by 1947 and then soon disappearing.

An intriguing train, commencing in summer 1908, was the 1.50pm SO Oxenholme-Ingleton L&NWR slow train, the tank engine running round at Low Gill to follow the southerly branch line from there — and having a return working at 3.30pm SO from Ingleton L&NWR station, bound for Tebay. The 1910-14 times were 2.20pm SO Kendal to Ingleton L&NWR, with two reversals, and 4.00pm SO (becoming 3.55pm SO) from Ingleton

L&NWR to Tebay. After absence during the war, the working emerged in late L&NWR days as 5.15pm (5.30pm FO) but settling down from February 1922 to be 5.05pm daily, Kendal to Ingleton, where it ran through over the viaduct to the Midland Railway's station, the L&NWR one having closed from 1 January 1917. This train ran until 1939; it was photographed from time to time by the enthusiasts of the interwar years. Its replacement during the decade after 1945 was a 5.0pm Oxenholme-Carlisle slow train.

A valuable local link was already provided, in the 1890s, out of the 4.15pm Manchester Exchange-Windermere express. It was the 6.35pm Oxenholme-Carlisle, all stations. It moved to 6.30pm Oxenholme-Penrith slow, 6.31pm by 1914 and during wartime, still connecting out of the 4.15pm ex-Manchester. After the war, it changed to connect out of the 5.00pm Manchester Exchange-Scotland express and was 7.30pm Oxenholme-Carlisle, all stations, a pattern continued until, at the end of the 1930s, the time was at 7.20pm, connecting out of the 6.15pm Preston-Glasgow (which train followed the 5.10pm Manchester-Windermere express). The time in the later 1940s and until disappearance in the late 1950s was 7.15pm, then 7.20pm — from its starting point at Oxenholme. It had given connection at Tebay into the last LNER train of the day to Kirkby Stephen (for Darlington) but the Tebay-Kirkby Stephen local service ended wef 1 December 1952 — reducing the importance of Tebay station — and the line closed entirely wef 22 January 1962, the same date when the route over Stainmore to Darlington was broken and local trains Penrith-Kirkby Stephen-Darlington ceased to run.

The branch Low Gill-Ingleton-Clapham lost its local passenger service from 1 February 1954 and was officially taken out of use from 26 July 1966 as a through route, although traversed on the odd occasion soon after that. By the end of the 1950s, only Tebay, Shap and Penrith stations remained open for passengers, between Oxenholme and Carlisle. Tebay and Shap were for a time served by the 6.00am Warrington-Carlisle and 10.35am Euston-Carlisle, while Tebay also had calls by 9.20am Crewe-Perth and 6.10pm SO Crewe-Carlisle. From 18 April 1966, the service was further curtailed and only 08.30 and 15.15 (new terminology) Carnforth-Carlisle trains (diesel multiple units) called at Tebay and Shap, while 17.05 Euston-Carlisle called at Tebay on Saturdays only. Both stations closed to passengers wef 1 July 1968.

The once busy Penrith-Keswick-Cockermouth-Workington route was a dead end branch Penrith-Keswick from 18 April 1966, worked on a 'one engine in steam' basis wef 4 December 1967; its focus was by this time almost solely on Carlisle, reached by through diesel multiple unit trains until final closure to passengers from 6 March 1972. The stations between Penrith and Carlisle had closed to passengers progressively: Wreay (nearest to Carlisle) wef 16 August 1943, Plumpton wef 31 May 1948; Calthwaite and also Southwaite wef 7 April 1952; it will be seen, therefore, that from as early as 1952 all the local trains which ran north of Penrith on the L&C main line were booked non-stop from that town to Carlisle.

And on the 'up'

On the up road, the 6.50am Carlisle-Oxenholme slow was already running by 1889-90, calling all stations, with smart timings and made up typically of six 6-wheeled carriages behind a 'Jumbo'. Departure became 6.30am and this continued right on to World War 1 era. The train connected at Oxenholme into the 8.10am (soon 8.00am) Windermere-Manchester express. Around 1906, it was held at Oxenholme for the 8.00am and 8.30am Windermere-Manchester expresses to go ahead and it went forward slow to Preston — but soon it again terminated at Oxenholme (with express and slow connections southward), then it took to running to Kendal. In 1916 it terminated at Oxenholme, with connection to Kendal, as well as Manchester. Through the 1920s and 1930s it was 6.25am ex-Carlisle and more than a 'local', being extended south and connecting at Acton Bridge into a Liverpool-Euston train. It entered the 1960s as 6.15am Carlisle-Crewe and concluded this period as 06.30 Carlisle-Carnforth. In 1981, trains leave Carlisle daily at 06.07 and 07.09 (07.21 SO) for Euston, calling at all present stations north of Warrington, so they have long antecedents.

The 9.30am Carlisle-Carnforth slow of the 1890s had a spell running through, slow, to Preston; then it was 9.55am to Carnforth, continuing through World War 1; 9.45am slow to Lancaster after that period, with adjustment to 9.50am and 9.43am, but disappearing for good in World War 2.

There was a 12.34pm Carlisle-Tebay slow, next stop Oxenholme and running to Kendal, in Edwardian days, but it ceased before 1914 and reappeared to run for a decade or so after the second war, as 1.50pm (then 1.51pm) Carlisle-Oxenholme, all stations. Also in the middle-day period, the 1.50pm Carlisle-Preston slow of the 1890s became 2.30pm Carlisle-Carnforth slow (connecting for a time into 4.20pm Windermere-Manchester Victoria), then 2.15pm Carlisle-Oxenholme, later back to a 2.30pm start, continuing during the World War 1 but then disappearing. A teatime up slow left Carlisle variously at 4.55pm (1890s) and 4.35pm — with a 4.55pm going farther afield — but was superseded about 1907 by 5.03pm Penrith-Lancaster slow, resumed after a wartime break as 4.50pm Penrith-Lancaster, becoming 5.00pm in 1923 (for a time back to 4.35pm *from Carlisle*)

and 5.15pm (*from Penrith once more*) lost with World War 2. For much of its career, this train was followed by another 'teatime' local departure; it started at Penrith 6.15pm all stations to Preston in the 1890s and was 6.15pm Penrith all stations to Oxenholme in 1946 (soon after that SO, then fading away) but during the intervening years it had taken many timings, some with lengthy lay-overs at points on its way south. A 'short' working originated in the 1920s and ran until 1939: 7.25pm Tebay-Oxenholme.

Wartime workers to Gretna

World War 1 led to the planning in 1915, and construction, of a vast explosives factory at Gretna and Dornock, northward of Carlisle; construction began in August 1915, with production starting before 1916 was out and full staffing from August 1917. There was an inflow of workers, including many from Ireland, and workmen's trains to suit shift-changing times were run by the Caledonian Railway and the Glasgow & South Western Railway; they went into the factory and Ministry of Munitions internal train services operated from an 'exchange station' beside the CR main line. A train was worked from Penrith at 5.20am, recalled as comprising a L&NWR 'Jumbo' on six six-wheeled carriages and making one of the fastest times of the day (23min) on the start-to-stop run to Citadel, en route Gretna (Mossband) station, which was close by the MM's 'Mossband Office Platform' — for internal connecting trains.

Examples of the CR's special 'Munition Works Workman's Ticket', valid between Gretna and Carlisle by workmen's trains only, have come to light. It would be interesting to see L&NWR examples.

A steam railmotor

Glancing farther south, a steam railmotor of the L&NWR, a 'one class' saloon carriage, with tiny locomotive enclosed in one end of the coach body, was probably put out of a job owing to the economies of 1917 — and found a niche at Lancaster. It put in two shifts daily, shuttling to and fro between Lancaster Castle station and Morecambe Euston Road. From February 1922, the fast 8.30am Windermere-Manchester residential service was resumed and the first job for the Lancaster 'motor' on weekdays was to run out to Grange-over-Sands and leave there with a 'business service' at 8.30am for Arnside, Silverdale, Carnforth and Lancaster, connecting into the 'Manchester'. It had a full day, taking in Carnforth (three times), Morecambe (once) and, southward, Bay Horse (three times). On Sundays, it put in a single shift, revenue earning between 1.25pm and 10.00pm; Bay Horse, Carnforth and Morecambe all figured, and the direct line, Hest Bank-Bare Lane was traversed. By the first year of the LMS, 1923, the 'motor' was still on the 8.30am from Grange, but from midday concentrated on coverage of the Lancaster-Glasson Dock passenger workings, then rounded off the day with the 7.20pm Lancaster-Arnside and 8.30pm Arnside-Lancaster. Short workings to Bay Horse had been given up by this time. The Sunday afternoon duties were to Carnforth and Morecambe. By 1927, the 'motor', which had remained faithful to Glasson, spent practically all its day on that branch (weekdays) and performed on Sundays on the Carnforth and Morecambe workings. Soon after this, probably wef July 1928, a train of three six-wheeled carriages, with conventional locomotive (2-4-0 'Engineer Lancaster' often on the first daily return workings; a 2-4-2 tank on the remainder) took over the Glasson line — which closed to passengers in 1930 — and the railmotor disappears from our ken. There was also a period of railmotor working on the Knott End line from Garstang, believed to be 1920-1930 (year of closing to passengers) without a break.

A private train on Shap Fell

There was also the 'private train' for the workmen of the Shap Granite Company, whose sidings adjoin the main line on the down side at Shap Summit, and still have rail connection there. The train probably originated in the mid-1880s, when the principal of the Company was expanding his own internal railway system. The train consisted of old L&NWR four- or six-wheeled carriages, at one time with wooden seats installed, but by 1939 there were two gas-lit carriages, including one or two first class compartments retained for use of office staff. During World War 2, it became reduced to a single bogie brake third vehicle and this is believed to have been its form for some time, but two coaches were noted in the 1950s. The 'regulars' had their own seats!

The train's journey was, in general, of 5min duration, from Shap station to Shap Summit, for an arrival variously between 6.40 and 7.20am, tending to be later over the years but also influenced by daylight hours, as was the return at 4.35 to 5.35pm, again with varying times (11.55am to 12.45pm, variously, on Saturdays).

In the early years of the 20th century, the train stabled overnight at Penrith and worked as empty stock to Shap station each morning and back likewise in the evening. By 1913, it was apparently stabling at Shap station overnight and this was the case in the 1920s and much of the 1930s. Rather strangely, a 1932 summer table shows it running from Shap 6.55am to Shap Summit (7.00-7.05am suggests a stop in the up loop, as it would not permit crossing to the private platform, on the down side) and on to Tebay, reached 7.13am, return being from Tebay 4.05pm to Summit (4.20-4.55pm) and on to Shap for 5.00pm. For a time during World War 2, the carriage was stabled overnight at Clifton & Lowther; this was convenient as a Penrith locomotive came out in the morning and shunted traffic, including army tanks for Lowther Park, then taking up the workers' duty. Stabling at Penrith was in vogue around 1945 and for a few years, indeed in 1947-48 passengers, including workmen, were conveyed ('unadvertised') at 6.00am from Penrith and back into Penrith at 5.35pm; a porter-guard worked the morning trip and the engine brought him back, with calls so that he could attend to the signal lamps on the road. After this, his status was porter-signalman, so that he could also work Harrisons' Sidings box. Stabling at Shap station was resumed, with both morning and evening trips covered by Tebay engines, usually 'Standard 4F' 0-6-0 tender type. In the morning, Shap provided the guard to Summit, after which he made his way to Harrisons' Sidings box for duty. There was a problem, however. It was simple to pick up the carriage(s) from the 'carriage siding' (cum cattle siding — its respective ends served different purposes), all at the up platform, run to summit and shunt right across to the private platform (down side). At teatime, on arrival at Shap station, after setting down, it was necessary to set back to the up road, then draw forward, detach, *couple with a shunting rope and haul the vehicle(s) into the siding* — fraught with hazard, so the engine often took the train to Penrith, brought it back on a goods about 10.00pm and put off the stock gracefully at Shap. The last trip was in autumn 1956.

Some special trains on the Carlisle Road

The West Coast postal special
From 1 July 1885, the Post Office reorganised its services and the 8.30pm Euston-Aberdeen down 'Special' (PO term) and the (then) 2.45pm Aberdeen-Euston up 'Special' were introduced. These trains, with PO staff apart from engine crew and guard, ran seven nights weekly and were travelling post office (TPO) services, made up of guards' brakes, mail stowage vans and mail sorting carriages. Typically, in summer 1914, a load of 11 vehicles down and 10 up was conveyed between London Euston and Carlisle; this formation included six sorting carriages. The up train today loads to 10 handsome vehicles, in blue and grey, with Royal Mail insignia. It has for long been made up of Euston-Aberdeen and Euston-Glasgow portions, Glasgow being regarded by BR as the main destination. Complementary and connecting services have been legion, varying over the years, but the up and down 'Specials' remain noteworthy in not conveying accommodation for passengers, railway parcels or other traffic. Between 21 September 1940 and 1 October 1945, the trains ran as 'bag tenders' but without sorting on their journeys. The daily sequence is said never to have been broken until snow caused suspension of the service from 29 January to 1 February 1947 and subsequently by discontinuance of Saturday evening departures after Saturday 2 October 1965 and of Sunday evening departures after Sunday 2 May 1976, this last with the abandonment of Sunday collections — and in recent years there have regrettably been suspensions due to strikes. It is the practice to run seven nights weekly, but without sorting, for about a fortnight during the period leading up to Christmas and the New Year.

Preston and Carlisle have always been amongst the principal stops of the 'Specials' and until 1914 (at least) Carnforth was an important call, with many connecting mails to be handled at that station. Sets of lineside apparatus, standards for picking up and nets for setting down mail bags, were installed at:

1. Lancaster — south of Castle station, the canal bridge and one overbridge to the south of the latter.
2. Carnforth — in cutting south of No 1 box and Crag Bank Road overbridge.
3. Penrith — well north of the station, No 3 signalbox, road overbridge and the footbridge beyond it.

The Carnforth apparatus would presumably be installed when it was decided to eliminate the station stop. Due to a vast increase in the PO's road operations, using fewer railheads, the employment of apparatus declined until 1971, when the up side apparatus at Penrith was the last to be used anywhere in British main line service. The GW Society, Didcot, inaugurated apparatus in 1979, but they do not employ 100mph electric working of their traffic. Apparatus well to the south of Tebay station has been recalled, from pre-1914.

The 8.30pm departure from Euston has been almost constant, sometimes 8.15pm on Sundays, '20.35' in recent electric days, and with electrification came routing (from Monday 6 March 1967) via Birmingham. The times at Crewe and Preston northbound have varied little in this century but the 1982 arrival in Carlisle is 40min earlier than in 1906 and 34min earlier than in 1971. Southbound, the time for calling at Carlisle is almost identical with 1906 and 8min later than in 1971. There is a Lancaster stop, up direction only, but Preston and Crewe times are close to those of tradition.

The Royal train
From 1867, the Queen usually travelled from Windsor to Ballater (for Balmoral) and back in spring and autumn, two return trips annually over Shap, in the LNWR Royal train. G. P. Neele, 'Superintendent of the line, L&NWR', recalled many late 19th century journeys. Preston station would be passed slowly, in hours of darkness, the station-master on the platform to see all well and bid a cheerful 'good morning' to Mr Neele, who travelled in one of the rearmost vehicles. The only stop onwards to Carlisle was at Oxenholme, where (wrote Neele) ' . . . the early dawn in May would be upon us; we pass along the platform generally to find all our travellers quietly sleeping, and to receive tidings from the district superintendent or his assistant, Mr Cattle or Mr Price, that all is clear through to Carlisle, and the pilot (a locomotive in advance) is running ahead at its proper interval. On the platform we shall look out for old Newbold, the Wolverton carriage foreman attendant, making his regular tour of the train while at rest, and get his assurance "all is running cool". Kendal lies asleep in the valley on the left hand — the swelling hills, rising above the mist, forming a charming picture. The Shap incline . . . has now to be faced, and . . . into Carlisle'. There, the CR's management, locomotives and crews took over most of the responsibility through to Aberdeen. On the journey of 24-25 August 1891, from Gosport (reached from Osborne House, Isle of Wight) to

Ballater, one of the axles of the Queen's night saloon ran hot and the attentions of the C&W staff were required at Wigan and again at Oxenholme ('in the midst of the heaviest rainstorm we have ever experienced on our night journeys'); they remedied the trouble without disturbing the sleeping Queen and the vehicle made the full trip devoid of further incident. The journey of 21-22 October 1901, return from Ballater to Euston in the first year of King Edward and Queen Alexandra, was made non-stop from Carlisle 1.30am to Crewe (South Junction), arr 4.48am, and this pointed to a new pattern of operation.

A vast number of local staff, from district officers and stationmasters to pw gangers and platelayers, were required to be on duty during the Royal journeys. In LMS days, the advance pilot engine was dispensed with but a notice of 1927 makes it clear that the train (northbound) was itself double-headed, engines being changed at Crewe and Carlisle on a day journey from Euston 10.15am to Edinburgh Princes Street, 6.35pm. The leading engine carried the traditional four headlamps and the rear vehicle two taillights. In general, night journeys have predominated and late summer-autumn have been usual for travel to and from Balmoral. The L&NWR Royal train has been modernised progressively and from May 1977 electric haulage and air brakes have been features of Royal journeys over Shap — and the two L&NWR-built passenger brake vehicles have been transferred to the National Railway Museum and steam-hauled railtours.

Railtours

Private special trains primarily for railway enthusiasts have traversed all or part of the Preston-Carlisle route, displaying a wide variety of motive power, rolling stock and itineraries. Something like 50 ran between 1954 and the nominal 'end of steam' in 1968. The pioneers appear to have been:

1 May 1954
'North Lancashire Rail Tour' from Preston to Oxenholme and back, taking in the branch lines to Longridge, Pilling, Glasson Dock, Sandside and Lancaster Old station, employing 2-6-4T No 42316 and a train with six 'club' carriages (including 815, the 'twin' of 814, which latter used to run in the Windermere and Manchester 'club train').

4 September 1955
'Northern Dales Rail Tour' — 4-4-0 compound No 41102 working from Manchester and emerging at Low Gill to run to Tebay, whence with fresh engines the route was over the NER lines by Stainmore to Teesside.

15 September 1956
'Pennine Diesel Railtour', using a dmu set of four cars, from Leeds, travelling inter alia between Hincaster Junction and Penrith.

29 May 1960
'Northern Fells Rail Tour' from Lancaster Castle to Glasson Dock, Clapham, Ingleton, Low Gill, Penrith, Kirkby Stephen, Tebay, Hincaster Junction, Arnside, Hest Bank and Morecambe Promenade — 2-6-0 No 42952 distinguishing itself with 73mph tender-first, down the Grayrigg bank.

Project 3 was promoted by the Railway Correspondence and Travel Society. The others were commissioned jointly by the Stephenson Locomotive Society and the Manchester Locomotive Society and the writer is happy to have been concerned intimately with their arrangement and execution, in all of which BR staff collaborated handsomely.

On 30 June 1963, 'A4' No 60023 *Golden Eagle* appeared between Tebay, Low Gill and Ingleton, southbound in course of a tour from Leeds for the RCTS. On 5 October 1963, No 46251 *City of Nottingham* made fine running from Crewe by the main line to Edinburgh Princes Street and return, on RCTS behalf. The same locomotive hauled the SLS Birmingham-Carlisle special of 12 July 1964. No 4472 *Flying Scotsman* came round Upperby curve off MR and NER routes and climbed to Penrith, before handing over to smaller locomotives for the CK&PR line, 2 April 1966, for SLS/MLS. 1 April 1967 was noteworthy for the first major public outing of No 4498 *Sir Nigel Gresley*, Crewe to Carlisle (and back via Ais Gill), after restoration for the 'A4' Preservation Society. Happily, 'Scotsman' and 'Sir Nigel' may still be seen at Carnforth, and actively working too. The beautifully turned out engines enumerated all provided a stirring sight on the Carlisle road.

Freight over Shap to Carlisle

Pattern of service — pre-Grouping and post-Grouping

The Lancaster & Carlisle line has never, in normal times, been a coal-carrying route. Its nearest collieries were those in West Cumberland and primarily met local needs, while Scotland was likewise generally self-supporting, yet not a significant exporter of coal to the south. Only during World War 1 was this balance upset; the fleet, in the Far North, then called for a succession of heavy coal trains from South Wales to the Highland line, styled 'Jellicoes' by the staff. Most of these ponderous assemblies of unbraked coal wagons had to be hauled — and banked — up the inclines to Grayrigg and Shap and cautiously conducted down the northern slopes. They did not reconcile happily with the operation of Anglo-Scottish expresses and hastening trains of merchandise ('fitted freights' in the terminology of the later LMS).

In the decade before 1914, there were about 15 through goods trains, Preston-Carlisle, in the down direction in each 24 hours, mostly titled 'express goods' or 'fast goods'. About two thirds of their number left their starting points from 7.00pm onwards and reached Carlisle between midnight and 5.00am. Their identities and times changed little in those years. Origins were Broad Street, Camden and Willesden in London; Aston (Birmingham); Bushbury (Wolverhampton), with nearby Bescot later favoured; Liverpool Road and Ordsall Lane in Manchester; Edge Hill in Liverpool. There were also trains made up at Crewe from many sources (comprising wagons from, for example, the Potteries, South and West Wales and the wide territories served by the Great Western Railway); likewise those made up at Warrington, Bamfurlong or Springs Branch (these last two yards sited to the south of Wigan). There were trains assembled at Ribble Sidings (down side of WCML south of the Ribble viaducts at Preston), or coming off the L&YR's East Lancashire line from Rose Grove (Burnley) or points beyond.

'Conditional' trains were run as required, notably from Holyhead conveying Irish cattle and from the L&NWR's Garston Dock on the Mersey, with block loads of bananas in ventilated vans. These last were essentially fully braked with the continuous vacuum brake. Progressively, more general goods vehicles were 'fitted' (with the vacuum brake) and these were marshalled next to the engine to provide a 'fitted head' to the train and place it in a higher classification, with higher booked speed and priority than accorded 'unbraked' trains.

Working instructions specified that 'specials with rough or unimportant traffic' were not to be run:

1. From Preston to L&C District: after 5.45pm until 4.00am or after departure of the 10.00pm and 11.50pm ex-Euston (namely the later and slower of the down night passenger trains which have been noted).

2. From L&C District to reach Preston after 8.00pm until after 3.30am.

This clearly sought to ease overnight congestion and to maintain the running speeds of the goods trains, which had to share the route with the night passenger expresses. Nevertheless, the differences in running speeds between the slower and faster goods and between the latter and the passengers were far greater than those between the tank trains, freightliners and sleeping car expresses of today. Accordingly, the timetables provided for some goods trains to be set back into refuge sidings or, more often, run into loops at several points between Preston and Carlisle for faster goods trains and passengers to overtake, while the faster goods were turned aside — less frequently — to give precedence to passengers. The goods vehicles were nearly all four-wheeled, of short wheelbase, with decidedly basic lubrication to the axle bearings (and some having grease-lubricated axleboxes); thus, it was imperative to examine every vehicle in a train at intervals in its journey and this examination was booked to be carried out intermediately between Ribble Sidings (Preston) and Upperby (Carlisle) at Carnforth and/or Tebay. Finally, many goods trains would call for bank engine assistance from Oxenholme to Grayrigg — sometimes at short notice, given by crowwhistles when passing a preceding signalbox or even when struggling into Oxenholme; and all goods trains were booked to stop at Tebay to take rear-end assistance to Shap Summit. Pity the poor signalmen. They had to draw on such sources of intelligence as timetable and telephone could provide, supplemented by their own experience and intuition, ensuring (if they controlled refuge loops or sidings) that a train was not allowed forward into the next section with insufficient 'margin' (in minutes) ahead of a faster following train. If delays occurred to the passenger expresses or prestigious goods trains, assuredly the memoranda would demand: 'Please explain . . . '.

Some of the goods trains had to be treated with exceptional respect. The very names of 'Camden' or 'Broad Street', passed along the wire, brooked no delay. Broad Street goods station was convenient for the City meat market at Smithfield. In 1913-14, the meat train from Scotland for London paused briefly in Citadel station, Carlisle (no diversion by the goods lines), picked up traffic speedily at Upperby Junction and at Penrith, called only from 8.15 to 8.20pm at Preston, and was away again to achieve early morning delivery in the markets. This train held its place for years; in 1963-64 it was made up with vans from slaughter houses at Broughton (in Peebles-shire), Biggar and Symington, picked up further vans at Lockerbie and (from the G&SW section) at Carlisle New Yard 2.29-3.11pm, where typically the 'Jubilee' 4-6-0 locomotive was changed, and was away with the title 4A08 to Preston No 1, then paused for relief crew and was on the road to Broad Street. Although the bulk of the Aberdeen fish traffic was conveyed by a succession of fitted trains over the East Coast route (memories of the North Eastern three-cylinder 4-4-2 and 4-6-0 engines tearing south through Alnmouth in the autumn dusk), the West Coast also had a competitive fish train over the vast distance from Aberdeen to London and additionally handled fish from Stranraer at one time.

High in prestige among the general merchandise trains was the 'Liverpool Road-Carlisle'. Liverpool Road was the first railway station in Manchester, 1830, and today is prospectively a museum of railway history. For many years, its name commanded the respect of traders and railway staff alike; the Carlisle goods left at 7.45pm in 1914, 7.20pm in 1925, 7.05pm in 1955 and 7.00pm in 1964, with arrivals in Carlisle correspondingly creeping forward from around 12.30am to 11.40pm over the years — in good time for wagons to go forward for morning delivery in the cities of Scotland. It was necessary to keep 'a step ahead' of the Midland's service from Manchester Ancoats to Carlisle via Hellifield and Ais Gill.

After the massive disturbance of traffics caused by World War 1 and ensuing economic problems came the railway amalgamation (1922-23) and reorganisation. By 1925, with some recovery by industry and before the strikes of 1926 and depression of 1929 onwards, there were about 18 down through goods trains booked over the L&C line to Carlisle in 24 hours, plus 'conditional' workings; some trains were recognisable from 1914, others not so. During the LMS regime, the appearance of the trains changed with the widespread adoption of containers — relatively small ones to permit carting in the towns and conveyance on short wheelbase four-wheeled railway wagons. Covered vans became rather more sophisticated, with oil axleboxes general, tighter couplings, anti-shock features and ventilation developed — and vacuum brakes fitted widely, and used. For many years now, it has been considered unsafe to run above 45mph with older type four-wheeled goods stock, but in the 1930s the fitted freights, composed of such stock (vans and container vehicles), tore down the winding Grayrigg bank with impunity, at all of 60mph; very impressive was the sight, sound and fury of their passage, if encountered at close quarters. No doubt the condition of the wagons deteriorated and so did the track; by the time permanent way maintenance had overtaken arrears, long-welded rails were widely installed and are unsuitable for the now out-dated vehicles.

In BR days, taking schedules of 1955-65, the number of booked through freight trains was about 22 in each 24 hours, plus as many as five or six 'conditional' paths for Fyffes' banana trains from Garston Dock. More through workings had appeared after the 1923 railway grouping, the L&NWR and CR being both in the LMS, along with MR and G&SWR, and the tendency continued into BR days. Various trains were made up at Oxley Sidings (Wolverhampton, Western Region) and Crewe Gresty Lane, a Morris Cowley-Bathgate (Company train for the motor industry) appeared, St Helens figured (according with the development of the glass industry) and there were such Anglo-Scottish titles as Camden-Buchanan Street, Edge Hill-Sighthill and Ashton-Gushetfaulds, all featuring Glasgow destinations.

The numbers of trains quoted are for Monday-Friday (with Saturday traffic progressively declining). It is interesting that on *Sundays* in 1925 about 18 down through goods were booked over the L&C; in 1964, just a solitary one. Typical timings of two of the faster goods trains (a 'Broad Street' and the 'Liverpool Road') from Preston to Carlisle were:

1. In 1906, 153min (including 10min at Tebay) and 176min (including five at Carnforth and nine at Tebay), respectively.
2. In 1964, 167min (including 4 and 20min for the stops) and 159min (including 2 and 5min stops).

By contrast, a particularly leisurely train overall was the 'Road Van Goods', leaving Lancaster at 12noon or 12.15pm, due Upperby 7.30pm (or 7.35pm) with many stops; this ran in L&NWR days but disappeared with LMS reorganisation.

The decline in freight traffic, dictated by the Beeching policies, set in around 1964, and has continued ever since. The up Scottish meat train, which has been described, was loading well in 1963 and providing a block load from Carlisle to London — but the traffic was driven away soon after that by swingeing increases in tariffs. Much the same happened in 1964-65 to the block-load fish traffic from Aberdeen to London.

It was April 1969 when Government approval was given to British Railways to proceed with wholesale changes in layout and re-signalling, between Weaver Junction and Glasgow. Approval of investment in electrification followed nearly a year later. However, BR had been seeking these approvals for a significant time and this was probably why a transfer of freight trains from the L&C route to the Settle and Carlisle line took place; by 1968-69, 15 freights of varied categories had been moved over to the Midland route — and the way was much clearer for civil engineering and permanent way modernisation over Shap. Prior to the late 1960s there had been little diversion of freights to the Midland line. After the big transfer, their numbers rapidly declined, due to loss of traffic.

By the time of completion of modernisation and electrification, May 1974, it was ruled that all freight trains over the

L&C line must be fitted throughout, this partly on account of removal of catch-points — designed to derail runaway vehicles on the banks — and partly in order to achieve high overall speed ranges. The ultimate aim was for retained trains to be permitted up to 75mph, alongside passenger trains allowed up to 90-100mph over much of the route.

Freight pattern today

In 1981-82, booked throughout freight workings between Preston and Carlisle by way of Shap total 14 daily (meaning that they run on at least five days each week), plus four others which are booked to run on two or three days weekly. Thus, for broad comparison with yesteryear, one may say that an average of about 16 through freights are booked daily over the L&C route. Amongst these, eight are freightliners (that is, wholly container-carrying), originating from freightliner terminals at Tilbury, Maritime and Millbrook (both Southampton), Pengam (Cardiff), Willesden, Dudley, Longsight (Manchester), Garston (Liverpool) — all to terminals in Scotland. There are three booked daily Company trains from Dee Marsh Junction to Ravenscraig, balancing the British Steel workings from Ravenscraig works (near Motherwell) to Shotton, which result from the recent ending of steel production at Shotton (near Chester); the level of demand has an obvious bearing on the number of these trains actually run. Only three daily booked workings between English and Scottish terminal or marshalling points — running by way of Shap — are available for more general rail-freight traffic. Other Company trains are booked less than five times weekly and represent the chemical, oil and motor industries; tank wagons and motor-vehicle wagons predominate. For steel, a Ravenscraig-Corby link has been established. Unusual, late 1981, were Margam-Cadder (Glasgow) block trains of coke.

There is a daily Hardendale-Ravenscraig and another on nominally four days weekly; these are Colvilles/British Steel Company trains conveying limestone from Hardendale quarries (just north of Shap Summit) to Ravenscraig for use in steel production. Train loads of granite ballast for use on BR come out of the sidings of Shap Granite Company at Summit, as required, and a modest amount of stone from Harrisons' Lime Works is secured in course of the Shap trip. Private sidings for a storage depot on the ironworks site at Carnforth have ceased to be used in 1981; they were reached from the Furness & Midland side, not direct from the main line. Carnforth Steamtown's industrial and also preservation activities produce traffic movements. South of Carnforth, basic services to and from the Furness coast line embrace two freight trains for Workington, two trains for Whitehaven Corkickle (for Albright & Wilson's chemical works via the incline there — but not running every day). The 17.12 (October 1981 time) Workington Yard-Dover 'Speedlink' express freight may be noted. There are several merry-go-round coal trains each day from the opencast coal point at Maryport, which commenced to despatch these block loads in autumn 1980; they are bound for Fiddlers Ferry Power Station (Warrington Low Level-Widnes line) and there is also mgr coal from NCB via the Whitehaven Harbour railway, conveyed to the same power station. An interesting feature of certain Furness line freights is the conveyance of the special vehicles carrying the exceedingly robust flasks containing irradiated fuel rods from base-load power stations to UKAEA's sidings at Sellafield; these vehicles have jogged to and fro happily since the 1960s, notwithstanding their unfortunate informal title of 'coffins'. With cessation of manufacture of pig iron at Workington — the last of the many iron and steel works in Furness and West Cumberland — in December 1980, traffic from there is reduced; rails are the principal product of the rolling mills which remain.

Heysham is terminal for a loaded Company train from Shell's Stanlow installations and also for an ICI train between Heysham Moss and Haverton Hill (adjoining Billingham-on-Tees); the first of these traverses the WCML south of Morecambe South Junction and the second runs over the short section between Hest Bank and Carnforth (for F&M line). The 'Shell' depot is likely to close in 1982.

The freight and coal trains running on and off the Furness or F&M lines are hauled by Class '40' or '47' diesel-electric locomotives, even when running on the WCML. So too are the trains out of Shap Granite Works and the Railway's own engineers' department ballast trains. More surprising is the rostering of one or two through freight workings for diesel-electric power and there has been an increasing tendency for diesel locomotives to appear — or be heard nocturnally on the banks — due to shortage of suitable electric locomotives. They are not popular with 'Control', as their performance lags below the standard set for the route. Whereas no passenger trains are booked for double heading under normal circumstances, some of the maximum-load freightliners are headed by two electric locomotives, thus obviating risk of wheelslip with loss of time and possible electrical damage.

Carlisle yards

The L&NWR sorting yard in Carlisle was Upperby (incorporating St Nicholas) and the Company's goods terminal station for town traffic was Crown Street, close beside Citadel station, on its east side. Apart from an incoming daytime 'pick-up' goods from Tebay, virtually all use of Upperby (St Nicholas) yard was for forming and despatching southbound goods trains.

Down goods trains off the L&C section normally diverged at Upperby Bridge Junction (No 13) box to the goods lines in the Upperby vicinity, just east of the main running lines, drew forward and set back any vehicles for detaching, into a couple of dead end roads (one became a through road in course of time); these vehicles could be tripped to Crown Street or London Road (NER). Many down trains required little detaching and were scheduled soon to be worked forward to the Caledonian yard, which could be either Viaduct or Kingmoor down sidings. Both were reached by the L&NWR through goods lines, passing under the passenger lines to reach Bog Junction box and by the lines of the Carlisle Goods Traffic Committee (CR, L&NWR, G&SWR, MR) via Rome Street box, past Dentonholme yard (located on the west side of the CGTC route) and Viaduct yard (on its east) to rejoin the passenger lines at Caldew Junction (No 3 box) en route Kingmoor; since 1943, there have been independent goods lines, with their own river bridge, which obviate this emergence on to the passenger lines. A few booked trains off the L&C route ran from Upperby Bridge Junction via London Road Junction to London Road yard; this being the NER, later LNER, yard, it was convenient for handling traffic bound for North East industry and to be worked over the Newcastle and Carlisle line — by NER locomotives.

The arrangements for arrivals in Carlisle changed little until opening of Carlisle (new) yard, sited well north of Kingmoor. The up and down yards at this new site opened on Monday 18 February 1963 and full operation was nominally achieved wef Monday 3 June 1963. Upperby yard closed from March, spread over a few months. The new yard, connecting lines and control equipment were beautifully laid out and construction had taken several years. By the time of completion, the decision had been taken by British Railways to run down their freight traffic and remodel the trains of the future to eliminate marshalling. Consequently, although the new yard replaced all the old sorting yards in Carlisle, it has never been used to full advantage; the down hump was taken out of use in 1974 and from then the up hump was used for both north and southbound traffic, and it too has been taken out of use wef 4 January 1982.

In general, until the 1963 opening of the present Carlisle yard, all up trains for the L&C were made up in Upperby (St Nicholas) yard, apart from perishable and other block loads which passed through Carlisle from north to south — some of which through workings were permitted via Citadel station. The Crown Street pilot engine, for long a 'Special Tank', a L&NWR saddle tank engine of venerable appearance, brought wagons to Upperby yard. The bulk of the traffic came, however, from the Caledonian line. There was a tendency for the early evening express goods trains from Glasgow and Edinburgh to call in Kingmoor up sidings only long enough to detach any traffic for the Midland line (or elsewhere, apart from the L&C), then running by the goods lines to Upperby. Here, the brake was hooked off and the train engine drew its load forward and set it back into one of the reception sidings, a group of four roads towards the west side of St Nicholas yard. The engine then picked up its brake and returned to Kingmoor. Alternatively — and this applied to a majority of the traffic from the north — trains were placed in Kingmoor sidings and there broken up as necessary, the L&C portions being 'tripped' to Upperby and placed in St Nicholas reception roads. Around the period of World War 1, the Caley had three nearly new 0-6-0 side tank engines, handsomely finished, to work these trips via the Joint Committee goods lines. The G&SWR, NBR, MR, NER and also M&CR 'tripped' traffic to Upperby (etc) as required, via the various goods lines and links.

The L&NWR, and LMS in its earlier days, employed tender locomotives of the 4-6-0 'Experiment' and 'Prince of Wales' classes for trip workings in Carlisle but they economically kept down the number of these duties by making the fullest use of Caledonian or other Companies' trip engines to take northbound (etc) traffic forward; sometimes, particularly if an incoming engine crew off the L&C were well short of their working day, the L&NWR/LMS train engine would take its load on to the Caledonian Viaduct

yard or other northern destination. Every train had its brake van; the L&NWR pooled theirs but the Scottish Companies were particular about the use of their vans. The Caledonian were very particular indeed; their vans, which often had the regular guard's name painted on them, had to be worked back precisely as rostered.

The St Nicholas yard, within the Upperby complex, comprised 20 dead-end roads and it can be seen on the enlargement of Carlisle layouts which is reproduced. To the west, it was bounded by the curve from Upperby goods lines to London Road Junction (and thus to the North Eastern and Midland yards and routes). From the west, there was the coal road, then the brake van sidings and the four reception roads (for holding traffic received from Crown Street or from other Companies yards and routes). Then followed two groups of roads for assembling southbound trains; each group was of seven sidings and each group was approached through a neck, the necks being parallel with one another and just north of the long footbridge which crossed all tracks from Upperby village to come down into Upperby shed yard by the old coal stage. For long, there was a 'signal cabin' between the humps which adorned the necks. Two or three L&NWR brake vans would be against the stops at the end of each road and wagons were propelled over the humps by 'Special Tanks', the points being set according to directions from the cabin and the wagons running down by gravity on to the vans in the sorting sidings. The yardmaster's office was immediately to the south, also the cabin from which representatives of the Railway Clearing House recorded each wagon. Particular roads were kept for forming of trains. Nos 1-7 of the western group ('No 1 side') were respectively for exchange traffic (39); Liverpool (34); Ordsall Lane and heavy traffic for Manchester (30); Springs Branch and St Helens (30); various goods traffic for Manchester (26); Preston and Preston & Wyre line (23); 'fitted loads' for Manchester, Liverpool and most of L&Y lines (23). The other group, ('No 2 side') embraced: East Lancashire (39); London (39); 'marshalling road' (40); heavy traffic for Crewe (46); Crewe, GW and Shrewsbury (39); Warrington (39); North Stafford and Trent Valley lines, and Birmingham (39) — the list reproduced being from LMS days, with siding capacity (number of four-wheeled wagons) shown. In the mid-1930s (circa), more modern 0-6-0 tank engines and flat working, without the humps, were introduced, and with the sorting sidings cabin removed. Reliefs for guards on outgoing trains were fixed between the yardmaster's office at Upperby and his opposite numbers at Tebay or Preston; reliefs were not available at Carnforth or Lancaster in L&NWR days.

Guards and enginemen from other parts of the L&NWR or LMS system were accommodated at the 'barracks' or hostel on the cliff above the Upperby engine sheds. Enginemen booked on for duty at the sheds just to the east and guards at the yard itself. Each engine in turn drew forward from the shed, then backed down over the hump (as long as the humps survived) on to its appointed train. Departure with the train was also over the hump, but little trouble was experienced; however, when the L&YR eight-coupled locomotives were used on the Rose Grove (Burnley) train, they had a nasty habit of derailing the leading pair of wheels in coming out over the hump; when this happened, it was necessary to set back again with great care, and usually the wheels took to the rails again.

Southbound trains emerged on to the main line at Upperby Bridge Junction (No 13) and were by then already embarked on 30 miles of almost continuous climbing to Shap Summit, starting with three miles of 1 in 131 to Wreay. In L&NWR days, there was a certain amount of banking of goods trains in rear from Upperby Bridge to Wreay. Use for this purpose of the somewhat rudimentary Webb 0-6-0 'Coal Engines', which had steam brake only, has been recalled. The engine was not coupled to the train and dropped off at Wreay, to be put across the road; sometimes it was held in the tip sidings until the way was clear back to Carlisle. The tip was significantly south of Wreay station, on the down side. It was available to the engineers for disposal of materials, but mainly used for loads of ash from Upperby engine sheds. It was in use from the first war, if not earlier. At one time, trips were made about twice weekly, with five or six 'ED' wagons and, on the site, the side doors were dropped and a gang shovelled out the ash; again, the small 'Coal' tender locomotives were common performers. After the signalbox at Wreay (up side) closed in 1935, replaced by intermediate block colour-light signals, the ground frame for access to the tip was released electrically from Southwaite box. The tip was eventually abandoned, although not until after 1945, and the land restored to cultivation; its later use has been mentioned in describing features of the route.

Other freight and mineral traffics

Goods and quarry traffic from or to the Keswick line converged or diverged at Penrith No 1 box. The onetime coke traffic from the NER for the Keswick line, via Eden Valley and Eamont Junctions, will be mentioned in dealing with North Eastern Railway incursions on the L&C line, likewise mineral traffics between Tebay, Hincaster Junction and Carnforth, which brought revenue but also inconvenient congestion to the L&NWR. The Ingleton branch goods traffic, worked from Tebay, included stone from a quarry with connection at Ingleton L&NWR station; and a through goods working of LMS and later days over the Ingleton line has still to be mentioned. The importance of Kendal as a goods depot and focal yard — with Liverpool goods and Wigan coal trains coming in, has been stressed in writing of the Windermere line and its layout. The depots at Windermere, Hincaster Junction and Milnthorpe were concerned with handling Westmorland gunpowder and its ingredients; a working from Carnforth covered the two latter sites. Milnthorpe, from later LMS days, produced dairy products for despatch, as did Garstang. Goods traffic to and from the Furness line, the Glasson Dock branch (L&NWR), the Midland (via Morecambe or Lancaster Green Ayre), the Knott End Railway and the wayside yards from Bay Horse southward are largely omitted from this review.

L&NWR and L&YR - collaboration

One thinks of the West Coast Main Line from Euston to Carlisle as being solely L&NWR property until the merger with the L&YR on 1 January 1922 and the wider LMS, formed 1 January 1923. However, the section from Euxton Junction to Dock Street Junction, 16 chains north of Preston main line station, being derived from the North Union Railway, was joint property of the L&NWR and L&YR. The same joint ownership applied to the Longridge and Wyre lines and part of the Preston Docks branch. Both Companies worked traffic over most of the lines in question and thus collaboration had long been prominent in the Euston-Hunts Bank relationship.

Still closer working developed. In summer 1901, the L&YR commenced to work a train through to Morecambe Euston Road with their own engine and carriages, the engine usually being No 630, a 2-4-2 side tank built in 1899, and the load about 165 tons; no stops were made between Preston and Lancaster. During the next one or two summers, L&YR locomotives and stock worked more frequently in and out of Morecambe. One suspects that the trains would be 'wakes week' Saturday workings from Lancashire towns and also day excursion trips. There may even have been workings from West Riding towns, in direct competition with the Midland. A L&NWR/L&YR working agreement of 1904 was followed by a wider one effective January 1905, providing for:

1. Use at discretion of Manchester Victoria, the L&YR station, for through trains of both Companies with destinations north of Preston;
2. The free running of L&YR passenger vehicles north of Preston; and
3. Some penetration by the L&YR in the working of goods traffic.

The progressive transfer of all-year Manchester-Scotland expresses from Exchange to Victoria station, commencing with the 9.50am down, has been discussed. A daily all-year business train from Windermere to *Manchester Victoria* commenced to run from the early 1900s, taking the L&YR route from Euxton Junction; it left Windermere at 8.00am, later 7.55am, and arrival was 10.15am, an excellent timing maintained down to World War 1 and into the war years. In 1922, it was 7.00am from Windermere, with portion from Morecambe, to Victoria, due 9.58am, but by then the train was not a L&YR locomotive duty.

In the timetable commencing 3 June 1905, there appeared a train of L&YR locomotive and carriages which left Preston at 7.45am and ran through to Windermere. That same summer an express with carriages from Liverpool and Manchester L&YR termini left Preston at 12.15pm for Windermere, also worked by a L&YR locomotive; maybe the engine working started the season on the 7.45am and transferred after a month or so to the 12.15pm. Its balancing working was at 4.20pm from Windermere, express to the L&YR line with that Company's locomotive. Next summer, 1906, the early train ran two days weekly, the 12.15pm down and 4.20pm up ran daily, but not with L&YR engines. However, in summer 1907, power was again provided by the L&YR for one down and one up working and this probably became an annual feature; Eric Mason well knew the up working, round about 1915, as 4.15pm ex-Windermere and he left photographic evidence. The 4.15pm or 4.20pm train, as distinct from the engine working, became an all-year feature; by the 1930s, it ran to Manchester Exchange.

A period has been recalled when, on summer Saturdays, *two* L&YR 7ft 3in wheeled 4-4-0 locomotives arrived at Oxenholme on successive down trains. The first train was for Windermere and was held at the down back platform face, while the second was for Keswick and arrived at the down main. The engines changed over between the trains and worked to Windermere and Penrith. This could have been around 1914 or in the period of merger, 1922-24.

Already, prior to 1905, the L&YR's spectacular Aspinall-designed prototype 7ft 3in 4-4-2 express locomotive No 1400 was reported to have made 'some trips to Carlisle with race specials'. More specifically documented was its run on 4 May 1905 with a train from Manchester to Carlisle and back for the racing fraternity; no record of load is thought to have survived but the banks were taken without assistance and running was throughout ahead of a reportedly easy schedule. Similar workings to Carlisle by L&YR engines on express passenger trains did not become a regular feature — nor, seemingly, even an occasional one — until amalgamation days.

With the agreement of 1905, a through L&YR express goods train at once began to run from the East Lancashire line to Carlisle by the L&C route and this continued right through to LMS days, apart from a period of suspension due to the first world war, and until at least the beginning of the second world war. In its early days it was 7.25pm Leeds L&YR via Rose Grove (Burnley) and Preston EL (passed 11.35pm) to Carlisle (arr 3.20am), with booked standing time of 29min at Oxenholme and 14min at Tebay. The up working was 2.05am Carlisle to Leeds by the same route, later becoming 2.15am. In the earlier years, L&NWR men from Carlisle Upperby shed, with their engine, worked alternate nights with the Rose Grove L&YR men, but after the first war Rose Grove had a monopoly, working six nights weekly in each direction. They used L&YR 0-8-0 'Coal' engines, with 4ft 6in wheels — both 30 class (unsuperheated) and 31 class (superheated), the latter having very large boilers and a somewhat top-heavy appearance. In fairly early LMS days, Rose Grove shed was provided with three ex-L&NWR unsuperheated 4-6-0 engines of the '19in Goods' class, having 5ft coupled wheels. They were primarily for the Carlisle jobs. Around 1925, the northbound train was leaving Rose Grove at 9.30pm and the engine was on Upperby shed by 4.00am and the crew away to the 'barracks'. At this period, the return working was booked away from Upperby yard at 2.15pm, so the Burnley men had a daylight run over Shap. They were nominally put 'inside' at Tebay for overtaking traffic but a clear run was not uncommon. Mr Tom Weavings, later a respected inspector of the motive power department, has recalled some rip-roaring runs on the '19in', when he fired to driver Ashworth Tattersall in the mid-1920s. The driver's aim was to approach Tebay and pass through the narrow, cavernous up platform so fast that, between the warning bells beginning to shrill on the platforms and the rush of engine and vans, time

did not permit effective defensive measures by the bookstall attendant. The engine crew would look back to see the lady surrounded in a cloud of fluttering newssheets, still struggling to place stones on them, while shaking a fist in the direction of the receding Rose Grove men. In 1926, Rose Grove secured five nearly new 2-6-0 'Crabs' and their '19in' engines departed.

Under the 1905 agreement, two other fast L&YR goods trains were introduced, one being a night train from Nelson to Carnforth and the other at 9.25am from Lostock Hall (just south of Preston on the EL line) to Carnforth. In the up direction there were balancing workings to Nelson and Bamber Bridge, but a 4.35pm Bay Horse-Bamber Bridge also appeared. Rose Grove men and engines worked the Rose Grove-Carnforth (this would be the 'Nelson') each way, certainly in LMS days.

An interesting service was instituted by the LMS, probably late in their era, usually worked by a Class '5' 4-6-0. In its 1955 form, the train was 11.55am MSX Bamber Bridge-Carlisle Viaduct Yard, Class 'H' freight, running via Blackburn, Hellifield and Settle Junction but thence by way of Ingleton (pass 3.20pm) and Low Gill (pass 4.04pm), then held as necessary for other traffic and nominally due by Carlisle No 13 box to the goods lines at 7.56pm. There was no balancing working by the WCML or Ingleton route.

Incursions by Derby

Penetrations by the Midland Railway into L&C territory during the 20th century resulted from agreements of 1908 (L&NWR/MR) and 1909 (L&NWR, L&YR and MR) for closer working.

In high summer of 1910, 1911 and 1912:

10.00am Leeds Wellington-Glasgow St Enoch corridor express (no restaurant car advertised in this portion of the train) was diverted to run daily, with MR locomotive, from Settle Junction via Ingleton, calling on the L&NWR only at Penrith 12noon-12.03pm, with a non-stop connection leaving Penrith 12.15pm daily for Keswick (arr 12.50pm); this connection was advertised as a through express from Leeds to Keswick.

10.30am Edinburgh Waverley-St Pancras restaurant car express was diverted to run daily, with MR power, via Penrith (calling 1.39-1.42pm) and Ingleton to Settle Junction and so to Leeds Wellington and St Pancras; the 12.35pm from Keswick was non-stop to Penrith (arr 1.15pm) and was advertised for Leeds, ostensibly conveying a through carriage, for attachment to the MR train. This up working by MR train gave a time from Penrith to St Pancras 9min faster than the best of the period to Euston.

Then, for a couple of months or so in summers of 1913 and 1914, a through carriage or carriages ran four days weekly from Leeds at 9.35am to Keswick, with calls on the L&NWR at Ingleton, Kirkby Lonsdale and Penrith, and a balancing up service left Keswick in middle day.

In summer 1922, commencing July, a through carriage from Leeds to Keswick was resumed, but via Carnforth, whence the L&NWR conveyed Leeds coaches to both Windermere and Keswick.

The LMS, in summer 1923 (commencing 9 June) reintroduced a service which ran four days weekly at 12.48pm (12.47pm in 1924) from Leeds Wellington via Ingleton, with calls on the L&NWR at Shap, Penrith and principal stations via Keswick to Workington. Coming up, the time was 9.10am Workington-Leeds, calling additionally at Tebay, where a portion (in rear) for Euston was detached, the MR portion proceeding first, via Ingleton. These workings continued until 1926, by then running SO in rather similar timings, but in summer 1927, the Keswick-Leeds had succumbed, while 'The Lakes Express' for Euston ran, complete with nameboards.

The time of 12.47pm reappeared in 1933, Leeds Wellington-Keswick, with times at Shap and Penrith almost identical with 1923-24 but this train was not introduced until August and ran FSO; outward, it was held at Penrith to join through carriages from York and Saltburn, which had come by the LNER route and were also bound for Keswick. In summer 1939, it was booked to run SO from 3 July until 9 September, as a through train Sheffield Midland 11.10am and Leeds Wellington 12.47pm to Keswick, calling inter alia at Shap, Penrith (4.06-4.13pm), then non-stop to terminate at Keswick at 4.53pm. Coming up, it left Keswick at 10.00am SO for Threlkeld, Penrith (10.52-10.57am) and Tebay, with no call at Shap, and onwards via Ingleton to reach Leeds at 2.05pm — not advertised as providing a through carriage to Sheffield. There were stops at Sedbergh, Kirkby Lonsdale, Ingleton and Clapham in both directions. It is not thought that any regular Leeds-Keswick passenger trains have been run in BR days.

The Midland exploited their link by the Wennington-Carnforth joint line in order to run to Barrow (a 'boat train') and Lake Side (Windermere), over Furness Railway tracks. They provided connections at Carnforth into L&NWR Windermere trains and, from July 1910, coaching stock was worked through in summer, taken on from Carnforth by L&NWR. In summer 1922, through carriages Leeds-Windermere via Carnforth and the L&C line were resumed; and in summer 1923 the midday Leeds-Keswick (four days weekly) conveyed carriages for Lake Side (FR) *and* Windermere (L&NWR), reached respectively at 4.10 and 4.15pm, the latter probably via Arnside, Sandside and Hincaster Junction. The service continued until 1939, but with many detail variations, latterly running SO; from 1924, the outward route was by main line from Carnforth to Windermere in all or most years. Up workings in the 1930s were, in general, via Sandside and Arnside and the chord line at Carnforth, with Nottingham as the objective by 1939.

Leeds-Windermere and return (but not Keswick) workings were restored on Saturdays in high summer commencing 11 July 1953 and last operated on 31 August 1963, but now by way of Arnside and Sandside in both directions. Taking summers of 1961 and 1962, the outward trip was a rear portion of the 11.14am Leeds City-Barrow by Carnforth chord line, detached at Arnside and eventually attached at Oxenholme to our old friend the 6.35am Euston-Windermere: arrival 2.50pm in 3hr 36min from Leeds. Even more amazing was the return trip, leaving Windermere at 11.10am and 'going off the map' after Oxenholme, as the times at Arnside and arriving Carnforth were all 'unadvertised'; eventually, Carnforth (23 miles from Windermere by main line) was left 100 minutes after the start. Thus, a time of all but four hours from Windermere to Leeds is explained. So effectively ended the association of the MR with the L&C line and the hopes engendered by the agreement of 1909.

It should be added that periodical blocks by snow and other causes on the Settle and Carlisle route have caused diversions via Carnforth (reverse) of Nottingham-Glasgow trains in recent years and that the threat of closure of the former MR route over Ais Gill is brought nearer by timetabling the Nottingham-Glasgow trains by a devious route from Sheffield to Manchester Victoria, thence Preston and the L&C main line, from May 1982.

The Furness Railway and the Lancaster & Carlisle line

The Furness Railway's operations were remarkably self-contained in pre-amalgamation times. During the first decade of the century, the Railway built up a useful stock of bogie non-corridor carriages and the trains were hauled by straightforward 4-4-0 locomotives of modest dimensions, running in general between Carnforth, Barrow-in-Furness and Whitehaven. In summer, there were scheduled workings of FR engines and carriages from Barrow and Grange to Morecambe Euston Road, traversing the L&C main line between Carnforth and Hest Bank and necessarily setting back at the latter place to attain access to the Morecambe line. Although the L&NWR made provision for similar workings off the FR to Lancaster Castle, these do not seem to have been normal. Carnforth was usually the frontier, apart from the working of through carriages (already mentioned) from the FR to Euston and Manchester; by 1910, the FR are understood to have contributed two corridor carriages to the through London service. In LMS days, and after, complete through trains between Barrow-in-Furness and the main line have been a daily feature.

The benefits of amalgamation which brought together the L&NWR and the Furness Railway and of LMS enterprise were seen and widely enjoyed by holiday-makers. A friend recalls from schooldays a family holiday at Morecambe, in August 1929. The LMS had by then received delivery of many comfortable 'open' carriages and a quota of kitchen cars to run with them. My friend's family booked for a round trip, including the (optional) provision of lunch and tea on the train. A 4-4-0 from FR stock headed a substantial train out of Morecambe (Euston Road) station, picking up passengers at most stations to Barrow. An hour was allowed for a stroll in Furness Abbey grounds. At Ravenglass, with two hours' break, the 15in gauge Ravenglass & Eskdale Railway provided a round trip to Dalegarth and back. At Workington, two L&NWR 0-6-0 'Cauliflowers' took over, onwards to Keswick — where another break was allowed to view the town and lake — then forward to Red Hills Junction and very, very cautiously down the 'North Eastern' flyunder and through to Eamont Junction, to join the L&C main line and return over Shap to Morecambe; memory is a trifle hazy at this stage but it is thought that the two 'Cauliflowers', after firing up and creating a huge smoke-pall on the NER link, took the train on to Shap Summit and one of them continued to Carnforth, whence the Furness 4-4-0 provided power to Morecambe. At Euston Road, the enginemen were stand-

ing with their backs to the firebox faceplate acknowledging the appreciative farewells of the passengers leaving the platform, after an arrival three minutes ahead of advertised time.

From about the same time the LMS developed 'holiday contract tickets', a weekly season for about 10s; a splendid example was the area which embraced all the L&NWR and FR passenger services north of Carnforth to Carlisle and indeed to Annan and Appleby. These 'seasons' gained in popularity through the years to 1939. On revival after the war years, their value has been progressively curtailed by closure of stations and whole routes, notably the CK&PR line, but 'rover' tickets with a still wider geographical coverage have in some degree supplanted them.

The introduction of diesel multiple unit trains in large numbers, around 1956-60, inspired enterprising use of otherwise-idle sets on Sundays. In July 1960, I joined in six-car set at Stockport Edgeley, which called at Manchester Victoria and then ran via Hindley No 1 to the Whelley line, joining the WCML at Standish Junction, taking the Furness line at Carnforth and the Dalton Junction — Park South cut-off to reach Ravenglass (for trip to and from Dalegarth by narrow gauge — less than two months before the crisis and sale involving that Railway), onwards to Keswick for teatime interval and home over Shap, necessarily running into Penrith and reversing direction there. A comparable trip, a month later, ran outward from Manchester to Carlisle (for lunchtime stop) by the Midland route, then south over Shap to Morecambe, finally Morecambe-Manchester in late evening.

The most consistent through passenger working by the FR was that between Grange and Kendal — occasionally originating at Barrow or Arnside and in some summers running through to Windermere. Grange-Kendal was an all-year service, dating from the opening of the Arnside-Hincaster Junction line, with its intermediate stations at Sandside and Heversham, and discontinued by the LMS from 4 May 1942, when Sandside station was closed to passengers and Heversham closed entirely. Typically, about a half dozen trains were run in each direction on mid-week days, the times fairly constant and slanted towards shop and school hours. Tank engines, believed at one time 2-4-2 side tanks, were normally employed by the FR and this was one of the three services for which the Company's shapely 4-4-2 side tanks were built in 1915-16. In LMS days, around 1930, FR 4-4-2 side tanks and older 0-6-2 side tanks, also small wheeled 4-4-0 tender engines, were on the trains, complemented by L&NWR-designed 4-4-2 'Precursor' tanks, on those trains worked by Oxenholme shed. The 'Precursor' tanks appeared to tower above the stock and indeed above the Furness locomotives. The use of the Sandside line for operating convenience by some Leeds-Windermere summer trains and by Furness line portions of occasional down WCML Windermere trains, also in summer, has been touched upon. The coke traffic via Sandside is about to be mentioned, along with the associated working of FR 0-6-0 locomotives over Grayrigg bank to Tebay.

The North Eastern on the North Western

Westward outlets from the Stainmore line

The North Eastern Railway's link with the Lancaster & Carlisle route at Tebay dated from 1861, that at Eden Valley Junction box from 1863 and the NER's double track curve from Eamont Junction box to Redhills on the Cockermouth, Keswick & Penrith Railway from 1866. The NER came over Stainmore summit (1,370ft od) between Barnard Castle in Durham and Kirkby Stephen in Westmorland; its physical and financial links had been with the old Stockton & Darlington Railway, whose 'long boiler' 0-6-0 mineral train locomotives were still seen at Tebay and traversing the WCML between Eden Valley and Eamont Junctions well into the 20th century. The NER men too brought something of the S&DR 'Quaker' spirit to their work in the west.

Coaching traffic from Tebay to Kendal

Although the prime purpose of the Stainmore line was to convey coke from the ovens of West Durham to the blastfurnaces of Carnforth, Furness and West Cumberland, the promoters had ideas of exporting ore and merchandise eastward and of carrying passengers. There were Kendal interests from the start of the project and the NER possessed running powers over the L&NWR for 'coaching traffic between Tebay and Kendal'. The L&NWR working appendix made provision for NER locomotive power on NER trains between these points.

Only three weeks after opening of the railway over Stainmore, on 29 August 1861 occurred a serious derailment of an eastbound evening passenger train on that line; it was a day excursion train of locomotive and eight vehicles, with 175 passengers, returning at 5.03pm from Windermere, 6.31pm (actual) from Tebay, bound for Darlington. Other excursions ran via Stainmore to Windermere but they do not seem to have been numerous after the early years of the present century; the need to run round the train or provide a substitute locomotive at Oxenholme was a deterrent.

By agreement between general managers George Gibb of the NER and Frederick Harrison of the L&NWR, one scheduled daily train was to be run through by the NER to Kendal; it commenced to run on 1 July 1897 and ceased wef 1 October 1908. The working was interesting, the NER passenger stock and guard, also NER engine and its crew, originating at Penrith and making a long round trip. Times varied a little but were approximately 7.18am Penrith-Kirkby Stephen, where the engine was turned before working Kirkby Stephen-Tebay (call at about 9.05-9.08am)-Oxenholme (arr about 9.35am), departing 5min

later to Kendal, reached about 9.45am. This would give residents of Appleby, Kirkby Stephen and Tebay a useful morning service, but, if using the 'through train' on return, they would have little time for business or shopping; departure was typically at 10.25am to Oxenholme, 10min allowed, then non-stop to Tebay (outward, calls had been made additionally at Low Gill and Grayrigg).

The return working tended to dally at Tebay, after which it ran in summer right through to Darlington, due, for example, at 1.10pm; left again at 3.10pm and ran as an express to Penrith, the duty ending there at 4.54pm, or thereabouts. In winter, the return from Oxenholme was to Kirkby Stephen, then direct to Penrith; here the crew were relieved but a late turn crew worked Penrith-Kirkby-Penrith and back with the same engine. The morning crew turned their engine at Oxenholme shed — presumably making a quick trip from Kendal to Oxenholme and back to achieve this — and the host Company debited 'sixpence per engine per time' for the privilege of turning on their table. In the early weeks of the working, the NER employed 2-4-0 rebuilds 1267 or 1268; these were 'Ginx's Babies', derived from distinguished-looking 4-4-0s of 1874. Soon, two '901' class 2-4-0s, usually 167 and 911, were allocated to Penrith in their stead. These were capable and reliable engines but on an unlucky day one of them broke a valve spindle and was disabled at Kendal. The NER men borrowed a L&NWR 'Special DX' 0-6-0 and duly ran Kendal-Oxenholme-Tebay-Kirkby Stephen with it; as the engine was equipped only to work vacuum braked stock and the NER set was air braked, a L&NWR porter travelled in the leading van, keeping in touch with the driver and applying the handbrake as necessary.

After the NER's through engine and carriage working to Kendal ceased in autumn 1908, the L&NWR ran a 9.10am Tebay-Kendal, in order to maintain the connection from Kirkby Stephen for shoppers, but on Saturdays only — and it continued until the earlier war years. They also introduced a daily 10.25am Kendal-Tebay (in the old NER path) and there was already a balancing 12.34pm Tebay-Kendal passenger; these two trains ran until summer 1911, inclusive.

There were no regular NER passenger workings in wartime but from summer 1920 a through NER passenger train again appeared, running daily. This was 12.38pm Darlington-Oxenholme, arr 3.08pm (with connection to Kendal and Windermere) and return (with connection from Kendal) Oxenholme 4.00pm to Darlington 6.50pm. A NER three-coach set was employed, with a Barnard Castle engine and crew; they and their engine had taken over from another Barnard Castle engine and men at their home station and they worked to Oxenholme and back.

This all-year carriage working continued for four years and the NER engine is recalled as coming on Oxenholme shed each afternoon to turn; the through *locomotive* working seems likely to have ceased after the first year or so of the four years. Early in 1923, engine 366 of '901' class and its Barnard Castle crew were climbing from Smardale to Sandy Bank, about eight miles short of Tebay, when a side rod came adrift at one end, damaged the firebox and seriously injured both men on the footplate due to the resulting escape of steam. During 1924-34, virtually the same timings applied to and fro on both railways, but the (by then) LNER train terminated at Tebay and the Barnard Castle engine sojourned there in mid-afternoon, while the LMS ran their own train to and from Oxenholme. There was a sequel, believed to be during the years 1938-39, when the 2.37pm Tebay-Oxenholme daily local and, probably, the 4.15pm Oxenholme-Tebay local were worked by a LNER three-coach set of carriages, with a Kirkby Stephen guard, who brought a LNER map along with him into this strange territory. This carriage working derived from inter-Company 'pooling' arrangements and search for economies, but the LNER engine did not work through.

The only significant later daily working of a comparable kind was introduced on 23 May 1949 and operated for about a couple of years. The handsome sets of Gresley corridor stock built by the LNER in the late 1930s for the Newcastle-Carlisle trains were still in use (what a contrast with today's juddering dmus on that service!). There were five of these sets in 1949-50 and, in daily rotation, they worked (with NE Region power):

(a) Carlisle 6.40am to Newcastle (8.50am), and back at 9.20am, due Carlisle 11.23am
(b) then, with LMR power, 1.51pm Carlisle-Oxenholme slow.
(c) At Oxenholme, the set of six was divided into two sets of three vehicles to work, respectively, the 5.00pm Oxenholme-Carlisle slow, due 6.25pm; and the 7.15pm Oxenholme-Carlisle slow, due 8.47pm; after which the set was re-formed and despatched to London Road NER sidings.

The LNER stock was distinctive and I recall making trips in it with the 1.51pm up and 7.15pm down on odd occasions in 1950. Clearly, this was an inter-regional economy measure of a sensible kind.

Boat train
In 1904, the Midland Railway transferred their connections for both Belfast and Douglas to Heysham, their new port. However, the Barrow Steam Navigation Company continued to sail at 2.15pm from Ramsden Dock, Barrow, bound for the Isle of Man and to sail inward from Douglas at 8.30am, to reach Ramsden Dock at 11.30am. A connecting train service between Newcastle upon Tyne and Barrow, for these sailings, was instituted from 15 July 1905 and ran until

9-11 September 1911. It has often been referred to as a through train but most of the time it was in fact a series of connections, the most interesting being those designed to bridge the gap between Tebay, Oxenholme and (via Sandside) the Furness Railway's main line, in each direction. The service was an all-year one but provision of through carriages was intermittent, daily in the first summer, primarily on Saturdays in the last summer. The NER advertised 9.30am Newcastle to Darlington (by a Cardiff train) and 10.32 Darlington to Tebay (arr 12.27pm); then came the L&NWR's 12.34pm Tebay-Kendal (used as far as Oxenholme, arr 12.51pm), with a FR connection at 1.01pm for Grange and thence Barrow Ramsden Dock, due 2.10pm. The service to the north east left Ramsden Dock at 12noon and was styled 'Douglas and Fleetwood Boat Train', as it gave, amongst others, a tourist connection off the Fleetwood-Barrow sailing for Lake Side (Windermere). A special connection was run from Ulverston non-stop to Oxenholme, 1.05pm.

This was followed by use of the 7.10am Euston-Carlisle (calling Oxenholme 1.41-1.46pm) to Tebay (2.06pm). Mr Knights (stationmaster?) was instructed that, if the 7.10am was running 10min or more late at Lancaster, he must arrange for 'a relief train from Oxenholme to Tebay to convey the through carriage'. Significantly, about this period, the NER were reputedly disinclined to await late connections. The NER train left Tebay at 2.15pm for Darlington, whence a Kings Cross-Newcastle train was advertised into Newcastle at 5.07pm.

The Newcastle to Barrow service continued almost unchanged right through to September 1911, apart from the more intermittent provision of a through carriage and arrivals advertised at Barrow Central station, in its latter years. Eastbound, the relevant sailing times changed and wef October 1908 Barrow Central was left at 8.45am, with connection from Grange at 10.00am via Sandside into the 10.25am Kendal-Tebay (10.40am from Oxenholme) to Tebay, and then by NER. As earlier noted, the 10.25am and the 12.34pm up from Tebay did not run after 1911, thus breaking the cross-country link — or it may be that NER-L&NWR-FR decided that the overall service, by this route, was not justified.

In 1931, a fence-rail near the Barrow glasshouse which contained the preserved locomotive 'Coppernob' was observed to be formed of a dilapidated blue carriage headboard lettered (it is thought, in gold) 'Newcastle-Barrow Through Carriage'.

It was not unknown for the NER to work excursion trains through with their own engines and crews (aided by conductors) to Windermere, touched on previously, and to the Furness line. There is a coloured picture of a NER 'C' 0-6-0 locomotive and six 6-wheeled vehicles, travelling westbound past Meathop Crag and nearing Grange-over-Sands; this was published in *The Railway Magazine* of May 1917 (facing page 305) and is likely to represent an excursion train in prewar years.

The 'Northern Belle'
The LNER showed notable enterprise, initiated in the difficult year 1933, by introducing the 'Northern Belle'.

This was a train of well-appointed stock, with vehicles for both day and night travel, and catering; it ran for several summers, providing a week-long railtour from and to Kings Cross, once each season. The itinerary, with emphasis on Scotland, varied the route but Stainmore, and Penrith, figured on occasion, and the LMS collaborated.

To the seaside on Saturdays

The LNER and LMS also cooperated in running through trains from Newcastle upon Tyne and intermediate points to Blackpool and Southport, by way of Stainmore and Tebay, where LMS motive power took over. Commencing in summer 1932, the destination was Blackpool and the train comprised five vehicles, but by summer 1933 there was also a portion for Southport, and presumably the train could be duplicated to meet demand. It ran on Saturdays during some six weeks of high summer, with a corresponding return service to the north east at the ensuing weekends. The pattern continued to 1939.

A Newcastle-Blackpool train was restored in summer 1946 but ran via Carlisle and the full length of the L&C route. It resumed in 1948, still via Carlisle for some years, but returned to the Stainmore route in 1953. However, from 1949, a combined South Shields and West Hartlepool train ran to Blackpool via Stainmore. Summer 1961 represented the peak of service. Three trains ran, respectively from South Shields, Darlington and Newcastle — calling at Kirkby Stephen round 10.40, 11.01 and 11.30am westbound and 1.56, 2.06 and 2.44pm eastbound. All changed engines at Tebay, usually in the NE (strictly 'up and down') platform southbound but routed northbound via Tebay down platform and No 2 box to No 3 box, where engines were changed on the line to Kirkby Stephen. This was the last year of junction status for Tebay.

Bound for the Priory

Unusual in character was a passenger train (unadvertised, but in working timetables) from Durham, by way of Bishop Auckland, Barnard Castle, Stainmore, Tebay, Oxenholme and Sandside to Ulverston. This ran to convey Durham miners to their convalescent home at Conishead Priory, near Ulverston, and bring them back a fortnight later. The service has been recalled as commencing 1933, indeed it first appears in the working timetable dated 18 July 1932, on alternate Mondays; the train itself made the return journey in the day, typically reaching Tebay at 11.08am outward and leaving at 2.39pm on the return run. It was a light train, and engines were changed at Tebay. No doubt the refreshment room was ready to provide for the wayfarers (when the Blackpools called, extempore tables were set out on the platform to supplement the accommodation). The working operated all the year round until interrupted by wartime. However, from May 1936, the runs were changed to alternate Fridays and the timings recast. They would suit the staff of the home better, as the men leaving made their homeward trip during the morning, the train leaving Tebay for Durham at 10.22am. Coming westward in the

afternoon, it reached Tebay (from Durham) at 3.43pm; the Barrow engine which had brought the morning working had sojourned on Tebay shed and was waiting to take the train on to Ulverston. It is believed that the service was resumed sometime in 1945, certainly it was running by May 1946, on alternate Fridays much as in the later 1930s. The crew from Barrow in the morning left their engine on Tebay shed and returned home passenger, a Tebay crew using the Barrow engine to work to Ulverston around teatime; the interval had lengthened, as times for the calls at Tebay were typically about 9.45am and 5.00pm. After the end of the 1961 summer season, this working would be the only regular one between Tebay and Kirkby Stephen, until its last fortnightly operation before final closure, effective 22 January 1962.

Special arrangements were made for visits by the committee of the Durham Miners' Welfare Association. LNER Sentinel steam railcar 'North Briton' from Heaton shed (Newcastle) ran empty to Durham and conveyed the committee throughout to Ulverston. Stops were made for refreshments and toilet purposes at Barnard Castle, Kirkby Stephen and Tebay; one might guess, also for water, and recuperation, to revive the 'Sentinel'. The LNER men worked throughout, with LMS conductor west of Tebay, and lodging at Barrow. An outward journey on Thursday, return on Saturday was on record, the car stabling at Barrow shed. On Friday 5 July 1935, an outward journey was made, with return on Sunday 7 July. On Sunday, 6 October 1935, I found the 'North Briton' on Barrow shed, around midday, and learned that it had come over on an excursion in connection with the miners — probably another committee visit. The green and cream Sentinel cars were an unusual feature on the main line between Tebay and Hincaster and on the FR, indeed also on their own Company's lines west of Barnard Castle. At Barnard Castle on 13 April 1936, I was told that a railcar was running *fortnightly* to the Furness line; perhaps there was some misunderstanding. 'North Briton' is known to have made 'committee' journeys during 1936-39.

Passengers to Penrith — and Keswick

The NER had running powers for all classes of traffic between Eden Valley Junction and Penrith (station and yard). Their daily passenger trains usually numbered five all year, plus an extra one in summer, during the early century years to 1914; they came down to basically four each way in the times of stringent LNER conomies, were up to five in winter 1935-36, six in summer 1938. The extra summer train was an 'express' from and to Darlington; in the years to 1914, it conveyed a through carriage York-Keswick (in Penrith 1.05-1.15pm down and 2.30-2.52pm up) and a Newcastle-Keswick vehicle also ran in the down express via Stainmore but was worked up in the 12.35pm from Keswick, at Penrith 1.15pm, leaving 1.40pm in a train to Darlington.

In earlier years the Eden Valley trains tended to run Penrith-Kirkby Stephen, connecting into Tebay-Darlington trains, while in LNER and BR times the pattern was reversed. The early departure of the engine stabled by the NER and LNER in the L&NWR shed at Penrith has been mentioned anent the Kendal working and was an advantageous feature of the service afforded Penrith folk. From 2 October 1939, this early departure was lost, never regained, and trains were four each way, three each way from 1 April 1940 until increased to four from 7 October 1946 but deteriorating to three in 1947 and still such in the days of dmus, which preceded withdrawal of service and closure of most of the Stainmore line, effective 22 January 1962. A short stub of line remained operational from Eden Valley Junction to Clifton Moor station, all easily visible from the WCML, but it closed from 6 July 1964 (traffic) and 16 May 1966 (final).

The NER/LNER/BR local passenger service into Tebay usually provided three trains daily, of which through workings on to the main line have been noted. There were two in and out during the 1939-45 years and most ensuing years until withdrawal wef 1 December 1952. NER goods into Penrith numbered two in early century, but the second became conditional and disappeared.

Among NER passenger locomotives at Penrith, the Fletcher-designed '901' class, mentioned on the Kendal passenger from the late 1890s, gave place in early LNER days to the '1463' (Tennant) type of 2-4-0s. Next, the NER's 4-4-0 'Waterburys' (neat inside-cylinder rebuilds) appeared, then came ex-Great Northern Railway 4-4-0s of LNER 'D3' class; there were six or seven in use on the Stainmore line in 1930-35 and they would not fit on Penrith turntable, so used the Redhills triangle for turning. Their successors were the ex-Great Eastern Railway Class 'E4' 2-4-0s, a half dozen allocated from 1936 for a few years; the last ones disappeared from the territory in 1942. The change from the GNR engines may have been influenced by derailment on the decrepit Redhills curve, finally abandoned soon afterwards. A 'G5' 0-4-4 tank figured at Penrith for a time in the 1930s. Officially, stabling of a LNER engine in Penrith shed (of the L&NWR) ceased wef 1 May 1939 and the early train was booked to be worked by a Kirkby Stephen engine — until that train was discontinued. The last 'E4' was gazetted away from Penrith shed on 17 June 1939, so the new arrangements may have been postponed some six weeks. The good old NER 5ft 1in-wheeled 0-6-0 engines, superheater rebuilds, gained a monopoly of Stainmore passenger workings, in and out of Tebay and Penrith. New '2MT' 2-6-0 engines of LMS design appeared from Darlington and Kirkby Stephen in late 1953, with various BR variants following, but diesel sets ran to Penrith in the last years, 1958-62.

Keswick was a favoured objective of excursions from the NER routes. A surviving notice shows three long-range trains on one day alone, Thursday 2 July 1903. All set out around 6.00-7.00am — from Stockton (private day excursion), Darlington (public day excursion) and Newcastle-Sunderland-Durham (also a public day excursion). All ran over Stainmore and times booked at 'Penrith' were respectively 9.35-9.50am, 10.00-10.10am and 10.51-11.00am. NER engine and men were to work each train throughout, accompanied by L&NWR pilotment from and to Penrith, the NER guard being signed

off at Penrith. Reference to 'Penrith' would mean Redhills curve, Eamont Junction-Redhills. The trains left Keswick between 6.50 and 7.20pm and left Eamont at 15-minute intervals; what a sight it would have been to see and hear them getting away over Eamont viaduct that summer evening, some 80 years ago. Mr J. W. Armstrong, with unrivalled knowledge of the Stainmore route engine workings, thanks to family associations back to his grandfather, supplemented by his own years of study and photography, tells of a couple of private excursions to Keswick in the early 1900s. His father worked from Leeds via York, Darlington and Stainmore, with a McDonnell '59' class 0-6-0 locomotive, akin to the Irish 'J15' of which preserved examples work today. His uncle worked from Hull, with a 'C' (LNER 'J21') 0-6-0. In each case the Redhills curve was taken and the crews took their engines to Cockermouth, to book off for a break before the return trip: as JWA remarks, a nice day's work, and one gathers that the enginemen enjoyed every minute of it. Tyneside and Wearside crews shared such outings, both to the CK&PR and to Windermere.

Coke via Cockermouth

The link from Eamont Junction, L&C main line, to Redhills Junction on the Cockermouth, Keswick and Penrith Railway was completed in 1866 by the North Eastern Railway and was always the property of the NER, later LNER. The NER met the cost of points and crossings, and signalling too, and it was not until November 1903 that their share of working expenses for Eamont Junction box was reduced from 100% to $^{13}/_{19}$ths. By that time the box, a blockpost on the L&C main line, had also controlled access to down loops for some years.

The object of the 'Redhills curve' was to enable coke trains which had come from West Durham via Stainmore, Kirkby Stephen, Eden Valley Junction and Eamont Junction to join the CK&PR and proceed to Cockermouth. Unlike the typical *coal* trains of private-owner wagons, these trains were formed of the NER's distinctive coke-carrying wagons, with high, straight sides, widening to the tops and in their later form nominally carrying 10½ tons. A train crew of the NER worked through, with that Company's brake van and locomotive, often two vans and two locomotives, which at the commencement of our period would commonly be long-boiler 0-6-0 tender engines of the '1001' family, giving place about that time to 'P' or 'P1' engines of Wilson Worsdell's neat and far more up-to-date outline.

The NER had a single-road stone engine shed, lengthened at some date, in the yard at Cockermouth. The traffic was worked westward from that place by the L&NWR, bound for the once numerous West Cumberland blastfurnaces. On the CK&PR, which was a joint railway with some autonomy but no locomotives or rolling stock, the NER had the right to work mineral traffic, as well as excursion trains, with their own stock; be it noted, the L&NWR had formal running powers for all their traffic, *with the exception of minerals*. In 1900, there were four or five trains daily to Cockermouth, conveying in the year about 220,000 tons of coke, a figure not equalled subsequently. In 1906, it was 122,000 tons with three trains booked daily (and one suspects that only two ran). After 1910, carryings by the route declined — down to 16,000 tons in 1913, with only one train booked each day, and that one running 'as required'.

Even wartime did not produce a significant revival in tonnages. In 1920, two trains were booked and then the running seems to have been spasmodic for several years but it recovered to be quite regular for some weeks in spring 1926 followed by total suspension, probably with the general strike of that summer, and never resumed apart from a spell in 1928; Cumbrian historian William McGowan Gradon understood that this last revival resulted from immobilisation of the Cumberland coke ovens by a local strike and lasted for a few months.

A scenic tour from Morecambe by an LMS train in summer 1929, traversing the Redhills curve southwards, has been identified, and probably there were others around that time. The curve had a most disconsolate look in the mid-1930s, although LNER (and other) engines used it for turning until the track was finally condemned; this was c1936-37.

Coke for Carnforth and Furness

The ironworks at Barrow-in-Furness dated from 1860 and called for coke by way of Stainmore and Tebay from opening of that route in 1861. Carnforth works dated from 1865, both Millom and Askam from 1866 and North Lonsdale (sited on a branch line near Plumpton Junction) from 1874. There was a heavy demand and the NER brought over trains akin to those bound for Cockermouth. However, those for Carnforth and Furness ironworks were taken over by L&NWR locomotives and crews at Tebay, and were then run to Carnforth, where wagons for the local works were detached and the Furness Railway provided power and train crew for onward transit of the major part of the traffic.

It is clear on any map that Carnforth was not on a direct route from Tebay to the Furness district of Lancashire. However, no haste was shown to achieve a more direct route. The Hincaster Junction-Sandside-Arnside link, mainly single track, was planned, authorised by the FR Act of 1867 and constructed in leisurely fashion during 1871-76; when built, it could offer a saving of 10 miles on each journey, loaded or empty, apart from wagons for Carnforth works, but there is no evidence that it was used by coke trains until well on in World War 1 — believed to be in 1917 — when the L&NWR were hard pressed to find line capacity for long-distance traffic. By early 1918, the NER trains were certainly booked via Sandside and they continued to use the line in LMS and BR days. Maybe, both L&NWR and FR wanted maximum mileage out of the business.

In 1900, 689,000 tons of coke were conveyed by Tebay and about a dozen trains ran daily in each direction, clearly the NER's 'single loads'. Six years later, the tonnage was much the same but only about six trains were booked, presumably each with 'double' (namely, two-engine) loads of 32 wagons westward over Stainmore — and from 1902 the NER introduced their powerful

0-8-0 locomotives of Class 'T', each hauling a double load, at first from Shildon to Tebay, then between Kirkby Stephen and Tebay only. These handsome engines were seen at Tebay until close on nationalisation, and the later superheated Q6 type appeared between Kirkby and Tebay in BR days. In LNER and BR times, many all-steel hopper type wagons infiltrated the coke trains and a full double load became somewhere between 20 and 30.

The pattern was five or six trains in 1913 and eight or nine in 1918, by then via the Sandside cut-off, and fluctuation was generally between these figures through LMS days; seven or eight were booked as late as 1953 but numbers soon declined after that. It was not usual to run on Sundays.

Askam went out of blast in 1919, Carnforth in 1931, North Lonsdale in 1938 (although a foundry operated until 1949), Barrow in 1963 and Millom (with the last blastfurnace in the territory) in September 1968. The coke traffic was down to two trains daily when diverted wef 4 July 1960 to make the long detour via Carlisle and Workington to Furness and thus by-pass the L&C main line. Note too that the Stainmore-Tebay line itself succumbed as a through route wef 22 January 1962 and Sandside-Hincaster Junction closed wef 9 September 1963.

Locomotive power for the coke trains over the L&C was the concern of Barrow FR and Tebay L&NWR engine sheds. The trains were always a problem for the L&C operating staff. As long as they ran all the way between Tebay and Carnforth, some 26 miles of difficult road was involved, booked southbound in 80min non-stop or northbound in 80-95min. In each direction, most runs were booked from about 4.00am, immediately after the succession of night fast freights and sleepers had been cleared. Even so, various 'coke' paths involved holding the trains in the loops at Oxenholme. A knowledgeable traveller of 1927 graphically recalls riding on the engines. After arrival at Tebay, where a number-taker from the Railway Clearing House recorded the wagons individually, the LMS (ex-FR) 0-6-0 locomotive was turned and watered and its fire was cleaned, then coupled up to a loaded train of 30-40 LNER highsided wagons and awaited a road south. Once over Grayrigg bank top, the tender brakes were screwed hard on and speed regulated by the steam brake on the engine, plus such help as the guard chose to give from his van. There were well-known positions on the winding descent of Grayrigg bank from which early sightings of distant signals could be secured, the most important being on the approaches to Oxenholme, where an up Windermere train could be standing in the platform. On summer Saturdays, there would often be a long wait in Oxenholme loop and expresses overtook, then the short downhill run to Hincaster Junction. The signalman was seen impatiently waving the slow-moving foreigner off his main line; if he was obliged to hold the 'coke' while down expresses passed, the up main would be totally blocked.

At Tebay, the stone-built NER engine shed with its four roads dated in its later form from 1878 and rather surprisingly closed from 31 October 1902, soon after receiving the 0-8-0 locomotives. From then on, NER locomotives seen at Tebay with coke trains usually belonged to Kirkby Stephen, Shildon or West Auckland sheds. Shildon closed wef 8 July 1935, West Auckland had closed wef 13 April 1931 but reopened on Shildon's closure and survived Stainmore's demise as a railway route. Kirkby Stephen, after a period with a single engine allocated, closed wef 13 (or more probably 20) November 1961. The London Midland Region of BR administered Kirkby Stephen shed from 1 February 1958 and the line thence to Tebay from an earlier date — 2 April 1950.

Loaded coke trains from the NER line at No 3 (Tebay Yard) box entered the sidings to their left, the engine was detached and the wagons dropped down by gravity to the 'south yard', alongside the station on the up side; here the engine to take the train forward to Furness was coupled up. The empties from Furness diverged from the main line at Tebay No 2 box by the goods junction and stopped clear to detach the van, then drew forward by No 3 box and set back the wagons into the empties sidings by the Lune; the locomotive came off here and went to the main line shed. Departure was from these sidings with the NE locomotive, with the train reformed if necessary. Local passenger trains off the NE line and, usually, the *southbound* Blackpool holiday trains carried the massive train staff from No 3 box and used the single track 'passenger line' to reach 'the Geordie platform', alternatively and rightly dubbed 'a grim cavern'.

The long-closed NER engine shed at Tebay stood well into LNER days, eventually becoming roofless; then a gaunt wall remained for years as a landmark for the cognoscenti travelling the WCML; eventually it disappeared, in 1960-61.

L&NWR incursions too

In the earlier years of our period, the L&NWR were known occasionally to venture on to the NER at Tebay with a through excursion. Such trains ran to Warcop, for Brough Hill horse fair; remarkably, the engines and crews, with NER conductor drivers, were sometimes required to take the empty stock right over Stainmore to Barnard Castle, for stabling and servicing during the day. Exceptionally, in 1901, Joseph Armstrong, grandfather of John Armstrong, acted as conductor to L&NWR men on a 'Special DX', an 0-6-0 about as antiquated as the NER '1001' varieties, going right through from Tebay over Stainmore to Barnard Castle with a passenger train; L&NWR vacuum-braked stock would be employed. Much later, 19 April 1954, 0-6-0 'Cauliflower' No 58412, in its last active year of life at Penrith, worked the 3.35pm Penrith-Darlington passenger train to Kirkby Stephen, due to failure at Penrith of the usual 'J21' engine.

An amusing reminiscence from the beginning of the century was of Joseph Armstrong and his very own and much-prized two-cylinder compound 0-6-2 tank engine of NER Class 'B' being enlisted to help in re-railing an old 'Wessie' engine at Tebay, aided by various NER stalwarts and their ramps. Finally, No 523 gave an almighty heave and the job was done. All members of both camps adjourned for refreshment at the 'Cross Keys', a hostelry near Tebay Church (and the NER houses and onetime shed), which welcomes hungry and thirsty folk to this day. No inter-Company debits resulted.

Locomotive sheds

Throughout the 'age of steam', the locomotive shed was the focal point for maintenance and operation of motive power for the railway. It was the local centre for a lively community of personable people. The tale of the men and their engines on the Lancaster and Carlisle route in steam days, and an evaluation of how machines and men measured up to demands of traffic, must wait for another time. A review is now presented of the steam sheds as such — their locations, premises and history. This covers sites at Preston, Lancaster, Carnforth, Oxenholme, Windermere, Tebay, Ingleton, Penrith and Carlisle (Upperby).

Other sheds whose engines and men were prominent on the section were those at Crewe (North and South) and Springs Branch (Wigan), with Patricroft (Manchester), Edge Hill (Liverpool), Warrington, Camden (London) and Polmadie (Glasgow) also represented in course of time.

Preston Engine Shed

The L&NWR adopted their final site for an engine shed at Preston in about mid-19th century; the North Union shed had been on the down side of their station, the Lancaster & Carlisle used a temporary wooden shed and the East Lancashire a substantial structure between the NU and EL stations (it later became a carriage shed, when the L&YR moved their engines to new premises at Lostock Hall, south of Preston). The L&NWR site was on the down side of the Fylde line at its divergence from the L&C route; the power signalbox is built in the area of the shed yard. By the 1890s the configuration implied at least three stages of development and remained essentially unchanged for another 40 years. The buildings provided 15 dead-end roads under cover, their lengths varying from 125 to 345ft. They were hemmed in by a small cotton mill and crowded streets of cottage property. A 60ft turntable and typical coal stage were on a westerly part of the site. In order to squeeze in a mechanical coaler and ash plant, the westerly shed building, with roads of unequal lengths, was demolished, leaving nine covered roads — in groups of three and six — by the end of the 1930s. The site was a constant embarrassment; the depot was inconvenient to work and the officials were assailed by complaints of smoke drifting into neighbouring premises. Approach on foot was past the barrack-like enginemen's hostel, through dingy alleys and yards.

Disaster struck these premises on 28 June 1960. At 11.00 that morning a fire was discovered. The brigade arrived in three minutes but were impeded by the devious access. The entire roof was destroyed. A breakdown train and 18 locomotives were inside the buildings. The train and five of the locomotives were successfully hauled out. Also, 15 barrels of oil were removed. Thirteen locomotives were badly scorched and had to be sent to main workshops. The track on six roads was buckled by heat. For some days afterwards much of the coaling, preparation and disposal of Preston engines was carried out by Lostock Hall depot. The disaster accelerated decline and Preston shed closed wef 11 September 1961; the Preston buildings were used for storing locomotives for some years after closure and observed newly razed in spring 1966. Duties were transferred to Lostock Hall shed, which survived to be one of the last three main line steam depots on British Railways, closed from 5 August 1968.

Lancaster L&NWR Engine Shed

The shed was in the angle between the Lancaster Old (L&PJ) and L&C lines, with access at No 1 box. Built in brick, probably around 1880, with two covered roads, it stood parallel with the 'Old Line'. A turntable (probably 42ft to the last) and short siding were in the wider area between the shed and the Carlisle main line. It closed in April 1934 and the former Midland Railway shed near Green Ayre station nominally absorbed its duties. The back portion of the shed, with water tank above it, survived for many years.

Carnforth Engine Sheds

Although Carnforth station was managed until the 1923 grouping by a joint station committee of the Furness Railway and L&NWR and an engine shed of 1861 had been built by that committee, the railways soon had their independent sheds, the L&NWR south of the station and the FR alongside it, both on the down side. The L&NWR shed was a building of two roads, built 1873 to a design typical of the period prior to Webb's standardisation. It held four locomotives under cover, with one outside road and a turntable road. It was supplemented, probably in the early 1890s, by a standard L&NWR structure with north-light ('saw tooth') roof; this building was placed west of the old shed and had six covered roads of a mere 105ft length, taking about 12 engines inside. There were two roads in the open to the west again, immediately under the cliff which bordered the property.

The 1873 shed was converted to provide an under-cover coal stage. The road nearest the main line accommodated the engines for coaling and the other road was raised to take wagons; clearly, not even a cabless 'Tater-roaster' saddle tank could safely climb under the roof so, prudently, the cautious propelling of wagons up under the roof was carried out with 'runners' interposed and entrusted only to the oldest drivers. In the 1930s, the outside 'ash' road was provided with a lead northward, from which a trail-back came in through an aperture made in the north wall of the 'coaling shed'. The turntable was 60ft diameter. The premises never had a wheel-drop, nor a mechanical coaling plant and looked to Preston for major work even after becoming a 'parent' depot in 1935.

The FR's gloomy stone-built shed, with six roads entering from its north end and four from the south, was closed by the LMS in 1925-26 and its engines distributed between the L&NWR and Midland sheds; the MR shed was a typical square built brick building with central turntable, nominally a 'roundhouse' — located away out on the F&M line, where it is clearly seen today from the WCML or A6 road, on the northern outskirts of the town of Carnforth.

A new motive power depot and facilities were included in the 1937 scheme for improvements at Carnforth. The signalling and station improvements were made in 1938-39 but, due to wartime stringency, the shed project was not tackled promptly. In 1941, the gaunt buildings of the FR shed, deserted since the mid-1920s, were eventually demolished. Colonel Rudgard, LMS superintendent of motive power, was brought down from his country headquarters at The Grove, outside Watford, and shown the worn-out drains and waterlogged pits of the L&NWR shed. Then, matters began to move; prisoner-of-war labour was brought in to dig foundations and pits on the site of the new shed — very much where the FR building had stood — and the new buildings were erected, having six spacious roads under cover and access at both ends. Opening was on 1 May 1944, 'somewhere in England'. The mechanical coaling and ash plants had been completed a year or two earlier, south of the new buildings, and brought into use. A 70ft turntable, north of the buildings, had been installed around 1939-40. Engines and staff moved at once from the L&NWR and MR sheds, which were closed; the former, being in a dangerous state structurally, was demolished within months.

The new shed was, in company with Rose Grove (Burnley) and Lostock Hall (near Preston), among the last main line steam sheds of British Railways and closed wef 5 August 1968 but, by the enterprise primarily of Doctor Peter Beet of Hest Bank, it soon started a new life as an operational museum of steam locomotive power, now titled Steamtown, Carnforth. The structure of the lofty mechanical coaler still provides a prominent landmark when nearing Carnforth in a southbound main line train.

Oxenholme Engine shed

From the 1850s, or a little earlier, there was an engine shed on the down side of the main line, to the south of Kendal Junction station, which became Oxenholme. The shed had a single through road, leading at its north end to a turntable and dead end siding. A larger shed was erected in 1880, absorbing the earlier site. It was of standard L&NWR design, in brick with north-light roof over its four roads, each

145ft long. It could take about 12 engines of the day and also replaced the small shed at Kendal — which had been on the down side of the branch, just short of the bridge over Sedbergh Road. One of the two roads west of the shed, by the railway boundary, ended on a turntable; this was close below the overline bridge which carries the then (1880) newly realigned road from Kendal to Old Hutton. A standard L&NWR coal stage was provided; a ground level road for engines and a raised road close alongside, to hold wagons of coal for manual shovelling, the whole 'roofed' by a prominent water tank. The incline up which coal trucks were propelled was a hazard of these stages, as an engine left on the incline propping up the trucks could easily run away and cause injury. The stage was used until the shed closed wef 18 June 1962, and so was the shed itself, although re-roofed c1938 in the contemporary LMS style with longitudinal smoke vents and gables. By March 1964 approach tracks were lifted but not those inside the empty shed, which itself was razed by 1967, although the isolated coal stage stood longer still. The shed sidings and turntable had been officially taken away wef 2/12/1963.

The setting of Oxenholme shed, beside the main line on its hillside shelf, with vista, was as dramatic as that of another delightful hillside engine shed, that outside Okehampton station on the edge of Dartmoor. A small plantation shielded the turntable, which was of only 42ft diameter; a 'Jumbo' or 0-6-0 tender engine, or 2-6-4T of later days, could be turned but larger engines sometimes had to be detached from their tenders by the fitters.

Windermere Engine Shed

Windermere engine shed, in stone, had one road, approached over a turntable, and was situated immediately to the left of the station train shed, as viewed when entering by rail. There was just one engine, believed to be a 'Crewe-type' 2-4-0 side tank in the 1860s and 1870s; normally a 4ft 6in 2-4-2 side tank from the 1890s until closure, a period during which a set of five 6-wheeled carriages was usual for the branch train. Old Duckett was the driver, with Jack Docker firing for many years but Bill Anderson being probably his last fireman, and there was a lad cleaner on night duty; Mr Duckett 'ran the shed'. Oxenholme covered all runs off the branch and also the evening trips. They provided a substitute engine when necessary. This was often a 'Cauliflower', unpopular with Mr Duckett and his mate because of the tender-first working.

Closing of Windermere as a running shed resulted from wartime stringency and is believed to have corresponded in date with the curtailed and recast branch train service of April 1918. From this date, almost the entire timetable could be worked by a 'shuttle', which started and finished daily at Oxenholme; this would be the early motor train (with engine and one or two carriages, having rod control from the driving compartment to the regulator and bell communication from driver to fireman), which is recalled as 'the miners' special', on account of its spartan appointments, and was probably in use until about the end of June 1919.

The shed building stood empty during the 1920s and could be used for oil or tackle brought down from Oxenholme on busy days. In time, it became a grain store, subsequently being adapted as offices. The 50-52ft turntable remained in use, a 60ft table being substituted in 1936, after which 'Black 5', '5X' and 'Scot' class 4-6-0 engines could be turned; the new table was virtually too late for the 'Claughtons'. The pre-1936 table was used both by locomotives of regular scheduled trains, such as 'Princes' and 'Compounds', and also by the 'Experiments', 'Princes', 'Crabs' and others arriving with excursion trains; these last three types would fit on with only one or two inches to spare and were thus badly balanced and difficult to turn. On summer Sundays, in LMS times, two or more sets of enginemen would be sent down from Oxenholme to Windermere. They relieved the engine crews on arriving excursions, set back the stock, which was then 'gravitated' to the station or sidings for stabling, turned, oiled and watered the engine and placed it on its train for standing during the afternoon; they had the fire in shape for return of the rested crew, who might be from sheds all over Lancashire or the Midlands. It should be noted that Oxenholme turntable was only 42ft diameter and thus unsuitable for 4-6-0 and 2-6-0 engines.

Tebay L&NWR Engine Shed

The shed was located on the down side of Tebay station, the site falling away to the Lune on the west; the river flows swiftly through the gorge. The premises dated from 1860-62, solidly built in stone, with five roads, two westerly ones of 100ft, under a gable, and three easterly ones of 150ft, covered by another gable; these roofs were hipped at their ends, incorporating glazing, and capped by long smokeventing clerestories. Locomotives left at the north end, with convergence near a coal stage and water point, erected 1873, and beyond this connection was to the down main line, near the foot of Shap incline — appropriate for emergence of bank engines. A covered track alongside the shed accommodated such items as tool vans or plough. A track outside the west wall gave the only (inconvenient) access to the 'north exchange sidings' and to rather poky carriage roads; stock would be required for the Ingleton train and at some periods for the Penrith school train and the quarry workers' train. A useful connection between shed and station led to the down refuge siding, which became a down goods loop in 1926. The turntable, 50ft diameter, was in the north west of the site and remained unchanged through the life of the site as an engine shed, although the LMS had had plans for a 60ft table and approach to it through the back of the shed building.

Like some other L&NWR sheds, this one housed its own gas producing works, south of the shorter shed tracks; its boiler house chimney was prominent and at one time two gasholders stood immediately south of the buildings. Gas for lighting was piped to the shed and its yard, the station premises and the odd lamp on the station approach. The houses in South Terrace — that is, the central one of the three terraces — had gas light and one can still see the pipes entering some of them just above pavement level. The market hall, behind the south cooperative store (the store being now Barnaby Rudge restaurant) was gas lit, so were the church and church institute.

Gas gave place to a public electricity supply and the works closed in 1936. After many years with negligible

structural change, drawings were prepared in 1947-49 and the shed itself rebuilt during 1949-50. Old stone arches were retained in the west wall, but most of the rest was new work, including a flat roof in reinforced concrete over four roads, in place of five. The shed offices were finished off in 1951-52. Following erection of a lofty mechanical coaling plant, the old coal stage was dismantled in September 1958. The new works of 1949-58 were not justified by events; the need for the depot was rapidly disappearing. After further decline, closure was on 6 May 1968; it had been only a stabling point since 1 January 1968. Demolition began on 7 December 1970 and was finished on 12 February 1971.

Ingleton L&NWR Engine Shed

Subsidiary to Tebay, it dated from 1861, but was rebuilt in 1899, in timber, with curved 'tin' roof. In early 20th century, there were two crews and the senior driver (in charge of the shed) was Charlie Ferguson. A 5ft 6in 2-4-2 tank was usual before the days of the 4-6-2 tank. The shed closed around the period 1923-25 but stood, with turntable operational, until at least the late 1930s.

Penrith Engine Shed

The shed was on the down side of the main line, significantly south of the station and set close against the boundary fence. Built with stone walls and infill brickwork, it was single ended, its two roads emerging at the south end. It was gabled longitudinally, with raised central vent, in the old L&NWR style. A short road beside the building accommodated wagons of locomotive coal; there was no proper coal stage. Outlet was at No 1 (Keswick Jn) box and from there locomotives could, by reversing, run north to the CK&P platform, EV bay, north end of station, carriage roads, or the 42ft turntable, without fouling the main lines (the goods yard was on the far side of the main running roads). A larger turntable was promised in LMS days, but never materialised. LNER 4-4-0s turned on the Keswick Jn-Redhills Jn-Eamont Jn triangle until its south west side fell into disuse. When, in BR days, LMS type '2MT' 2-6-0s were employed, they had to be rostered to and from Carlisle in order to turn for a trip to the Keswick line and often ran tender first to and from Keswick. The shed had been built in 1865, under pressure from the semi-independent CK&PR with an understanding that the S&DR might use it. An extension of 1873 led to extra rent paid by the CK&PR with the NER contributing. It was closed wef 18 June 1962, noted deserted in 1964, razed by 1967.

Carlisle (Upperby) L&NWR Engine Shed

Investigation today on the ground at Upperby holds for the industrial archaeologist something akin to the thrills known to those who explore Roman sites in the City of London, with evidence of successive eras and their evolution. The western boundary is the L&C main line and that in the north the NER (original Newcastle and Carlisle Railway) line. To the east is the bluff on which today stand premises of Radio Carlisle and on the south east is the steep bank of the river — the Petterill — and that too has a tale to tell.

As the 20th century opened, the L&NWR locomotive department buildings and layout at Upperby were already essentially in the form shown by the LMS line diagram (Carlisle enlargement), which is dated 1928. Note the southerly convergence of routes culminating at No 13 (Upperby Bridge Jn) signalbox, also the obvious routes from the engine shed northwards, alternatively by-passing Carlisle Citadel station on the goods lines or joining the down main line at No 12 box and reaching the Citadel.

On the diagram of 1928 is depicted the massive carriage shed, standing on ground reclaimed by diversion and straightening of the river Petterill, and building of a retaining wall, all carried out well before the 20th century. The plan shows a parallel outside carriage road, then four more parallel roads in the open; two of these had been added since 1900 to allow more stabling for locomotive department purposes. Next, again, is the locomotive workshop, 450ft long and 50ft wide, with three roads inside, lofty, with curved-topped windows in the upper walls and overhead travelling crane, the entire building also on the reclaimed ground. Its use was for 'general' — meaning, major — repairs to locomotives, relieving the pressure on the main workshops at Crewe, and this work was done until about 1925-26, the time of modernisation at Crewe. Nevertheless, significant repair work continued at Upperby workshop until 1931. The 1928 plan is slightly misleading as, after 1900 but well before the 1920s, the workshop had been lengthened at its outer end, as seen on photographs.

Abutting on the workshop was the huge engine shed, with groups of three, four and four stabling roads, each group under a long gabled roof with hipped ends, the three groups being partially separated from one another by walls of open stone arches with brick infill. Accommodation was nominally for 48 engines, in the days of older, smaller locomotives than those which in time stabled here. This running shed building had essentially been in existence in 1865 but between 1873 and 1876 it was converted from fitting shops to engine sheds and equipped with pits between the rails of each of its 11 covered roads.

A long range of buildings behind the sheds, built on a NW-SE axis, with splayed SE end, had been an old boiler shop and workshops in 1873 but modified in the 1873-76 project to provide a tender shop and fitting shops. The ensuing diversion of the river to provide ground for the locomotive shops and carriage shed took it well away from the splayed end of the long buildings, which had been built originally in that form to align with the sweeping curve of the old river bank.

The position of the 60ft turntable was consistent in 20th century. Additionally, Carlisle was well provided with triangular layouts suitable for turning locomotives, useful when Pacifics appeared from 1933 onwards. Indeed, these locomotives always used London Road table until the 70ft table in the 1948 shed was available. The coal stage was close to the NW corner of the engine sheds, accessible to the turntable road. Although retained for many years, the stage was largely superseded c1917 by an early mechanical coaling plant, built by nearby Cowans Sheldon & Company, a modest-sized structure with bunker and prominent conveyor; it was south of the turntable but north of the coal stage. The mechanical plant survived to the end of steam power at Upperby. The plant is illustrated in *The Railway Magazine*, December 1919, but with no indication of the date of erection.

After the lofty locomotive repair workshop ceased to be used for 'CME' purposes, all the buildings at Upperby were allowed by the LMS to decline into a sorry state. By 1936, the centre shed block of four roads was roofless, although the flanking sections of three and four roads remained roofed. Rebuilding and remodelling were taken in hand speedily after World War 2. Drawings were prepared during 1946-48 and a huge round locomotive shed of concrete construction was built in 1947-48, with its stalls radiating from a new 70ft turntable. The whole obliterated the site of the lofty workshop with its three roads and the engine sheds of 11 roads. The westerly five roads of the carriage shed became engine accommodation. The easterly nine roads were deprived of roofs and became eight open carriage sidings. Drawings for wheeldrop and amenity buildings were not prepared until 1957 and they were then put in hand. The former offices had to come down to make room for the round shed and the new block housed the shedmaster (the present-day maintenance engineer is installed here) and also the canteen. A new stores building with rail access adjoined the round shed closely on its south west; it now survives as a plant and machinery shop, with overhead electrical wiring train stabled alongside, roughly on the alignment of the former steam locomotive coaling plant and coalstage. Following a short useful life, the shed closed wef 1 January 1968. The modern round building, together with the area of Upperby locomotive yard, was used by the electrification contractors (c1971-74), but the building then became progressively derelict and was razed in 1978-79, its outline however being traceable on the ground.

Nowadays, the two outside carriage roads on the river bank have disappeared. The easterly tracks in the onetime L&NWR carriage shed have been further spaced out as seven open-air carriage sidings, but with the back end gable extant. The five tracks which were roofed as part of the steam facilities are now spaced out to provide four carriage maintenance roads, a good building under a new roof but retaining old-world workshop premises at its northern end, against the original back wall. At the back of this carriage shop, then a carriage shed, one remembers the typical L&NWR gas works, often as it seemed with a decrepit 'Cauliflower' engine on the very brink of the river bank, immobile but providing steam boiler power for the gas works.

On Gallows Hill, above the sheds, and towards the London Road was Harraby Hill workhouse (marked on maps of 1865). By the end of the century this was Harraby Hill House, and, with additions, it became the L&NWR trainmen's hostel, or 'Barracks', not too well spoken of by the older hands. The LMS in their latter days replaced it by a new hostel — and by a metamorphosis that is now the nucleus of a large 'Motel', with Radio Carlisle adjoining and rather more prominent from the WCML.

Epilogue — age of steam
A happy memory by one of Upperby's top link drivers dates from a morning in the mid-1950s. He was working home from Euston in the normal way. At Camden shed, he was

provided with one of the last two 'Duchess' Pacifics, built at Crewe in 1947: No 46256 *Sir William A. Stanier, FRS*. At Euston, quite a company had assembled to send off J. W. Street, who had been brought along and introduced; he was to join the enginemen and travel on the locomotive to Carlisle, without company of an inspector. It transpired that Mr Street had retired in 1936, at age 60, from driving on the Great Western Railway from Old Oak Common sheds, London. He was a contemporary in years of Sir William Stanier and their friendship went back to Sir William's early years at Swindon, 1892-99, and his evening lectures for

enginement at 'Willesden Tech', 1904-05, a period when Sir William was preparing the move from Westbourne Park to the new Old Oak depot. Mr Street was author of *I drove the Cheltenham Flier* (published 1951) and other works and was travelling at the instance of his old friend, then long retired as CME of the LMS. Mr Street enjoyed every minute of his run. He commented to the driver that the vista from the footplate at Oxenholme towards Windermere was one of the finest seen on his travels at home and abroad. He stayed overnight at Carlisle and rode back next day on the engine of the up 'Royal Scot' train.

Alternating current over the Westmorland Fells, 1974-1981

From steam to electricity

In the days of Stamp and Stanier, typically 1937-39, the LMS moved away from the concept of many small engine sheds, each with its territory and its out-and-back engine workings. There were fewer locomotives. There were complex rosters, much re-manning en route and lengthened periods away from home depot, backed by examinations and maintenance centralised in each motive power district. The same principles were further extended in the diesel interregnum. Meanwhile, the rosters for the driver (with or without fireman or 'second man') became more basic on the WCML, designed to bring a driver home within each turn of duty and thus normally involving an out-and-back trip, for example Carlisle to Preston and back, but on different footplates. The AC electric locomotives, some in service since 1960, have carried the process farther still, especially since May 1974, when Preston-Carlisle-Glasgow was added to the Euston-Birmingham/Liverpool/Manchester/Preston routes.

Available motive power, 1981-82

At the time of writing (December 1981), the 10 electric locomotives of Class 84 have been withdrawn. Classes 82 and 83 nominally number 21 but about a third are in fact laid aside. Classes 81 (22 in stock) and 85 (40) are available for work up to 100mph but tend to be used on secondary duties. Class 86/0 (20) retain axle-hung traction motors and are capable locomotives but limited to 80mph out of consideration for the track. Classes 86/3 (19) with flexible wheels, 86/2 (58) with new bogie frames and prominent flexicoil suspension and 86/1 (3) with 87-type bogies are all 100mph locomotives. So are 87 (35) and the thyristor-controlled locomotive No 87.101 *Stephenson*. In order to cover most of the loco-hauled traffic on the whole of the WCML electrified principal routes, the 86/3, 86/2, 86/1 and 87 locomotives achieve an average of about 175,000 miles per annum by each locomotive and effectively pay allegiance to Willesden (London) depot. Individual locomotive records are kept there and major scheduled examinations and maintenance (between visits to main works at Crewe) are carried out. The other depots on the system are at Crewe, Longsight (Manchester), Shields (Glasgow) and Carlisle, this last being the 'Traction Depot' at Kingmoor, on the down side of the Caledonian main line, where both diesel and electric work is undertaken. These depots share the more frequent but less onerous examinations of electric locomotives.

The loads

The daytime passenger trains traversing Preston-Carlisle (apart from a few diesel-electrically hauled for Barrow and those DMU-operated for Barrow and Windermere) are normally worked by 100mph AC locomotives. Most loads vary between 9 and 12 vehicles, usually 100mph air-conditioned stock of marks 2d (1970) and later, set weights ranging from about 300 Imperial tons tare for 9 coaches to 400 tons for 12. Sleeping car trains may be heavier but only run up to 80 or 90mph. Freightliner trains of 10 loaded bogie flat vehicles are typically around 475 tons including average load of merchandise. 'Full' freightliner trains of 20 vehicles double this and are *usually* double-headed, either with multiple-unit operation by one driver or rostered in tandem, in which latter case the driver of the second locomotive gives assistance as needed; two locomotives drawing power in this way do not rob one another of current. The freightliner speed limit is 75mph. Other freights have limits of 60mph or 45mph. Among the heaviest currently are steel-carrying and can load to well over 1,000 tons throughout between Ravenscraig and Shotton, always double-headed. All trains are air-braked throughout, this being a requirement as catch-points were eliminated at the time of electrification of the heavily graded Lancaster and Carlisle line.

Power output — adhesion — a 'down' run

Both timings and daily routine performance are far superior to those immediately preceding them, with steam or diesel power. The Class 87 locomotives are rated at 5,000hp (at 87mph) and weigh only 82 tons — carried, like all the others, on two 4-wheeled bogies. There are adhesion problems; these become apparent mainly on the L&C route, and in Scotland. This is where life on the footplate in the 1980s touches that in past eras and it provides one of the reasons why the AC electric driver must be as observant of his steed as was his predecessor of his 'Jumbo'. And just as the 'Jumbo' driver and his mate would sight their tall semaphore distant signals at the earliest moment when descending the winding banks, so the high prevailing speeds today call for prompt sighting of colour-light signals — and for adherence to speed restrictions uphill as well as down.

'Mushy' leaves have always provided a hazardous carpet at autumn on Grayrigg bank and likewise on much of the southbound ascent from Eamont Junction to Shap. The problem is complemented by the film which commonly forms on the exposed sections of the route from the mists of Shap — and Beattock — inclines. Typically, on locomotive

No 86.224 recently, with a load of (only) nine coaches, making the stops northward from Preston, the notorious re-start from Oxenholme to Hay Fell — 1 in 104, 124, 131, prevailing — on a wet and windy October day through the plantations, a light touch by the driver was called for, with constant coaxing as slipping was felt. The initial re-start had itself been exceptionally careful, registering only 25% on the notch indicator. This meant that the controller was moved sufficiently up the 38 available notches to tap 25% of the 1,500V (approx) AC available from the main transformer. The controller was then eased gently up the scale until at Hayfell box (site), about $3\frac{1}{4}$ miles, 70% voltage was being tapped, with 650A and 70mph registered. The problem was overcome and at Grayrigg summit speed was allowed to fall from 78 to 75mph for the restricted curve onwards to Low Gill. Even leaving Penrith that morning, with the grade slightly falling but the train on the curve, there was significant slipping.

Running on the 'up'

A couple of 'up' runs were made from Carlisle on successive days, with different trains but each with a load of 10, about 340 tons tare, and non-stop to Preston. It was a pleasure to accompany the same Crewe driver on each occasion and to see how he tackled nominally identical circumstances but with entirely different conditions on the rail-heads. The locomotives were successively Nos 87.020 and 86.250 — *North Briton* and *The Glasgow Herald*. On the first day the weather was squally, but with relatively 'clean' conditions on the rails. Beyond Upperby No 13 (site) and the neutral section, the controller was soon moved up past the 100% notch into 'field diversion' (weak field), which introduces resistances in parallel with the traction motor field circuits, thus increasing the current for acceleration — giving 1,000A briefly, falling to 800A, with speed 85mph passing Brisco (80mph and 90mph restrictions curtailed further acceleration). Again, after the 70mph limit on Penrith curve and caution on Eamont curve, maximum power was seen and felt at 'field divert' and 1,100A, slightly eased to 100% tapping with 600-800A by Eden Valley Junction, impressively producing 100mph on the 1 in 125 up by Clifton & Lowther. Thrimby curves were taken at 75mph and all the other restrictions closely observed, plus a lengthy pw slack to 20mph after Oxenholme No 1 (site), where speed should have been nearer 90; once on the level, 100mph was registered at Burton & Holme, 105 past Carnforth, 70 limit through Lancaster Castle. Speed was 70mph, rising, past Lancaster No 1 (site, on curve at bank top) with 'field divert' and 950A giving spectacular acceleration again to 100mph past Oubeck ($1\frac{3}{4}$ miles from No 1). Time to Preston stop was $69\frac{3}{4}$min, against 69 (including 4min allowance in timing for pws, etc) booked, so in conditions of no slipping and three powerful accelerations but with special caution over an embankment slippage and the long, badly-placed pws after Oxenholme, there was little in hand.

Next day, with loco No 86.250, it was again blustery, but wet withal and in contrast slipping occurred on all crucial sections, namely Carlisle to Brisco. Penrith (pass) to Eden Valley Junction and from near Harrisons to Shap Summit. With a brief exception, the highest power applied was 80%

notching with 600-750A and speed 80mph falling to 78mph sustained, on 1 in 125 up. Incidentally, there is no 'field divert' facility on Class 86. The Oxenholme slack was the same as the day before and likewise no hint of adverse signals. 70min were taken overall, very creditable on a difficult day.

Tentative conclusions — and the future?

The indications are that 69min southbound from Carlisle to Preston non-stop is just about right as an all-weather timing for Class 86/2 or 87 locomotives, if allowance is to be included for up to 5min of pw or other out-of-course checks. Looking to the future, one could visualise a development of the Class 87, mounted with articulation on three power bogies, completing the mastery of Locke's gradients and the APT tilting technique straightening out his curves.

Freightliner and the speed factor

The enormous difference made by a lowering of the 100mph objective to 75mph over this road is seen when travelling with a freightliner — for example, a down run with No 85.025 on the Millbrook (Southampton)-Coatbridge: 10 freightliner flats, loaded weight 480 tons. The train's permitted speed of 75mph was maintained for a large part of the start-to-stop run from Preston station to Carlisle Citadel; as most of the many line speed restrictions are 70mph or above, they proved of little hindrance. The highest output noted was 85%, with 500A, passing Oxenholme. There was a little slipping in a hailstorm near Scotsman's bridge on Shap incline, with slight easing, also a pws to 20mph for about $\frac{1}{4}$-mile at Shap Summit and a lengthy 20mph slowing at the slipped embankment, on the approaches to Carlisle's outer suburbs. The timetable allowed $97\frac{1}{2}$min (inclusive of 8min margin) and the time taken was 86min (including the two lengthy 20mph slacks). There was far more in hand on this schedule, with 480 tons, than on the 69min southbound schedule with 340 tons.

Refinements of technique

Because overspeeding through wheelslip can do serious electrical damage, as well as damage to the rails, the later classes of AC locomotives have electrical detection for slip which, if not forestalled by the driver, automatically notches down on the tap-changer and thus reduces power to the rectifiers and (DC) traction motors. Power and speed can be lost progressively by the sequence: acceleration; weight transfer from leading to rear axle of each power bogie; slipping; automatic notching down; slipping; more notching down; speed falling . . . Probably this happened, in most unfavourable circumstances, viewed recently from the rear of an up train. Locomotive No 87.020 (*quo vide, ante*) was hauling dead loco No 86.261 *Driver John Axon, GC* and a near maximum load of 12 bogies. Restarting from the platform road at Lancaster Castle, directly on the mile of 1 in 98 up, the train came to a painful stand 3min 17sec after starting, restarted 1min 15sec later but took 11min 30sec from the station to topping the mile at No 1 box (site) and joining the 'Old Road' (as it is known) onwards to Preston. Only 15 min 35 sec were taken from No 1 to Preston stop!

Sand is nominally available but not favoured. In addition to careful manual use of the controller, such as described, there is available an anti-slip button, which gives a partial braking (by conventional application of the blocks to the tyres); its use is believed to be effective in minimising loss of power and speed when accelerating from rest but is *not* a permitted practice if the slipping develops at speed. Locomotive No 87.101 *Stephenson* — and the advanced passenger trains (APT) — have the benefit of thyristor control, giving infinite gradations of power, in association with separate excitation of each traction motor; wheelslip is automatically and rapidly detected and corrected on each traction motor individually, thus contributing to trouble-free acceleration.

It is interesting to note that Class 85, 86 and 87 locomotives are equipped with rheostatic (electrical) braking on the locomotive, which operates concurrently with air braking on the train, through the medium of a combination brake valve, the effect being akin to the combination brake valve on a steam locomotive which could simultaneously apply the steam brake to the loco and vacuum brake to its train. Use of a 'rheo' brake contributes to locomotive availability by prolonging the life of the brake blocks. At low speeds, or in the event of failure of the 'rheo' brake, an air brake on the locomotive automatically takes over.

Proved reliability

The AC locomotives of Class 86 (with variants) and 87 have proved highly reliable, indeed planned availability stands currently (with reason) around 80%; this takes account of normal maintenance and overhauls in main workshops as well as occasional failures. 'Failures' of the powerful AC locomotives are as likely to be mechanical as electrical in character, for example in drive gearing or, more particularly, by cracking of cross beams or other parts of the fabricated frames of power bogies — just as has been known in BR's larger diesel-electric locomotives, and probably the world over.

Windstorm

Electric locomotives are dependent on their power supplies.

One thinks of overhead line equipment on the fells of the L&C route as eliminating the problems which have afflicted the SR and LT in conditions of ice and snow, thus achieving the reliability of supply to which we became accustomed in course of regular travel on the MSJ&AR and the Woodhead route. There were, however, various occasions, chiefly in the strong winds of early 1962, when the then newly-installed overhead line equipment between Crewe and Manchester suffered damage due to cross winds, the equipment being blown out of line and 'hooked' down by moving pantographs. The problem was largely overcome at the time by improving the rigidity of registration assemblies; and massive balance weights appeared at intervals.

For the electrification north of Weaver Junction, including the L&C route, there was strong pressure to keep down capital costs and a new and less expensive design of overhead line equipment was adopted, while at the same time special attention was paid to those areas where high winds were anticipated. Nevertheless, from time to time severe windstorm has caused damage. Perhaps the worst occasion was during a heavy storm on the night of Sunday 16 December 1979, which only abated in the late evening of Monday 17 December. This caused problems on the L&C line and a serious incident on the Esk viaduct a few miles to the north of Carlisle. My own homeward journey was completed on foot from Lancaster to Carnforth on a course near to the main line.

The extremely high winds on these occasions affected exposed locations such as the Solway approaches and also places where the hills produced a funnelling effect and increased wind velocity locally. Remedial action has been taken in these areas by improving the supporting and registration arrangements and increasing the tension on the wiring; it is hoped that these measures have helped towards eliminating the problem but events in all recent winters, and especially 1982–3 have demonstrated that it still exists. One looks forward to continued technical and commercial success, with even greater reliability and performance.

The folk of the Lancaster and Carlisle Railway

Right: The cheerful staff of Oxenholme station, in July 1981, including the ladies who operate the much-appreciated 'railbar'. *HDB*

Below: *The brothers Gordon* at Carlisle, September 1981. From left to right: *Frank Gordon*, who joined the L&NWR at Upperby shed in 1917, fired also at Huddersfield shed, and retired from Upperby in 1967 as a top-link driver of 'Duchesses' and diesel-electric locomotives; *George Gordon*, who joined the LMS at Kingmoor shed and is senior traction inspector, Carlisle, and concerned with power from 'Black 5s' to AC electric; *John Gordon*, who worked in Upperby yard from 1916 and ended his career at Longridge, today a talented artist of railway and other subjects.
Courtesy 'Cumberland News'

Acknowledgements

I wish to thank my friends old and new who have so helpfully answered my many questions, readily discussing their own findings and recollections as contribution to my quest for railway lore and history, between Preston, Windermere and Carlisle. They include:

Harvey Airey, Dr Michael Andrews, J. G. Altham, C. A. Appleton, J. W. Armstrong, G. J. Aston, Alfred Bailey, Edward Bateson, Ernest Beetwell, F. H. Bell, Michael Bentley, G. J. Biddle, G. C. Bird, Dennis Boardley, C. E. Box, Allan Brackenbury, W. A. Brown, Joseph Capstick, O. F. Carter, R. M. Casserley, Brian Chadwick, C. R. Clinker, J. G. Coates, Fred Consterdine, D. E. Cookson, Edgar Corless, Walter Coward, Roy Cutler, J. D. Darby, W. B. Darnell, Thomas Davidson, W. N. Davies, John Dearden, Percy Duff, Alan Earl, John Edgington, Harold Ellis, W. Fawcett, N. Fields, Edward Foster, R. D. Foster, E. H. Fowkes, E. W. Gilmour, Frank Gordon, George Gordon, J. R. Gordon, Arthur Grayland, Jack Hall, John Hammond, A. M. Harvey, William Hennigan, Alastair Heslop, Major J. W. B. Hext, William Hoggarth, Frank Hodgson, Frank Holmes, G. O. Holt, Kenneth Hoole, Harry Horton, F. R. Johnson, Owen Jones, G. N. King, Brian Lord, Geoffrey Lord, Willis Machell, Clem Major, Mrs Diana Matthews, J. F. McEwan, R. S. and Mrs McNaught, Julian Mellentin, W. Milburn, Joseph Mitchell, E. K. Nelson, Thomas Oversby, Techwin Parry, George Pattinson, J. D. Petty, G. H. Platt, Miss Phyllis Porritt, Frank Proctor, Brian Reed, Sid Ridley, J. E. Roberts, R. Roberts, P. W. Robinson, Harold and Mrs Satterthwaite, H. S Simpson, J. L. Slater, D. L. Smith, J. A. Sommerfield, Kenneth Stokes, John Strange, H. E. Swainbank, H. V. Swainbank, Commander George Taylor, D. F. Tee, Thomas Thewlis, Paul and Dorothy Vogt, C. Vincent, A. St G. Walsh, Thomas Weavings, Mr and Mrs Whitaker, Preston Whiteley, G. D. Whitworth, D. E. Willink, Mrs J. Woodhouse, W. B. Yeadon and W. J. Young.

Among these folk are those whose memories carried us back to the faraway days of 1914-18, and even earlier, on the line. There are also those present-day researchers who have read through sections of my drafts and contributed to content and accuracy. Arthur Chambers has drawn maps, as well as helping from TPO Society sources. Doug Rendell has meticulously and professionally copied and presented many old photographs.

Much appreciated help has come from British Railways, including Messrs Carter and Lickfold at Euston and Peter Halsall at Preston; R. H. Blyth and colleagues (S&T, Manchester, Preston and Carlisle); A. King and colleagues (civil engineering, Preston); W. S. Taylor and colleagues (mechanical and electrical engineering and rolling stock, Derby); Messrs Cramer, Kay and Duncan at Carlisle and motive power inspectors Arthur Morris, George Hesketh, Herbert Moore and, of course, George Gordon. And I must mention Cowans Sheldon & Company Ltd and James Cropper & Company Ltd, also Ripley School and the Windermere & Bowness Civic Society.

Great help has been received from Record Offices and their archivists at Carlisle Castle, Kendal, Preston and Kew and reference librarians at Carlisle (Tullie House), Kendal, Lancaster, Preston (Harris Library), Manchester (Central Library), National Railway Museum (York) and Ian Allan's headquarters. Published works consulted include:

Crewe to Carlisle (Brian Reed, 1969)
Main line over Shap (David Joy, 1967)
Chronological list of the railways of Lancashire (M. D. Greville, 1953)
The Lancaster & Preston Junction Railway (M. D. Greville and G. O. Holt, 1961)
Guide to the Lancaster & Carlisle Railway (1859)
The track of the Royal Scot (LMS route book No 3, probably c1930)
Register of closed passenger stations and goods depots (C. R. Clinker, 1978, and supplement)
Railway reminiscences (G. P. Neele, 1904)
The Kendal & Windermere Railway (Julian Mellentin, 1980)
The Premier Line (O. S. Nock, 1952)
Railways around Lancaster (K. Nuttall and T. Rawlings, 1980)
The Preston & Longridge Railway (Norman Parker, 1972)
The Garstang & Knott End Railway (R. W. Rush and M. Price, 1964)
The Furness Railway (W. McGowan Gradon, 1946)
The Lowgill Branch (R. G. Western, 1971)
A history of the Cockermouth, Keswick & Penrith Railway (W. McGowan Gradon, 1948)
Forgotten railways of North West England (John Marshall, 1981)
The North Eastern Railway (W. W. Tomlinson, 1914)
The Stainmore Railway (K. Hoole, 1973)
Locomotives of the North Eastern Railway (O. S. Nock, 1953)
RCH junction diagrams (various)

The changing face of Carnforth; North Western engineman; and *Hazards of the footplate* (all by J. E. Roberts, 1974-80)

AC electric locomotives of British Railways (Brian Webb and John Duncan, 1979)

LMS engine sheds, L&NWR (Chris Hawkins and George Reeve, 1981)

The great age of steam on Windermere (G. H. Pattinson, 1981)

Paper: A taste of freedom (Arthur Barker and John Huggon, 1964)

Papers on Windermere (Dr John Marshall and colleagues, Lancaster University)

Papers on the Summit Branch canal (Railway & Canal Historical Society)

Journals

The Railway Magazine (1897-1981), including work of R. E. Charlewood (published and unpublished)

Modern Railways (in particular, signal diagrams published 1973-74)

Cumbrian Railways Association; Stephenson Locomotive Society;

Railway Correspondence and Travel Society; London & North Western Railway Society; *The Westmorland Gazette.*

HDB

LANCASTER AND CARL[ISLE]

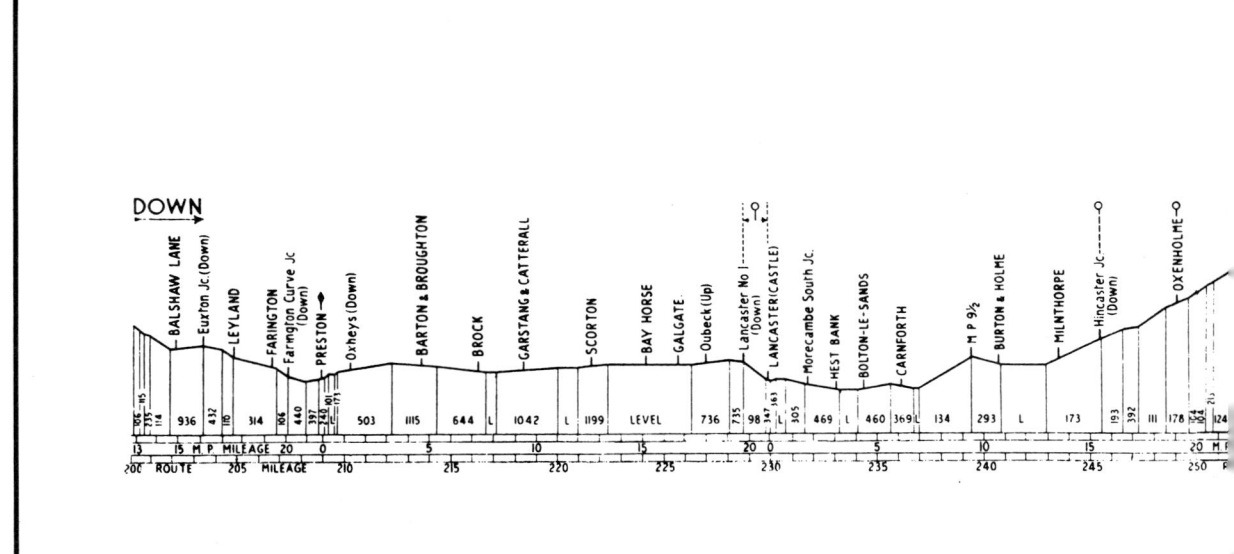

SOUTH -PORT · BLACK -POOL · FLEET -WOOD · KNOTT END · LINDAL · LAKESIDE · MORECAMBE · HEYSHAM · CARNFORTH · FR · FR

LEYR · LEYR · LEYR · LEY&LNWR · KER · FEMUR · LANCASTER · MR · MILN- THORPE

CHORLEY · PRESTON · LEY&LNWR · LONG- RIDGE · GARSTANG & CATTERALL · BAY HORSE · LNWR

BENTHAM · MR · INGLETON

```
SCALE OF MILES.
0     5     10    15    20
```

THIS MAP IS NOT IN
ONLY TO GIVE AN OV[ERVIEW]

DOWN →

BALSHAW LANE · Euxton Jc. (Down) · LEYLAND · FARINGTON · Farington Curve Jc (Down) · PRESTON → · Oxheys (Down) · BARTON & BROUGHTON · BROCK · GARSTANG & CATTERALL · SCORTON · BAY HORSE · GALGATE · Oubeck (Up) · Lancaster No 1 (Down) · LANCASTER (CASTLE) · Morecambe South Jc. · HEST BANK · BOLTON-LE-SANDS · CARNFORTH · M P 9½ · BURTON & HOLME · MILNTHORPE · Hincaster Jc (Down) · OXENHOLME

106 · 233 · 114 · 936 · 432 · 314 · 104 · 440 · 397 · 248 · 503 · 1115 · 644 · L · 1042 · L · 1199 · LEVEL · 736 · 735 · 98 · 147 · 161 · 205 · 469 · L · 460 · 369 · 134 · 293 · L · 173 · 193 · 392 · 111 · 178 · 104 · 124

13 · 15 M P MILEAGE 20 · 0 · 5 · 10 · 15 · 20 0 · 5 · 10 · 15 · 20 M P
200 ROUTE · 205 MILEAGE · 210 · 215 · 220 · 225 · 230 · 235 · 240 · 245 · 250